Contents

||||||||||||||||||||||||||||||||||||||||||
✔ **KU-755-539**

HOW TO USE THIS BOOK

Communicating in a foreign language doesn't have to be difficult – you can convey a lot with just a few words (plus a few
gestures and a bit of mime). Just remember: keep it simple.
Don't try to come out with long, grammatically perfect sen-
tences when one or two words will get your meaning across.

Inside the back cover of this book is a list of All-purpose
phrases. Some will help you to make contact – greetings,
'please' and 'thank you', 'yes' and 'no'. Some are to get people to
help you understand what they're saying to you. And some are
questions like 'do you have . . . ?' and 'where is . . . ?', to which
you can add words from the Dictionary at the back of the book.

The book is divided into sections for different situations, such
as Road travel, Shopping, Health and so on. In each section
you'll find

- Useful tips and information
- Words and phrases that you'll see on signs or in print
- Phrases you are likely to want to say
- Things that people may say to you

Many of the phrases can be adapted by simply using another
word from the Dictionary. For instance, take the question
¿Está lejos el aeropuerto? (Is the airport far away?). If you want
to know if the *station* is far away, just substitute **la estación** (the
station) for **el aeropuerto** to give **¿Está lejos la estación?**

All the phrases have a simple pronunciation guide underneath
based on English sounds – this is explained in Pronunciation
(page 5).

If you want some guidance on how the Spanish language
works, see Basic grammar (page 172).

There's a handy reference section (starts on page 182) which contains lists of days and months, countries and nationalities, general signs and notices that you'll see, conversion tables, national holidays, useful addresses and numbers.

The 5,000-word Dictionary (page 202) comes in two sections – Spanish–English and English–Spanish.

A concise list of numbers is printed inside the front cover for easy reference, and right at the end of the book is an Emergencies section (which we hope you *won't* have to use).

Wherever possible, work out in advance what you want to say – if you're going shopping, for instance, write out a shopping list in Spanish. If you're buying travel tickets, work out how to say where you want to go, how many tickets you want, single or return, etc.

Practise saying things out loud – the cassette that goes with this book will help you to get used to the sounds of Spanish.

Above all – don't be shy! It'll be appreciated if you try to say a few words, even if it's only 'good morning' and 'goodbye' – and in fact those are the very sorts of phrases that are worth learning, as you'll hear them and need to use them all the time.

If you'd like to learn more Spanish, BBC Books also publishes *When in Spain, Get by in Spanish* and *España Viva*. BBC phrase books are also available for the following languages: French, German and Italian. Future titles include Arabic, Greek, Portuguese and Turkish.

The authors would welcome any suggestions or comments about this book, but in the meantime, have a good trip – **¡buen viaje!**

PRONUNCIATION

You don't need perfect pronunciation to be able to communicate – it's enough to get the sounds approximately right and to stress the words in the correct place. If you want to hear real Spanish voices and practise trying to sound like them, then listen to the cassette.

Spanish pronunciation is very regular – you can tell how a word is pronounced from the way it's written, once you know what sound each letter (or group of letters) represents. A pronunciation guide is given with the phrases in this book – the system is based on English sounds, as described below.

Many Spanish consonants are pronounced in a similar way to English. The main differences are with **c, g, h, j, ll, ñ, qu, r, v, z**.

Spanish vowels are pronounced the same wherever they occur (unlike English where each vowel can be pronounced in several distinct ways).

For the Spanish alphabet, see page 8.

Stress

Except in the cases listed below, Spanish words are stressed on the last but one syllable: *tengo*, *gustan*, *España*, *excursiones*. The exceptions are:
1 If a word ends in a consonant other than **n** or **s**, the stress is on the last syllable: *Madrid*, *acampar*, *español*.
2 If there is a written accent, the stress is where the accent is: *estación*, *Málaga*, *café*.
In this book, a stressed syllable is shown in the pronunciation guide by bold type: *estathyon*, *tengo*.

Vowels

	Approx. English equivalent	Shown in book as	Example	
a	a in 'cat'	a	nada	*nada*
au	ow in 'cow'	ow	autobús	*owtoboos*
ai, ay	i in 'pile'	iy	hay	*iy*
e	e in 'met'	e	cena	*thena*
ei, ey	ay in 'say'	ay	veinte	*baynte*
i	ee in 'meet'	ee	amigo	*ameego*
i (unstressed)	y in 'yet'	y	gracias	*grathyas*
o	o in 'lot'	o	como	*komo*
oi, oy	oy in 'boy'	oy	soy	*soy*
u	oo in 'moon'	oo	una	*oona*
u (before another vowel)	w in 'wet'	w	cuenta	*kwenta*
			muy	*mwee*
but in que, qui, gue, gui	not pronounced	–	quién	*kyen*
		–	guerra	*gerra*

Consonants

	Approx. English equivalent	Shown in book as	Example	
b	b in 'but'	b	baño	*banyo*
c followed by e or i	th in 'thick'	th	cenar	*thenar*
c otherwise	c in 'can'	k	cama	*kama*
ch	ch in 'church'	ch	noche	*noche*
d	d in 'dog'	d	donde	*donde*
f	f in 'feet'	f	fonda	*fonda*
g followed by e or i	Scottish ch in 'loch'	hh	gente	*hhente*

g otherwise	g in 'got'	g	gamba	*gamba*
h	always silent	–	hora	*ora*
j	Scottish ch in 'loch'	hh	hijo	*eehho*
k	k in 'kit'	k	kilo	*keelo*
l	l in 'lock'	l	libro	*leebro*
ll	lli in 'million'	ly	llama	*lyama*
m	m in 'mat'	m	mano	*mano*
n	n in 'not'	n	nombre	*nombre*
ñ	ni in 'onion'	ny	mañana	*manyana*
p	p in 'pack'	p	pera	*pera*
qu	k in 'kit'	k	que	*ke*
r	rolled as in Scottish accent	r	cara	*kara*
rr	strongly rolled	rr	perro	*perro*
s	s in 'set'	s	solo	*solo*
except before m, b	z in 'zoo'	z	mismo	*meezmo*
t	t in 'tin'	t	tengo	*tengo*
v	b in 'bat'	b	vino	*beeno*
x	x in 'six'	x	excursión	*exkoor-syon*
y	y in 'yet'	y	yo	*yo*
except y (and)	ee in 'meet'	ee	y	*ee*
z	th in 'thick'	th	plaza	*platha*

7

Note

d between vowels and at the end of words often sounds more like 'th' in 'other', but for the sake of simplicity it's shown as d throughout this book

c and z: in Southern Spain these are often pronounced 's' rather than 'th'

ll is often pronounced more like the 'y' in 'you'

THE SPANISH ALPHABET

In the Spanish alphabet, **ch** and **ll** are treated as separate letters, and there is an extra letter **ñ** – these follow **c**, **l** and **n** respectively in dictionaries and so on. The letters **k** and **w** are only found in words borrowed from other languages.

Spelling

How is it spelt?
¿Cómo se escribe?
komo se eskreebe

B and **V** sound almost the same in Spanish so, when spelling a word out, you can distinguish between them by saying **B como Barcelona** or **V como Valencia**.

Letter	Pronounced	Letter	Pronounced
A	*a*	N	*ene*
B	*be*	Ñ	*enye*
C	*the*	O	*o*
CH	*che*	P	*pe*
D	*de*	Q	*koo*
E	*e*	R	*ere*
F	*efe*	S	*ese*
G	*hhe*	T	*te*
H (hache)	*ache*	U	*oo*
I	*ee*	V	*oobe*
J (jota)	*hhota*	W (uve doble)	*oobe doble*
K	*ka*	X (equis)	*ekees*
L	*ele*	Y (i griega)	*ee gree-ega*
LL	*elye*	Z (zeta)	*theta*
M	*eme*		

GENERAL CONVERSATION

● The phrases **buenos días**, **buenas tardes** and **buenas noches** are used at different times of day. **Buenos días** means 'good morning' (or literally 'good day') and is used up to lunchtime – Spanish lunchtime that is. After that, until around 9 p.m. or nightfall, it's **buenas tardes** – which therefore means both 'good afternoon' and 'good evening'. **Buenas noches** can be used as a greeting late in the evening, as well as to say 'goodnight'.

Hola means 'hello', and is often used together with one of the phrases above, e.g. **hola, buenos días**.

Adiós (goodbye) can also be used with one of the phrases above, e.g. **adiós, buenas tardes**, or with a phrase like **hasta luego** (see you later) – **adiós, hasta luego**.

● Spaniards shake hands when they meet and when they say goodbye. Women, and men and women (though not two men) often exchange kisses on both cheeks.

● Spaniards use the words **señor**, **señora** and **señorita** far more often than English-speakers say 'sir', 'madam' or 'miss' – it isn't as formal-sounding in Spanish.

● When you're talking to someone in English you vary your tone of voice and your way of saying things depending on whether you're addressing them formally, showing respect, or in a more casual way (as with a friend or member of the family).

In Spanish, there's an extra way of making this distinction – by using different words to say 'you' and different endings on verbs. One way is more formal, the other more casual. There's a further explanation of this on page 177, but all you need to be aware of is that in this book we have used the more formal way, on the assumption that you will mostly be talking to people you don't know. The formal word for 'you' is **usted** (*oosteth*).

People may address *you* in the informal way (this is quite general among younger people). The informal word for 'you' is **tú** (*too*). You may notice an s on the ends of verbs, e.g. **¿quieres?** instead of **¿quiere?** (would you like?); **¿tienes?** instead of **¿tiene?** (do you have?); and you may also hear **¿te gusta?** instead of **¿le gusta?** (do you like it?).

Greetings

Hello
Hola
ola

Good morning
Buenos días
bwenos deeas

Good afternoon/evening
Buenas tardes
bwenas tardes

Good evening/goodnight
Buenas noches
bwenas noches

Goodbye
Adiós
adyos

See you later
Hasta luego
asta lwego

(Hello), how are things?
(Hola), ¿qué tal?
ola ke tal

How are you?
¿Cómo está usted?
komo esta oosteth

Fine, thanks
Bien, gracias
byen grathyas

And you?
¿Y usted?
ee oosteth

Introductions

My name is . . .
Yo me llamo . . .
yo me lyamo . . .

This is . . .
Este/Esta es . . .
este/esta es . . .

This is Mr Brown
Este es el señor Brown
este es el senyor . . .

This is Mrs Clark
Esta es la señora Clark
esta es la senyora . . .

This is my husband/son
Este es mi marido/hijo
este es mee mareedo/eehho

This is my boyfriend/fiancé
Este es mi amigo/novio
este es mee ameego/nobyo

This is my wife/daughter
Esta es mi mujer/hija
esta es mee moohher/eehha

This is my girlfriend/fiancée
Esta es mi amiga/novia
esta es mee ameega/nobya

Pleased to meet you
Mucho gusto
moocho goosto

Talking about yourself and your family

(*see* Countries and nationalities, *page 187*)

I am English
Soy inglés (*If you're a man*)
soy eengles
Soy inglesa (*If you're a woman*)
soy eenglesa

I am Scottish
Soy escocés/escocesa
soy eskothes/eskothesa

I am Irish
Soy irlandés/irlandesa
soy eerlandes/eerlandesa

I am Welsh
Soy galés/galesa
soy gales/galesa

I live in London
Vivo en Londres
beebo en londres

We live in Newcastle
Vivimos en Newcastle
beebeemos en . . .

I am a student
Soy estudiante
soy estoodyante

I am a nurse
Soy enfermero (*male*)/
enfermera (*female*)
soy enfermero/enfermera

I work in . . .
Trabajo en . . .
trabahho en . . .

I work in an office/factory
**Trabajo en una oficina/
fábrica**
*trabahho en oona ofeetheena/
fabreeka*

I work for a computer
company
**Trabajo en una compañía de
ordenadores**
*trabahho en oona kompanyee-a
de ordenadores*

I am unemployed
Estoy en paro
estoy en paro

I am single
Soy soltero (*male*)/**soltera**
(*female*)
soy soltero/soltera

I am married
Estoy casado/casada
estoy kasado/kasada

I am separated
Estoy separado/separada
estoy separado/separada

I am divorced
Estoy divorciado/divorciada
*estoy deeborthyado/
deeborthyada*

I am a widower/widow
Soy viudo/viuda
soy byoodo/byooda

I have a son/a daughter
Tengo un hijo/una hija
tengo oon eehho/oona eehha

I have three children
Tengo tres hijos
tengo tres eehhos

I don't have any children
No tengo hijos
no tengo eehhos

I have one brother
Tengo un hermano
tengo oon ermano

I have three sisters
Tengo tres hermanas
tengo tres ermanas

I'm here with my husband/
wife
**Estoy aquí con mi marido/
mujer**
*estoy akee kon mee mareedo/
moohher*

I'm here with my family
Estoy aquí con mi familia
estoy akee kon mee fameelya

I'm here on holiday
Estoy aquí de vacaciones
estoy akee de bakathyones

I'm here on business
Estoy aquí de negocios
estoy akee de negothyos

I speak very little Spanish
Hablo muy poco español
ablo mwee poko espanyol

My husband/wife is . . .
Mi marido/mujer es . . .
mee mareedo/moohher es . . .

My husband is a bus-driver
**Mi marido es conductor de
autobús**
*mee mareedo es kondooktor
de owtoboos*

My wife is an accountant
Mi mujer es contable
mee moohher es kontable

My husband/wife works
in . . .
**Mi marido/mujer trabaja
en . . .**
*mee mareedo/moohher
trabahha en . . .*

My son is five years old
Mi hijo tiene cinco años
*mee eehho tyene theenko
anyos*

My daughter is eight years
old
Mi hija tiene ocho años
mee eehha tyene ocho anyos

You may hear

¿Cómo se llama (usted)?
komo se lyama (oosteth)
What is your name?

¿De dónde es?
de donde es
Where are you from?

¿Qué hace?
ke athe
What do you do?

¿En qué trabaja?
en ke trabahha
What job do you do?

¿Qué estudia?
ke estoodya
What are you studying?

¿Está usted casado/casada?
esta oosteth kasado/kasada
Are you married?

¿Tiene hijos?
tyene eehhos
Do you have any children?

¿Cuántos años tienen?
kwantos anyos tyenen
How old are they?

¿Cuántos años tiene?
kwantos anyos tyene
How old is he/she?

Es muy simpático/guapo
es mwee seempateeko/gwapo
He is very nice/good-looking

Es muy simpática/guapa
es mwee seempateeka/gwapa
She is very nice/pretty

¿Tiene hermanos?
tyene ermanos
Do you have any brothers and sisters?

¿Es éste su marido/novio/amigo?
es este soo mareedo/nobyo/ameego
Is this your husband/fiancé/boyfriend?

¿Es ésta su mujer/novia/amiga?
es esta soo moohher/nobya/ameega
Is this your wife/fiancée/girlfriend?

¿Adónde va usted?
adonde ba oosteth
Where are you going?

¿Dónde se queda usted?
donde se keda oosteth
Where are you staying?

¿Dónde vive usted?
donde beebe oosteth
Where do you live?

Talking about Spain and your own country

I like Spain (very much)
Me gusta mucho España
me goosta moocho espanya

Spain is very beautiful
España es muy bonita
espanya es mwee boneeta

It's the first time I've been to
Spain
**Es la primera vez que vengo a
España**
*es la preemera beth ke bengo a
espanya*

I come to Spain often
Vengo mucho a España
bengo moocho a espanya

Are you from here?
¿Es usted de aquí?
es oosteth de akee

Have you ever been to
England?
**¿Ha estado alguna vez en
Inglaterra?**
*a estado algoona beth en
eenglaterra*

Scotland/Ireland/Wales
Escocia/Irlanda/Gales
eskothya/eerlanda/gales

Did you like it?
¿Le gustó?
le goosto

You may hear

¿Le gusta España?
le goosta espanya
Do you like Spain?

**¿Es la primera vez que viene
a España?**
*es la preemera beth ke byene a
espanya*
Is this your first time in
Spain?

¿Cuánto tiempo se queda aquí?
kwanto tyempo se keda akee
How long are you here for?

¿Qué piensa de . . . ?
ke pyensa de . . .
What do you think of . . . ?

¿Qué piensa de Andalucía?
ke pyensa de andaloothee-a
What do you think of
Andalucía?

Habla muy bien el español
abla mwee byen el espanyol
Your Spanish is very good

Likes and dislikes

I like . . .
Me gusta/gustan . . .
me goosta/goostan . . .

I don't like . . .
No me gusta/gustan . . .
no me goosta/goostan . . .

I like it
Me gusta
me goosta

I don't like it
No me gusta
no me goosta

I like football
Me gusta el fútbol
me goosta el footbol

I don't like beer
No me gusta la cerveza
no me goosta la therbetha

I like swimming
Me gusta nadar
me goosta nadar

I don't like playing tennis
No me gusta jugar al tenis
no me goosta hhoogar al tenis

I like strawberries
Me gustan las fresas
me goostan las fresas

Do you like it?
¿Le gusta?
le goosta

Do you like ice cream?
¿Le gusta el helado?
le goosta el elado

Talking to a child

What's your name?
¿Cómo te llamas?
komo te lyamas

How old are you?
¿Cuántos años tienes?
kwantos anyos tyenes

Do you have any brothers
  and sisters?
¿Tienes hermanos?
tyenes ermanos

Invitations and replies

Would you like a drink?
¿Quiere tomar algo?
kyere tomar algo

I'd love to
Me encantaría
me enkantaree-a

Yes, please
Sí, por favor
see por fabor

That's very kind of you
Es usted muy amable
es oosteth mwee amable

No, thank you
No, gracias
no grathyas

Please leave me alone
Por favor, déjeme en paz
por fabor dehheme en path

You may hear

¿Quiere(s) . . . ?
kyere(s) . . .
Would you like . . . ?

¿Quiere(s) tomar algo?
kyere(s) tomar algo
Would you like a drink?

¿Quiere(s) comer algo?
kyere(s) komer algo
Would you like something
to eat?

¿Qué hace(s) esta noche?
ke athe(s) esta noche
What are you doing tonight?

¿Quiere(s) venir a . . . ?
kyere(s) beneer a . . .
Would you like to come
to . . . ?

¿Quiere(s) ir a bailar?
kyere(s) eer a biylar
Would you like to go dancing?

¿Quiere(s) venir al cine?
kyere(s) beneer al theene
Would you like to come to
the cinema?

¿Quiere(s) venir a cenar?
kyere(s) benir a thenar
Would you like to come to
dinner?

¿A qué hora nos encontramos?
a ke ora nos enkontramos
What time shall we meet?

¿Dónde nos encontramos?
donde nos enkontramos
Where shall we meet?

¿Tiene(s) fuego?
tyene(s) fwego
Have you got a light?

Good wishes and exclamations

Congratulations!
¡Enhorabuena!
enorabwena

Happy Birthday!
¡Feliz cumpleaños!
feleeth koomple-anyos

Merry Christmas!
¡Feliz Navidad!
feleeth nabeedad

Happy New Year!
¡Feliz Año Nuevo!
feleeth anyo nwebo

Good luck!
¡Buena suerte!
bwena swerte

Enjoy yourself!
¡Que se divierta!
ke se deebyerta

Have a good journey!
¡Buen viaje!
bwen byahhe

Cheers!
¡Salud!
salood

Enjoy your meal!
¡Que aproveche!
ke aprobeche

Bless you! (*when someone sneezes*)
¡Jesús!
hhesoos

If only!/I wish I could!
¡Ojalá!
ohhala

What a pity!
¡Qué pena!/¡Qué lástima!
ke pena/ke lasteema

Talking about the weather

The weather's very good
Hace muy buen tiempo
athe mwee bwen tyempo

The weather's very bad
Hace muy mal tiempo
athe mwee mal tyempo

It's a wonderful day
Hace un día estupendo
athe oon dee-a estoopendo

It's hot, (isn't it?)
Hace calor, (¿no?)
athe kalor (no)

It's cold, (isn't it?)
Hace frío, (¿no?)
athe free-o (no)

Phew, it's hot!
¡Qué calor!
ke kalor

I (don't) like the heat
(No) me gusta el calor
(no) me goosta el kalor

It's very windy
Hace mucho viento
athe moocho byento

Is it going to rain?
¿Va a llover?
ba a lyober

ARRIVING IN THE COUNTRY

● Whether you arrive by air, road or sea, the formalities (passport control and Customs) are quite straightforward; the only document you need is a valid passport.

● You will probably not need to say anything in Spanish unless you are asked the purpose of your visit, or have something to declare at Customs. If you need to say what you have to declare (rather than just showing it), look up the words you need in the Dictionary. EC duty-free allowances apply – you can get a leaflet with the details at your point of departure.

You may see

Aduana	Customs
Artículos que declarar	Goods to declare
Bienvenido	Welcome
CE	EC
Control de pasaportes	Passport control
Nada que declarar	Nothing to declare
Otros pasaportes	Other passports

You may want to say

I am here on holiday
Estoy aquí de vacaciones
estoy akee de bakathyones

I am here on business
Estoy aquí de negocios
estoy akee de negothyos

It's a joint passport
Es un pasaporte familiar
es oon pasaporte fameelyar

I have something to declare
Tengo algo que declarar
tengo algo ke deklarar

I have this
Tengo esto
tengo esto

I have two bottles of whisky
Tengo dos botellas de whisky
tengo dos botelyas de weeskee

I have two cartons of
cigarettes
**Tengo dos cartones de
cigarrillos**
*tengo dos kartones de
theegarreelyos*

I have a receipt (for this)
Tengo un recibo (para esto)
tengo oon retheebo (para esto)

You may hear

Su pasaporte, por favor
soo pasaporte por fabor
Your passport, please

Sus documentos, por favor
soos dokoomentos por fabor
Your documents, please

**¿Cuál es el objeto de su
visita?**
*kwal es el obhheto de soo
beeseeta*
What is the purpose of your
visit?

**¿Está usted de vacaciones o
de negocios?**
*esta oosteth de bakathyones o
de negothyos*
Are you here on holiday or
business?

**¿Cuánto tiempo va a
quedarse en España?**
*kwanto tyempo ba a kedarse
en espanya*
How long are you going to
stay in Spain?

**Por favor, abra esta bolsa/
maleta**
*por fabor abra esta bolsa/
maleta*
Please open this bag/
suitcase

Por favor, abra el maletero
por fabor abra el maletero
Please open the boot

Tenemos que registrar el coche
tenemos ke rehheestrar el koche
We have to search the car

¿Tiene usted más equipaje?
tiene oosteth mas ekeepahhe
Do you have any other
luggage?

**Hay que pagar impuestos
sobre esto**
iy ke pagar eempwestos sobre esto
There is duty to pay on this

**Venga usted conmigo/con
nosotros**
*benga oosteth konmeego/kon
nosotros*
Come with me/with us

DIRECTIONS

● Some general maps are available from the Spanish National Tourist Office (address, page 198). A wide range of road maps and some more specialised maps, e.g. for walkers, are obtainable from bookshops and specialist mapsellers.

In Spain, the Spanish *Instituto Geográfico Nacional* publishes numerous maps at different scales, but they are not always easy to obtain and they can be unreliable. Local tourist offices can provide town plans and regional maps.

● When you need to ask the way somewhere, the easiest thing is just to name the place you're looking for and add 'please', e.g. **¿Granada, por favor?** Or you can start with 'where is . . . ?': **¿dónde está . . .?**

● The question 'Where is the nearest (petrol station/bank)?' is rather complicated in Spanish, so instead just ask 'Is there (a petrol station/bank) around here?': **¿Hay (una gasolinera/un banco) por aquí?**

● If you're looking for a particular address, have it written down. In Spain, addresses are written with the street name first and the number afterwards, e.g. **Calle de Cervantes, 73**. An address for a flat may also have the number of the floor and of the flat, e.g. **Calle de Cervantes, 73, 2°–4 (2°** means 2nd, i.e. 2nd floor, and **4** is the number of the flat).

● When you're being given directions, listen out for the important bits (such as whether to turn left or right), and try to repeat each bit to make sure you've understood it correctly. If you can't understand anything, ask the person to say it again more slowly, prompting with **Otra vez** ('Again') if necessary.

You may see

Al/A la . . .	To the . . .
Alcázar	Castle, fortress
Avenida (Avinguda in Catalan)	Avenue
Ayuntamiento	Town hall
Calle (Carrer in Catalan)	Street
Calle peatonal	Pedestrian precinct
Castillo	Castle
Catedral	Cathedral
Glorieta	Square
Iglesia	Church
Museo	Museum
Palacio	Palace
Paseo (Passeig in Catalan)	Avenue
Paso de peatones	Pedestrian crossing
Paso subterráneo	Subway
Peatón/Peatones	Pedestrians
Plaza (Plaça in Catalan)	Square
Rua (Galician)	Street
Zona peatonal	Pedestrian precinct

You may want to say

Excuse me (please)
Perdone (por favor)
perdone (por fabor)

More slowly
Más despacio
mas despathyo

Pardon?
¿Cómo?
komo

Again
Otra vez
otra beth

Can you repeat that, please?
¿Puede repetirlo, por favor?
pwede repeteerlo por fabor

I am lost
Me he perdido
me he perdeedo

Where are we?
¿Dónde estamos?
donde estamos

Where does this road/street
lead to?
**¿Adónde lleva esta carretera/
calle?**
*adonde lyeba esta karretera/
kalye*

Is this the right way to
Zaragoza?
**¿Es éste el camino de
Zaragoza?**
*es este el kameeno de
tharagotha*

Can you show me on the map?
¿Puede enseñarme en el mapa?
pwede ensenyarme en el mapa

The station, please?
¿La estación, por favor?
la estathyon por fabor

The (town) centre, please?
**¿El centro (de la ciudad), por
favor?**
*el thentro (de la thyoodad) por
fabor*

The road to Barcelona,
please?
**¿La carretera de Barcelona,
por favor?**
*la karretera de barthelona por
fabor*

How do I/we get to . . . ?
¿Cómo se llega a . . . ?
komo se lyega a . . .

How do I/we get to Granada?
¿Cómo se llega a Granada?
komo se lyega a granada

How do I/we get to the airport?
¿Cómo se llega al aeropuerto?
komo se lyega al iyropwerto

How do I/we get to the beach?
¿Cómo se llega a la playa?
komo se lyega a la pliya

Where is . . . ?
¿Dónde está . . . ?
donde esta . . .

Where are . . . ?
¿Dónde están . . . ?
donde estan . . .

Where is this? (*if you've got
an address written down*)
¿Dónde está esto?
donde esta esto

Where is the tourist office?
**¿Dónde está la oficina de
turismo?**
*donde esta la ofeetheena de
tooreezmo*

Where is the Post Office?
¿Dónde está Correos?
donde esta korre-os

Where is this office/room?
**¿Dónde está este despacho/
habitación?**
*donde esta este despacho/
abeetathyon*

Where are the toilets?
¿Dónde están los servicios?
donde estan los serbeethyos

Is it far?
¿Está lejos?
esta lehhos

Is the airport far away?
¿Está lejos el aeropuerto?
esta lehhos el iyropwerto

How many kilometres
away?
¿A cuántos kilómetros?
a kwantos keelometros

How long does it take (on
foot/by car)?
**¿Cuánto se tarda (andando/
en coche)?**
*kwanto se tarda (andando/en
koche)*

Is there a bus/train?
¿Hay un autobús/un tren?
iy oon owtoboos/oon tren

Can I/we get there on foot?
¿Se puede ir andando?
se pwede eer andando

Can I/we get there by car?
¿Se puede ir en coche?
se pwede eer en koche

Is there . . . ?
¿Hay . . . ?
iy . . .

Is there a bank around
here?
¿Hay un banco por aquí?
iy oon banko por akee

Is there a supermarket in
the village?
**¿Hay un supermercado en el
pueblo?**
*iy oon soopermerkado en el
pweblo*

You may hear

Se ha equivocado usted
se a ekeebokado oosteth
You've made a mistake

Estamos aquí
estamos akee
We are here

Aquí
akee
Here

Allí, Allá, Ahí
alyee, alya, a-ee
There

Por aquí
por akee
This way

Por allí/allá/ahí
por alyee/alya/a-ee
That way, Along there

A la derecha
a la derecha
(To the) right

A la izquierda
a la eethkyerda
(To the) left

Recto, Todo recto, Todo derecho
rekto, todo rekto, todo derecho
Straight on

La primera (calle)
la preemera (kalye)
The first (street/turning)

La segunda (calle)
la segoonda (kalye)
The second (street/turning)

La tercera (calle)
la terthera (kalye)
The third (street/turning)

A mano derecha
a mano derecha
On the right-hand side

A mano izquierda
a mano eethkyerda
On the left-hand side

Al final de la calle
al feenal de la kalye
At the end of the street

Al otro lado de la plaza
al otro lado de la platha
On the other side of the square

En la esquina
en la eskeena
On the corner

Abajo
abahho
Down/downstairs

Arriba
arreeba
Up/upstairs

Debajo de
debahho de
Under

Encima de
entheema de
Over

Antes del semáforo
antes del semaforo
Before the traffic lights

Después de la catedral
despwes de la katedral
After/Past the cathedral

Enfrente de
enfrente de
Opposite

Delante de
delante de
In front of

Detrás de
detras de
Behind

Al lado de
al lado de
Next to

Cerca de
therka de
Near, Close to

Está en la plaza mayor
esta en la platha miyor
It's in the main square

Al llegar a la Calle de Cervantes
al lyegar a la kalye de therbantes
When you get to the Calle de Cervantes (Cervantes Street)

Hacia la catedral
athya la katedral
Towards the cathedral

Hasta el semáforo
asta el semaforo
As far as the traffic lights

(No) está lejos
(no) esta lehhos
It's (not) far away

Muy lejos, Bastante lejos
mwee lehhos, bastante lehhos
Very far, Quite far

Está cerca
esta therka
It's close by

Muy cerca, Bastante cerca
mwee therka, bastante therka
Very close, Quite close

Está a cinco minutos
esta a theenko meenootos
It's five minutes away

Está a veinte kilómetros
esta a baynte keelometros
It's twenty kilometres away

Tiene que coger el autobús/ tren
tyene ke kohher el owtoboos/ tren
You have to catch the bus/ train

Está en el tercer piso
esta en el terther peeso
It's on the third floor

La primera/segunda puerta
la preemera/segoonda pwerta
The first/second door

Coja usted el ascensor
kohha oosteth el asthensor
Take the lift

You may also hear words like these, sometimes with the word **usted** (*oosteth*), the word for 'you':

Vaya . . .
biya . . .
Go . . .

Siga . . .
seega . . .
Carry on/Go on . . .

Baje . . .
bahhe . . .
Go down . . .

Suba . . .
sooba . . .
Go up . . .

Doble/Gire/Tuerza . . .
doble/hheere/twertha . . .
Turn . . .

Tome/Coja . . .
tome/kohha . . .
Take . . .

Pase por . . .
pase por . . .
Go along/over . . .

Cruce . . .
kroothe . . .
Cross . . .

ROAD TRAVEL

● Consult the motoring organisations or Spanish National Tourist Office for information on driving in Spain. An international driving licence and Green Card insurance may not be technically necessary, but check their advice. A bail bond is advisable, and you must carry your vehicle registration document.

● You drive on the right in Spain. Traffic from the right has priority on roads, even on roundabouts. Seatbelts are compulsory outside towns. Crash helmets are compulsory for both drivers and passengers of motorbikes and scooters.

● Speed limits are generally:
60 km per hour in towns, 90 or 100 km per hour on ordinary roads, and 120 km per hour on motorways.

● Main roads are labelled as follows:

A **(Autopista)** Motorway
N **(Carretera Nacional)** National highway (those numbered with Roman numerals, e.g. N-IV, start from Madrid)
C **(Carretera Comarcal)** Provincial or secondary road

● You have to pay a toll **(peaje)** on motorways. The road surface of un-numbered roads and some C roads, particularly in rural areas, can be very variable, and mountain roads can be dangerous in winter. Spain is a mountainous country so roads are often twisty – journeys can often take longer than you'd think from looking at a map.

● The main grades of petrol are **super** (4-star) and **normal** (2-star). Unleaded petrol **(gasolina sin plomo)** is becoming more widely available. Diesel **(gasóleo** or **gas-oil)** is easily obtainable.

Petrol stations are not generally self-service, so you'll need a few words of Spanish. Outside towns, petrol stations can be few and far between, so fill up whenever possible. Few petrol stations accept credit cards.

● Parking in towns and cities can be difficult because of traffic congestion. Some car parks have an attendant, and there are meters and underground car parks in some cities.

In a Blue Zone (**Zona Azul**) parking time is limited and you must display a parking disc or ticket to show the time you parked – they are available from hotels, town halls and tobacconists.

If you park illegally you are likely to be fined and you may also have your car towed away by the municipal **grúa** (tow truck). If you do have it towed away, contact the municipal police (**Policía Municipal**) to find out where to collect it.

● You can arrange car hire in Britain with the large international firms. They also have offices at airports and elsewhere in Spain (and there will often be someone who speaks English). There are local companies too in most towns and cities – look for the sign **Alquiler de coches**. You may be able to hire mopeds and bicycles, especially in tourist areas.

● In case of breakdown, there are emergency telephones on motorways and some other main roads.

If you have to tell a mechanic what's wrong with your vehicle, the easiest way is to indicate the part affected and say 'this isn't working': **esto no funciona**. Otherwise, look up the word for the appropriate part (see page 39).

You may see

Aduana	Customs
Alquiler de coches	Car hire
Alto	Stop
Aparcamiento (vigilado/ subterráneo)	(Supervised/underground) car park
Atención	Caution
Atención al tren	Beware of the train
Autopista (de peaje)	(Toll) motorway
Calzada deteriorada	Uneven road surface
Calle peatonal	Pedestrian precinct
Callejón sin salida	Cul-de-sac, no through road
Camino cerrado	Road closed
Cañada	Cattle track
Carril de bicicletas	Bicycle path
Ceda el paso	Give way
Centro urbano/ciudad	Town/city centre
Circule por la derecha	Keep right
Cruce peligroso	Dangerous crossroads
Cuidado	Take care
Curva peligrosa	Dangerous bend
Dejen paso libre/Dejar libre la salida	Allow free access
Despacio	Slow
Desviación/Desvío	Deviation
Dirección prohibida	No entry
Dirección única	One-way street
Encender las luces (en túnel)	Use headlights (in tunnel)
Escalón lateral	Ramp
Escuela	School
Estación de servicio	Service/petrol station
Estacionamiento (prohibido/ reglamentado)	Parking (prohibited/ limited)
Final de autopista	End of motorway
Obras	Road works

31

Ojo al tren	Beware of the train
Paso a nivel	Level crossing
Paso de ganado	Cattle crossing
Paso de peatones	Pedestrian crossing
Peaje	Toll
Peatones	Pedestrians
Peligro	Danger
Prioridad a la derecha	Priority to the right
Prohibido adelantar	No overtaking
Prohibido aparcar/detenerse	No parking
Prohibido el paso	No entry
Puerto cerrado	Mountain pass closed
Puesto de socorro	First-aid post
RENFE	Spanish Railways
Salida	Exit
Salida de camiones	Lorry exit
Salida de fábrica	Factory exit
Taller (de reparaciones)	Repair shop
Uso obligatorio cinturón de seguridad	Seatbelt compulsory
Vado permanente	In constant use
Vehículos pesados	Heavy goods vehicles
Velocidad limitada	Speed limit
Viraje peligroso	Dangerous bend
Zona azul	Blue zone
Zona peatonal	Pedestrian precinct

You may want to say

Petrol

Is there a petrol station
around here?
¿Hay una gasolinera por aquí?
iy oona gasoleenera por akee

4-star
Super
sooper

2-star
Normal
normal

Unleaded petrol
Gasolina sin plomo
gasoleena seen plomo

Diesel
Gasóleo/Gas-oil
gasoleo/gasoyl

20 litres of 4-star, please
Veinte litros de super, por favor
baynte leetros de sooper por fabor

1000 pesetas' worth of
unleaded, please
**Mil pesetas de gasolina sin
plomo, por favor**
*meel pesetas de gasoleena seen
plomo por fabor*

Fill it up with 4-star/2-star
Lleno de super/normal
lyeno de sooper/normal

A can of oil/petrol
Una lata de aceite/gasolina
oona lata de athayte/gasoleena

Water, please
Agua, por favor
agwa por fabor

Can you check (the pressure
in) the tyres?
**¿Puede comprobar (la
presión de) los neumáticos?**
*pwede comprobar (la presyon
de) los ne-oomateekos*

Can you change the tyre?
¿Puede cambiar el neumático?
pwede kambyar el ne-oomateeko

Can you clean the windscreen?
¿Puede limpiar el parabrisas?
pwede limpyar el parabreesas

Where is the air, please?
¿Dónde está el aire, por favor?
donde esta el iyre por fabor

How does the car wash work?
**¿Cómo funciona el lavado
automático?**
*komo foonthyona el labado
owtomateeko*

How much is it?
¿Cuánto es?
kwanto es

Parking

Where can I/we park?
¿Dónde se puede aparcar?
donde se pwede aparkar

Can I/we park here?
¿Se puede aparcar aquí?
se pwede aparkar akee

How long can I/we park here?
**¿Cuánto tiempo se puede
 aparcar aquí?**
*kwanto tyempo se pwede
 aparkar akee*

How much is it per hour?
¿Cuánto es por hora?
kwanto es por ora

A parking disc/ticket, please
**Un disco/Una tarjeta de
 aparcamiento, por favor**
*oon deesko/oona tarhheta de
 aparkamyento por fabor*

Hiring a car

(*see* Days, months, dates, *page 182*)

I want to hire a car
Quiero alquilar un coche
kyero alkeelar oon koche

A small car, please
Un coche pequeño, por favor
oon koche pekenyo por fabor

A medium-sized car, please
Un coche mediano, por favor
oon koche medyano por fabor

A large car, please
Un coche grande, por favor
oon koche grande por fabor

An automatic car, please
Un coche automático, por favor
oon koche owtomateeko por fabor

For three days
Por tres días
por tres dee-as

For a week
Por una semana
por oona semana

For two weeks
Por dos semanas
por dos semanas

From . . . to . . .
De/Desde . . . a/hasta . . .
de/dezde . . . a/asta

From Monday to Friday
De lunes a viernes
de loones a byernes

From 10th August to 17th August

Desde el diez de agosto hasta el diecisiete de agosto

dezde el dyeth de agosto asta el dyetheesyete de agosto

How much is it?

¿Cuánto es?

kwanto es

Per day/week

Por día/semana

por dee-a/semana

Per kilometre

Por kilómetro

por keelometro

Is mileage (kilometrage) included?

¿Está incluido el kilometraje?

esta eenkloo-eedo el keelometrahhe

Is petrol included?

¿Está incluida la gasolina?

esta eenkloo-eeda la gasoleena

Is insurance included?

¿Está incluido el seguro?

esta eenkloo-eedo el segooro

Comprehensive insurance cover

El seguro a todo riesgo

el segooro a todo ree-esgo

My husband/wife is driving too

Mi marido/mujer conduce también

mee mareedo/moohher kondoothe tambyen

Do you take credit cards?

¿Aceptan tarjetas de crédito?

atheptan tarhhetas de kredeeto

Do you take traveller's cheques?

¿Aceptan cheques de viaje?

atheptan chekes de byahhe

Can I leave the car in Barcelona?

¿Puedo dejar el coche en Barcelona?

pwedo dehhar el koche en barthelona

Can I leave the car at the airport?

¿Puedo dejar el coche en el aeropuerto?

pwedo dehhar el koche en el iyropwerto

How do the controls work?

¿Cómo funcionan los mandos?

komo foonthyonan los mandos

Breakdowns and repairs

(*see* Car and bicycle parts, *page 39*)

My car has broken down
El coche está estropeado
el koche esta estrope-ado

Is there a garage around here?
¿Hay un garaje por aquí?
iy oon garahhe por akee

Can you telephone a garage?
¿Puede llamar a un garaje?
pwede lyamar a oon garahhe

Can you send a mechanic?
¿Puede mandar un mecánico?
pwede mandar oon mekaneeko

Can you tow me to a garage?
¿Puede remolcarme hasta un garaje?
pwede remolkarme asta oon garahhe

Do you do repairs?
¿Hacen reparaciones?
athen reparathyones

I don't know what's wrong
No sé lo que pasa
no se lo ke pasa

I think . . .
Creo que . . .
kre-o ke . . .

It's the clutch
Es el embrague
es el embrage

It's the radiator
Es el radiador
es el radyador

It's the brakes
Son los frenos
son los frenos

The car won't start
El coche no quiere arrancar
el koche no kyere arrankar

The battery is flat
La batería está descargada
la bateree-a esta deskargada

The engine is overheating
El motor se calienta
el motor se kalyenta

It's losing water/oil
Pierde agua/aceite
pyerde agwa/athayte

It has a puncture
Tiene un pinchazo
tyene oon peenchatho

I don't have any petrol
No tengo gasolina
no tengo gasoleena

The . . . doesn't work
El/La . . . no funciona
el/la . . . no foonthyona

Can you repair it (today)?
¿Puede repararlo (hoy)?
pwede repararlo (oy)

I need a . . .
Necesito un/una . . .
netheseeto oon/oona . . .

When will it be ready?
¿Cuándo estará listo?
kwando estara leesto

Is it serious?
¿Es algo importante?
es algo eemportante

How much will it cost?
¿Cuánto costará?
kwanto kostara

You may hear

Petrol

¿Qué desea?
ke dese-a
What would you like?

La llave, por favor
la lyabe por fabor
The key, please

¿Cuánto quiere?
kwanto kyere
How much do you want?

Parking

No se puede aparcar aquí
no se pwede aparkar akee
You can't park here

Es gratuito
es gratweeto
It's free

Son cien pesetas por hora
son thyen pesetas por ora
It's 100 pesetas an hour

Hay un aparcamiento por ahí
iy oon aparkamyento por a-ee
There's a car park over there

No se paga
no se paga
You don't pay

Hiring a car

¿Qué clase de coche quiere?
ke klase de koche kyere
What kind of car do you want?

¿Por cuánto tiempo?
por kwanto tyempo
For how long?

¿Por cuántos días?
por kwantos dee-as
For how many days?

(El precio) son cinco mil/
treinta mil pesetas
*(el prethyo) son theenko meel/
traynta meel pesetas*
(The price) is 5000/30 000
pesetas

Por día
por dee-a
Per day

Por semana
por semana
Per week

¿Quién conduce?
kyen kondoothe
Who is driving?

Su carné/permiso de
conducir, por favor
*soo karne/permeeso de
kondootheer por fabor*
Your driving licence, please

¿Cuál es su dirección?
kwal es soo deerekthyon
What is your address?

Aquí tiene las llaves
akee tyene las lyabes
Here are the keys

Por favor, devuelva el coche con el depósito lleno
por fabor debwelba el koche kon el deposeeto lyeno
Please return the car with a full tank

Por favor, devuelva el coche antes de las seis
por fabor debwelba el koche antes de las says
Please return the car before six o'clock

Si la oficina está cerrada, puede dejar las llaves en el buzón
*see la ofeetheena esta therrada pwede dehhar las lyabes en el
boothon*
If the office is closed, you can leave the keys in the letterbox

Breakdowns and repairs

¿Qué le pasa?
ke le pasa
What's wrong with it?

¿Puede abrir el capó?
pwede abreer el kapo
Can you open the bonnet?

No tengo los repuestos necesarios
no tengo los repwestos nethesaree-os
I don't have the necessary parts

Tendré que pedir los repuestos
tendre ke pedeer los repwestos
I will have to order the parts

Estará listo para el próximo martes
estara leesto para el proxeemo martes
It will be ready by next Tuesday

Costará diez mil pesetas
kostara dyeth meel pesetas
It will cost 10 000 pesetas

Car and bicycle parts

Accelerator	**El acelerador**	*athelerador*
Air filter	**El filtro de aire**	*feeltro de iyre*
Alternator	**El alternador**	*alternador*
Battery	**La batería**	*bateree-a*
Bonnet	**El capó**	*kapo*
Boot	**El maletero**	*maletero*
Brake cable	**El cable de freno**	*kable de freno*
Brake fluid	**El líquido de frenos**	*leekeedo de frenos*
Brake hose	**La tubería del freno**	*tooberee-a del freno*
Brakes (front/rear)	**Los frenos (delanteros/ traseros)**	*frenos (delanteros/ traseros)*
Carburettor	**El carburador**	*karboorador*
Chain	**La cadena**	*kadena*
Choke	**El stárter**	*starter*
Clutch	**El embrague**	*embrage*
Cooling system	**El sistema de refrigeración**	*seestema de refreehherathyon*

Disc brakes	Los frenos de disco	*frenos de deesko*
Distributor	El distribuidor	*deestreebweedor*
Electrical system	El sistema eléctrico	*seestema elektreeko*
Engine	El motor	*motor*
Exhaust pipe	El tubo de escape	*toobo de eskape*
Fanbelt	La correa de ventilador	*korre-a de benteelador*
Frame	El cuadro	*kwadro*
Front fork	La horquilla delantera	*orkeelya delantera*
Fuel gauge	El indicador de nivel	*eendeekador de neebel*
Fuel pump	La bomba de gasolina	*bomba de gasoleena*
Fuse	El fusible	*fooseeble*
Gearbox	La caja de cambios	*kahha de kambyos*
Gear lever	La palanca de cambio	*palanka de kambyo*
Gears	Las marchas	*marchas*
Handbrake	El freno de mano	*freno de mano*
Handlebars	El manillar	*maneelyar*
Headlights	Los faros	*faros*
Heater	La calefacción	*kalefakthyon*
Horn	La bocina	*botheena*
Ignition	El encendido	*enthendeedo*
Ignition key	La llave de contacto	*lyabe de kontakto*
Indicator	El intermitente	*eentermeetente*
Inner tube	La cámara de aire	*kamara de iyre*
Lights (front/rear)	Las luces (delanteras/ traseras)	*loothes (delanteras/ traseras)*
Lock	La cerradura	*therradoora*
Oil filter	El filtro de aceite	*feeltro de athayte*
Oil gauge	El manómetro de aceite	*manometro de athayte*
Pedal	El pedal	*pedal*
Points	Los contactos	*kontaktos*
Pump	La bomba	*bomba*
Radiator	El radiador	*radyador*

Radiator hose (top/bottom)	El tubo flexible (superior/inferior)	*toobo flexeeble (sooperyor/eenferyor)*
Reversing lights	Las luces de marcha atrás	*loothes de marcha atras*
Rotor arm	El rotor del distribuidor	*rotor del deestreebweedor*
Saddle	El sillín	*seelyeen*
Silencer	El silenciador	*seelenthyador*
Spare wheel	La rueda de recambio	*rweda de rekambyo*
Spark plugs	Las bujías	*boohhee-as*
Speedometer	El velocímetro *or* El cuentakilómetros	*velotheemetro kwentakeelometros*
Spokes	Los radios	*radee-os*
Starter motor	El motor de arranque	*motor de arranke*
Steering	La dirección	*deerekthyon*
Steering wheel	El volante	*bolante*
Transmission (automatic)	La transmisión (automática)	*transmeesyon (owtomateeka)*
Tyre (front/rear)	El neumático (delantero/trasero)	*ne-oomateeko (delantero/trasero)*
Valve	La válvula	*balboola*
Warning light	La lámpara indicadora	*lampara eendeekadora*
Wheel (front/rear)	La rueda (delantera/trasera)	*rweda (delantera/trasera)*
Wheel rim	La llanta	*lyanta*
Window	La ventanilla	*bentaneelya*
Windscreen	El parabrisas	*parabreesas*
Windscreen washer	El limpiaparabrisas	*leempyaparabreesas*
Windscreen wiper	El lavaparabrisas	*labaparabreesas*

TAXIS

● You can hail taxis in the street, or find them at a taxi rank – look for a sign with a white T on a dark blue background. Taxis that are free have the sign **LIBRE**, or in Catalunya you'll see the Catalan word **LLIURE**.

● Taxis have meters, but it's a good idea to ask what the fare will be approximately, especially if you are going some distance. Extras for luggage, airport pick-ups, etc. may not be shown on the meter. A tip of 10% or so is usual.

● Write down clearly the address of your destination if it's at all complicated so that you can show it to the taxi driver. In Spanish, addresses are written with the street name first and the number afterwards, e.g. **Calle de Cervantes, 73**.

You may want to say

(*see also* Directions, *page 22*)

Is there a taxi rank around here?
¿Hay una parada de taxis por aquí?
iy oona parada de taxees por akee

I need a taxi
Necesito un taxi
netheseeto oon taxee

Can you order me a taxi?
¿Puede pedirme un taxi, por favor?
pwede pedeerme oon taxee por fabor

Immediately
Ahora mismo
a-ora meezmo

For tomorrow at nine o'clock
Para mañana a las nueve
para manyana a las nwebe

To go to the airport
Para ir al aeropuerto
para eer al iyropwerto

To the airport, please
Al aeropuerto, por favor
al iyropwerto por fabor

To the station, please
A la estación, por favor
a la estathyon por fabor

To the Hotel Victoria, please
Al Hotel Victoria, por favor
al otel biktoree-a por fabor

To this address, please
A esta dirección, por favor
a esta deerekthyon por fabor

Is it far?
¿Está lejos?
esta lehhos

How much will it cost?
¿Cuánto va a costar?
kwanto ba a kostar

I am in a hurry
Tengo prisa
tengo preesa

Stop here, please
Pare aquí, por favor
pare akee por fabor

Can you wait (a few minutes), please?
¿Puede esperar (unos minutos), por favor?
pwede esperar (oonos meenootos) por fabor

How much is it?
¿Cuánto es?
kwanto es

There is a mistake
Hay un error
iy oon error

On the meter it's 700 pesetas
En el contador son setecientas pesetas
en el kontador son setethyentas pesetas

Keep the change
Quédese con el cambio
kedese kon el kambyo

That's all right
Está bien
esta byen

Can you give me a receipt?
¿Puede darme un recibo?
pwede darme oon retheebo

For 1000 pesetas
Por mil pesetas
por meel pesetas

You may hear

Está a diez kilómetros
esta a dyez keelometros
It's 10 kilometres away

**Costará aproximadamente
dos mil pesetas**
*kostara aproxeemadamente
dos meel pesetas*
It will cost approximately
2000 pesetas

**(Son) mil ochocientas
pesetas**
*(son) meel ochothyentas
pesetas*
(It's) 1800 pesetas

Hay un suplemento
iy oon sooplemento
There is a supplement

Para el equipaje
para el ekeepahhe
For the luggage

Para cada maleta
para kada maleta
For each suitcase

Para el aeropuerto
para el iyropwerto
For the airport

AIR TRAVEL

● Spain has over 30 airports served by international and domestic flights. There are regular shuttle services between Madrid and Barcelona.

● At airports and airlines offices you'll generally find someone who speaks English, but be prepared to say a few things in Spanish.

● Approximate flight times from Madrid to some other main cities:
Barcelona – 55 minutes
Bilbao – 50 minutes
Seville – 50 minutes
Valencia – 45 minutes
Palma de Mallorca – 1 hour
Canary Islands – 2½ hours

● Approximate distances from main airports to city centres:
Madrid – 16 km (10 miles)
Barcelona – 10 km (6 miles)
Bilbao – 9 km (5½ miles)
Malaga – 8 km (5 miles)
Seville – 12 km (7½ miles)
Valencia – 10 km (6 miles)
Palma de Mallorca – 9 km (5½ miles)
Tenerife-Norte – 13 km (8 miles)
Tenerife-Sur – 61 km (37 miles)

You may see

Abróchense los cinturones	Fasten seatbelts
Aduana	Customs
Aeropuerto	Airport
Alquiler de coches	Car hire
Artículos a declarar	Goods to declare
Autobuses (al centro ciudad)	Buses (to the town/city centre)
Cambio	Bureau de change
CE	EC
Control de pasaportes	Passport control
Demora	Delay
Embarcación	Boarding
Entrada	Entrance
Entrega de equipajes	Luggage reclaim
Facturación	Check-in
Hora local	Local time
Huelga	Strike
Información	Information
Llegadas	Arrivals
Nada que declarar	Nothing to declare
No fumar	No smoking
Otros pasaportes	Other passports
Pasajeros	Passengers
Puerta	Gate
Retraso	Delay
Sala de embarque	Departure lounge
Salida (de emergencia)	(Emergency) exit
Salidas	Departures
Servicios	Toilets
Tienda libre de impuestos	Duty-free shop
Vuelo	Flight

You may want to say

(*see also* Numbers, *page 200;* Days, months, dates, *page 182;* Time, *page 185*)

Is there a flight (from Madrid) to Bilbao?
¿Hay algún vuelo (de Madrid) a Bilbao?
iy algoon bwelo (de madreed) a beelbow

Today
Hoy
oy

This morning/afternoon
Esta mañana/tarde
esta manyana/tarde

Tomorrow (morning/afternoon)
Mañana (por la mañana/tarde)
manyana (por la manyana/tarde)

Do you have a timetable of flights to Barcelona?
¿Tiene un horario de vuelos para Barcelona?
tyene oon oraryo de bwelos para barthelona

What time is the first flight to Barcelona?
¿A qué hora sale el primer vuelo para Barcelona?
a ke ora sale el preemer bwelo para barthelona

The next flight
El próximo vuelo
el proxeemo bwelo

The last flight
El último vuelo
el oolteemo bwelo

What time does it arrive (at Barcelona)?
¿A qué hora llega (a Barcelona)?
a ke ora lyega (a barthelona)

A ticket/Two tickets to Seville, please
Un billete/Dos billetes para Sevilla, por favor
oon beelyete/dos beelyetes para sebeelya por fabor

Single
Ida solamente
eeda solamente

Return
Ida y vuelta
eeda ee bwelta

1st class/Business class
En primera clase/En clase preferente
en preemera klase/en klase preferente

47

Economy class
En clase económica
en klase ekonomeeka

Which gate is it?
¿Qué puerta es?
ke pwerta es

For the eleven o'clock flight
Para el vuelo de las once
para el bwelo de las onthe

Is there a delay?
¿Hay alguna demora?
iy algoona demora

I want to change/cancel my reservation
Quiero cambiar/anular mi reserva
kyero kambyar/anoolar mee reserba

Where is the luggage from the flight from London?
¿Dónde está el equipaje del vuelo de Londres?
donde esta el ekeepahhe del bwelo de londres

What is the number of the flight?
¿Cuál es el número del vuelo?
kwal es el noomero del bwelo

My luggage is not here
Mi equipaje no está
mee ekeepahhe no esta

What time do I/we have to check in?
¿A qué hora hay que hacer la facturación?
a ke ora iy ke ather la faktoorathyon

Is there a bus to the centre of town?
¿Hay un autobús al centro de la ciudad?
iy oon owtoboos al thentro de la thyoodad

You may hear

¿Quiere un asiento de ventanilla?
kyere oon asyento de bentaneelya
Would you like a seat by the window?

¿Quiere un asiento al lado del pasillo?
kyere oon asyento al lado del paseelyo
Would you like a seat on the aisle?

¿Fumadores o no fumadores?
foomadores o no foomadores
Smoking or non-smoking?

Embarcación a las . . .
embarkathyon a las . . .
The flight will board at . . . (time)

Puerta número siete
pwerta noomero syete
Gate number seven

Su billete, por favor
soo beelyete por fabor
Your ticket, please

Su pasaporte, por favor
soo pasaporte por fabor
Your passport, please

Su tarjeta de embarque, por favor
soo tarhheta de embarke por fabor
Your boarding card, please

¿Cómo es su equipaje?
komo es soo ekeepahhe
What does your luggage look like?

¿Tiene la etiqueta?
tyene la eteeketa
Do you have the reclaim tag?

Announcements you may hear over the airport public address system

Words to listen for include:

El vuelo	*bwelo*	Flight
Con destino a	*kon desteeno a*	Bound/destined for
Embarcación (inmediata)	*embarkathyon (eenmedyata)*	Boarding (now)
Pasajero(s)	*pasahhero(s)*	Passenger(s)
Puerta	*pwerta*	Gate
Retraso/Demora	*retraso/demora*	Delay
Salida	*saleeda*	Departure
Última llamada	*oolteema lyamada*	Last call

TRAVELLING BY TRAIN

● The Spanish State railway company is **RENFE** (*renfay*), and it has a network of around 13000 km of track. There are RENFE offices in every city where you can get information and book tickets. (You can also get information and tickets in many travel agencies.)

There are also some non-RENFE lines in parts of the country, e.g. the narrow gauge FEVE network in the north.

● There are various types of trains, including:
Talgo, **Intercity**, **Electrotrén** and **TER** – fast, inter-city trains
Rápido – express, stopping at main stations
Expreso – long distance night trains
And there are several types of more local, slow, stopping trains
– **automotor**, **ómnibus**, **tranvía**, etc. You'll see these listed on timetable boards, but you don't need to name them when buying tickets.

● There are also some luxury excursion trains, including the **Al-Andalus Expreso**, which tours Andalucía, and the **Transcantábrico**, which travels through northern Spain.

● On some long-distance routes there is an **Auto-expreso** service which allows you to take your car on the train. Prices vary according to the length of the car. There is also a **Motoexpreso** service for motorbikes.

● You can take bicycles on trains, but only where there's a luggage van.

● Rail travel is relatively cheap, though fares vary from one type of train to another (faster ones generally cost more), according to the date of travel, and the type of passenger. Children under four travel free, and for half-fare from ages four to twelve. Fares are cheaper on **Días Azules** (Blue Days), and other discounts include:

Tarjeta Turística (Tourist Card) – available only to visitors to Spain (and obtainable in the UK); gives unlimited travel over a period (8, 15 or 22 days)

Tarjeta Joven (Youth Card) – available to people under 26; entitles the holder to reduced fares

(Information about other European railcards is obtainable from British Rail.)

● It is a good idea to buy tickets in advance for long-distance trains. If you do, you also have to book a seat, sleeper or couchette on a specific train.

● Don't rely too heavily on printed timetables or information boards – if you ask, you may find out about different connecting trains, and you can make sure you're getting on the correct train (there is often no indication on the platform of where the next train is going).

● Work out in advance what you're going to ask for (1st or 2nd class, single or return, adult or child tickets, particular trains, reservations, etc.). If you ask for just 'a ticket' (**un billete**), it'll be assumed that you want a single unless you specify 'return' (**ida y vuelta**).

You may see

Andén/A los andenes	Platform/To the platforms
Auto-expreso	Car-train
Billetes	Tickets
Cantina	Buffet
Coche-cama	Sleeping-car
Consigna (de equipajes)	Left luggage
Demora	Delay
Destino	Destination
Diario	Daily
Días azules	Cheap travel days
Días laborables	Mondays to Saturdays
Domingos y festivos	Sundays and holidays
Entrada	Entrance
Horarios de trenes	Train timetables
Huelga	Strike
Jefe de estación	Station-master
Literas	Couchettes
Llegadas	Arrivals
Multa por uso indebido	Penalty for misuse
Objetos perdidos	Lost property
Procedencia	Where from
Prohibido asomarse (a la ventana)	Do not lean out (of the window)
RENFE (Red Nacional de Ferrocarriles Españoles)	Spanish Railways
Reservas	Reservations
Retraso	Delay
Sala de espera	Waiting room
Salida	Exit; departure
Servicios	Toilets
Taquilla	Ticket office
Trenes de cercanías	Suburban trains
Trenes de largo recorrido	Main line trains
Venta anticipada	Advance booking
Venta inmediata	Tickets for immediate use

You may want to say

Information

(*see* Time, *page 185*)

Is there a train to Malaga?
¿Hay un tren para Málaga?
iy oon tren para malaga

Do you have a timetable of trains to Algeciras?
¿Tiene un horario de trenes para Algeciras?
tyene oon oraryo de trenes para alhhetheeras

What time . . . ?
¿A qué hora . . . ?
a ke ora . . .

What time is the train to Ronda?
¿A qué hora sale el tren para Ronda?
a ke ora sale el tren para ronda

What time is the first train to Vigo?
¿A qué hora sale el primer tren para Vigo?
a ke ora sale el preemer tren para beego

The next train
El próximo tren
el proxeemo tren

The last train
El último tren
el oolteemo tren

What time does it arrive (at Vigo)?
¿A qué hora llega (a Vigo)?
a ke ora lyega (a beego)

What time does the train from Irun arrive?
¿A qué hora llega el tren de Irún?
a ke ora lyega el tren de eeroon

The train to Valencia, please?
¿El tren para Valencia, por favor?
el tren para balenthya por fabor

Which platform does the train to Valencia leave from?
¿De qué andén sale el tren para Valencia?
de ke anden sale el tren para balenthya

Does this train go to Tarragona?
¿Este tren va a Tarragona?
este tren ba a tarragona

Do I/we have to change trains?
¿Hay que cambiar de tren?
iy ke kambyar de tren

Where?
¿Dónde?
donde

Tickets

(*see* Time, *page 185;* Numbers, *page 200*)

One/two to Granada, please
Uno/dos para Granada, por favor
oono/dos para granada por fabor

One ticket/Two tickets to
Cordoba, please
**Un billete/Dos billetes para
Córdoba, por favor**
*oon beelyete/dos beelyetes para
kordoba por fabor*

Single
Ida solamente
eeda solamente

Return
Ida y vuelta
eeda ee bwelta

For one adult/two adults
Para un adulto/dos adultos
para oon adoolto/dos adooltos

(And) one child/two
children
(Y) un niño/dos niños
(ee) oon neenyo/dos neenyos

First/second class
En primera/segunda clase
en preemera/segoonda klase

For the 10.00 train to San Sebastian
Para el tren de las diez para San Sebastián
para el tren de las dyeth para san sebastyan

For the Talgo/Ter to Valencia
Para el Talgo/Ter para Valencia
para el talgo/ter para balenthya

I want to reserve a seat/two seats
Quiero reservar un asiento/ dos asientos
kyero reserbar oon asyento/dos asyentos

I want to reserve a sleeper
Quiero reservar una cama
kyero reserbar oona kama

I want to reserve a couchette
Quiero reservar una litera
kyero reserbar oona leetera

I want to book tickets on the car-train to Madrid
Quiero reservar billetes en el auto-expreso para Madrid
kyero reserbar beelyetes en el owto expreso para madreed

For the car and two passengers
Para el coche y dos pasajeros
para el koche ee dos pasahheros

The car is a Seat Ibiza
El coche es un Seat Ibiza
el koche es un se-at eebeetha

Can I take my bicycle on the train?
¿Puedo llevar mi bicicleta en el tren?
pwedo lyebar mee beetheekleta en el tren

55

How much is it?
¿Cuánto es?
kwanto es

Is there a supplement?
¿Hay algún suplemento?
iy algoon sooplemento

Left luggage

Can I leave this?
¿Puedo dejar esto?
pwedo dehhar esto

Until three o'clock
Hasta la tres
asta la tres

Can I leave these two suitcases?
¿Puedo dejar estas dos maletas?
pwedo dehhar estas dos maletas

What time do you close?
¿A qué hora cierran?
a ke ora thyerran

On the train

I have reserved a seat
He reservado un asiento
e reserbado oon asyento

I have reserved a sleeper/
couchette
He reservado una cama/litera
e reserbado oona kama/leetera

Is this seat taken?
¿Está ocupado este asiento?
esta okoopado este asyento

Do you mind if I open the
window?
¿Le importa si abro la ventana?
le eemporta see abro la bentana

Where is the restaurant car?
¿Dónde está el coche-restaurante?
donde esta el koche restowrante

Where is the sleeping-car?
¿Dónde está el coche-cama?
donde esta el koche kama

Excuse me, may I get by?
Perdone, ¿puedo pasar?
perdone pwedo pasar

Do you mind if I smoke?
¿Le importa si fumo?
le eemporta see foomo

Where are we?
¿Dónde estamos?
donde estamos

Are we at Ronda?
¿Estamos en Ronda?
estamos en ronda

How long does the train
stop here?
**¿Cuánto tiempo para el
tren aquí?**
*kwanto tyempo para el
ten akee*

Can you tell me when we
get to Aranjuez?
**¿Puede avisarme cuando
lleguemos a Aranjuez?**
*pwede abeesarme kwando
lyegemos a aranhhweth*

56

You may hear

Information

(*see* Time, *page 185*)

Sale a las diez y media
sale a las dyeth ee medya
It leaves at half past ten

Llega a las cuatro menos diez
lyega a las kwatro menos dyeth
It arrives at ten to four

Hay que cambiar de tren en Bobadilla
iy ke kambyar de tren en bobadeelya
You have to change trains at Bobadilla

Es el andén número cuatro
es el anden noomero kwatro
It's platform number four

Tickets

(*see* Time, *page 185;* Numbers, *page 200*)

¿Para cuándo quiere el billete?
para kwando kyere el beelyete
When do you want the ticket for?

¿Cuándo quiere viajar?
kwando kyere byahhar
When do you want to travel?

¿Ida solamente o ida y vuelta?
eeda solamente o eeda ee bwelta
Single or return?

¿Cuándo quiere volver?
kwando kyere bolber
When do you want to return?

¿Fumador o no fumador?
foomador o no foomador
Smoking or non-smoking?

Sólo hay primera clase
solo iy preemera klase
There's only first class

(Son) seiscientas cincuenta pesetas
(son) saysthyentas theenkwenta pesetas
(It's) 650 pesetas

Hay un suplemento de mil doscientas pesetas
iy oon sooplemento de meel dosthyentas pesetas
There is a supplement of 1200 pesetas

57

BUSES AND COACHES

● As well as town and city bus services, there are many buses between towns and villages. In most cases you pay the driver as you get on, though tickets for some long-distance services can be bought at bus station ticket offices.

● If you intend to use the buses a lot in a town or city, you can buy **un bonobús**, a multiple-journey ticket, which you can buy at newspaper stands or bus company kiosks and offices. There is usually one fixed fare in towns and cities. Children under four travel free. There are no half-fares.

You may see

Autocar	Coach
Coche de línea	Long-distance coach
Entrada	Entrance
Entrada por la puerta delantera	Enter by the front door
Estación de autobuses	Bus station
Lleve el importe preparado	Have the correct money ready
No fumar	No smoking
No hablar con el conductor	Do not talk to the driver
Parada (de autobús)	Bus stop
Parada discrecional	Request stop
Salida por la puerta central	Exit by the centre door
Salida (de emergencia)	(Emergency) exit

You may want to say

Information

(for sightseeing bus tours, see Sightseeing, *page 134)*

Where is the bus stop?
¿Dónde está la parada del autobús?
donde esta la parada del owtoboos

Where is the bus station?
¿Dónde está la estación de autobuses?
donde esta la estathyon de owtobooses

Is there a bus to the beach?
¿Hay un autobús para la playa?
iy oon owtoboos para la pliya

What number is the bus to the station?
¿Qué número es el autobús para la estación?
ke noomero es el owtoboos para la estathyon

Do they go often?
¿Salen con frecuencia?
salen kon frekwenthya

What time is the bus to Marbella?
¿A qué hora sale el autobús para Marbella?
a ke ora sale el owtoboos para marbelya

What time is the first bus to Cuenca?
¿A qué hora sale el primer autobús para Cuenca?
a ke ora sale el preemer owtoboos para kwenka

The next bus
El próximo autobús
el proxeemo owtoboos

The last bus
El último autobús
el oolteemo owtoboos

What time does it arrive?
¿A qué hora llega?
a ke ora lyega

Where does the bus to the town centre leave from?
¿De dónde sale el autobús para el centro de la ciudad?
de donde sale el owtoboos para el thentro de la thyoodad

Does the bus to the airport leave from here?
¿El autobús para el aeropuerto sale de aquí?
el owtoboos para el iyropwerto sale de akee

Does this bus go to Jerez?
¿Este autobús va a Jerez?
este owtoboos ba a hhereth

I want to get off at the Prado Museum
Quiero bajar en el museo del Prado
kyero bahhar en el moose-o del prado

Can you tell me where to get off?
¿Puede avisarme dónde bajar?
pwede abeesarme donde bahhar

Is this the right stop for the cathedral?
¿Es ésta la parada para la catedral?
es esta la parada para la katedral

The next stop, please
La próxima parada, por favor
la proxeema parada por fabor

Can you open the door, please?
¿Puede abrir la puerta, por favor?
pwede abreer la pwerta por fabor

Excuse me, may I get by?
Perdone, ¿puedo pasar?
perdone pwedo pasar

Tickets

One/two to the centre, please
Uno/dos para el centro, por favor
oono/dos para el thentro por fabor

Where can I buy a multiple ticket?
¿Dónde puedo comprar un bonobús?
donde pwedo comprar oon bonoboos

A multiple ticket, please
Un bonobús, por favor
oon bonoboos por fabor

How much is it?
¿Cuánto es?
kwanto es

You may hear

El autobús para el centro sale de esa parada, de ahí
el owtoboos para el thentro sale de esa parada de a-ee
The bus to the centre leaves from that stop there

El cincuenta y siete va a la estación
el theenkwenta ee syete ba a la estathyon
The 57 goes to the station

Salen cada diez minutos
salen kada dyeth meenootos
They go every 10 minutes

Sale a las diez y media
sale a las dyeth ee medya
It leaves at half past ten

Llega a las tres y veinte
lyega a las tres ee baynte
It arrives at twenty past three

Puede comprar un bonobús en un quiosco
pwede comprar oon bonoboos en oon kyosko
You can buy a multiple ticket at a newspaper stand

Se paga al conductor
se paga al kondooktor
You pay the driver

¿Baja usted aquí?
bahha oosteth akee
Are you getting off here?

Tiene que bajar en la próxima parada
tyene ke bahhar en la proxeema parada
You have to get off at the next stop

Tenía que bajar (una parada) antes
tenee-a ke bahhar (oona parada) antes
You should have got off (one stop) before

UNDERGROUND TRAVEL

● The underground is called **El metro**, and there are systems in Madrid, Barcelona and Valencia. There is a fixed fare for any distance so you only need to say how many tickets you want. You can buy a ticket valid for ten journeys at any **metro** ticket office.

● Children under four travel free. There are no half-fares.

You may see

Entrada	Entrance
Línea 1	Line 1
Metro	Underground
No fumar	No smoking
Salida (de emergencia)	(Emergency) exit

You may want to say

Is there an underground station around here?
¿Hay una estación del metro por aquí?
iy oona estathyon del metro por akee

Do you have a map of the underground?
¿Tiene un plano del metro?
tyene oon plano del metro

One/Two, please
Uno/Dos, por favor
oono/dos por fabor

A ticket for ten journeys, please
Un billete para diez viajes, por favor
oon beelyete para dyeth byahhes por fabor

Which line is it for Atocha station?
¿Qué línea es para la estación de Atocha?
ke leene-a es para la estathyon de atocha

Which stop is it for the Sagrada Familia?
¿Qué parada es para la Sagrada Familia?
ke parada es para la sagrada fameelya

Does this train go to Moncloa?
¿Este metro va a Moncloa?
este metro ba a monklo-a

Where are we?
¿Dónde estamos?
donde estamos

Is this the stop for the Retiro Park?
¿Es ésta la parada para el Parque del Retiro?
es esta la parada para el parke del reteero

You may hear

Es la línea número dos
es la leene-a noomero dos
It's line number two

Es la próxima parada
es la proxeema parada
It's the next stop

Tenía que haber bajado (una parada) antes
tenee-a ke aber bahhado (oona parada) antes
You should have got off (one stop) before

BOATS AND FERRIES

● There are long-distance ferry and some hovercraft services between mainland Spain and the Balearic Islands, the Canary Islands and North Africa. There are also inter-island ferry services.

You may see

Aerodeslizador	Hovercraft
Barcos	Boats
Bote salvavidas	Lifeboat
Camarotes	Cabins
Embarcadero	Pier
Ferry	Car ferry
Hidroplano	Hydrofoil
Muelle	Quay
Paseos por la bahía	Trips round the bay
Puerto	Port, harbour
Salvavidas	Lifebelt
Transbordador	Ferry

You may want to say

Information

(*see* Time, page 185)

Is there a boat to Ibiza (today)?
¿Hay un barco para Ibiza (hoy)?
iy oon barko para eebeetha (oy)

Is there a car ferry to Menorca?
¿Hay un ferry para Menorca?
iy oon ferree para menorka

Are there any boat trips?
¿Hay algunas excursiones en barco?
iy algoonas exkoorsyones en barko

What time is the boat to Fuerteventura?
¿A qué hora sale el barco para Fuerteventura?
a ke ora sale el barko para fwertebentoora

What time is the first boat?
¿A qué hora sale el primer barco?
a ke ora sale el preemer barko

The next boat
El próximo barco
el proxeemo barko

The last boat
El último barco
el oolteemo barko

What time does it arrive?
¿A qué hora llega?
a ke ora lyega

What time does it return?
¿A qué hora vuelve?
a ke ora bwelbe

How long does the crossing take?
¿Cuánto dura la travesía?
kwanto doora la trabesee-a

Where does the boat to Mahón leave from?
¿De dónde sale el barco para Mahón?
de donde sale el barko para ma-on

Where can I buy tickets?
¿Dónde puedo comprar los billetes?
donde pwedo comprar los beelyetes

What is the sea like today?
¿Cómo está el mar hoy?
komo esta el mar oy

Tickets

(*see* Numbers, *page 200*)

Four tickets to Formentera, please
Cuatro billetes para Formentera, por favor
kwatro beelyetes para formentera por fabor

Two adults and two children
Dos adultos y dos niños
dos adooltos ee dos neenyos

Single
Ida solamente
eeda solamente

Return
Ida y vuelta
eeda ee bwelta

I want to book tickets for the ferry to Mahón
Quiero reservar billetes para el ferry para Mahón
kyero reserbar beelyetes para el ferree para ma-on

For a car and two passengers
Para un coche y dos pasajeros
para oon koche ee dos pasahheros

I want to book a cabin
Quiero reservar un camarote
kyero reserbar oon kamarote

For one person
Para una persona
para oona persona

For two people
Para dos personas
para dos personas

How much is it?
¿Cuánto es?
kwanto es

On board

I have reserved a cabin
He reservado un camarote
e reserbado oon kamarote

I have reserved two berths
He reservado dos literas
e reserbado dos leeteras

Where are the cabins?
¿Dónde están los camarotes?
donde estan los kamarotes

Where is cabin number 20?
¿Dónde está el camarote número veinte?
donde esta el kamarote noomero baynte

Can I/we go out on deck?
¿Se puede salir a cubierta?
se pwede saleer a koobyerta

You may hear

Hay barcos los martes y los viernes
iy barkos los martes ee los byernes
There are boats on Tuesdays and Fridays

El barco para Fuerteventura sale a las nueve
el barko para fwertebentoora sale a las nwebe
The boat to Fuerteventura leaves at nine o'clock

Vuelve a las cuatro y media
bwelbe a las kwatro ee medya
It returns at half past four

El barco para Mahón sale del embarcadero número dos
el barko para ma-on sale del embarkadero noomero dos
The boat to Mahón leaves from pier number two

El mar está en calma
el mar esta en kalma
The sea is calm

El mar está embravecido
el mar esta embrabetheedo
The sea is rough

AT THE TOURIST OFFICE

● There are tourist information offices in most towns and cities – look for the sign **Turismo**. There will often be someone who speaks English.

Tourist offices have leaflets about sights worth seeing, lists of hotels, town plans and regional maps, and can supply information about opening times and local transport. They can also book hotel rooms for you.

● Opening hours are generally 10 a.m. to 1 p.m. and 4 p.m. to 7 p.m., Mondays to Fridays, and 10 a.m. to 1 p.m. on Saturdays.

You may want to say

Where is the tourist office?
¿Dónde está la oficina de turismo?
donde esta la ofeetheena de tooreezmo

Do you speak English?
¿Habla usted inglés?
abla oosteth eengles

Do you have . . . ?
¿Tiene . . . ?
tyene . . .

Do you have a plan of the town?
¿Tiene un plano de la ciudad?
tyene oon plano de la thyoodad

Do you have a map of the area?
¿Tiene un mapa de la región?
tyene oon mapa de la rehhyon

Do you have any leaflets?
¿Tiene algunos folletos?
tyene algoonos folyetos

Do you have a list of hotels?
¿Tiene una lista de hoteles?
tyene oona leesta de oteles

Do you have a list of campsites?
¿Tiene una lista de campings?
tyene oona leesta de kampeengs

Can you recommend a cheap hotel?
¿Puede recomendarme un hotel barato?
pwede rekomendarme oon otel barato

Can you book a hotel for me, please?
¿Puede reservarme un hotel, por favor?
pwede reserbarme oon otel por fabor

Can you recommend a traditional restaurant?
¿Puede recomendarme un restaurante tradicional?
pwede rekomendarme oon restowrante tradeethyonal

Where can I/we hire a car?
¿Dónde se puede alquilar un coche?
donde se pwede alkeelar oon koche

What is there to see here?
¿Qué hay de interés aquí?
ke iy de interes akee

Do you have any information about . . . ?
¿Tiene información sobre . . . ?
tyene eenformathyon sobre . . .

Where is the archaeological museum?
¿Dónde está el museo arqueológico?
donde esta el moose-o arkeolohheeko

Can you show me on the map?
¿Puede enseñarme en el mapa?
pwede ensenyarme en el mapa

When is the museum open?
¿Cuándo está abierto el museo?
kwando esta abyerto el moose-o

Are there any excursions?
¿Hay excursiones?
iy exkoorsyones

You may hear

¿En qué puedo ayudarle?
en ke pwedo iyoodarle
Can I help you?

¿Es usted inglés/inglesa?
es oosteth eengles/eenglesa
Are you English?

¿Alemán/alemana?
aleman/alemana
German?

¿De dónde es usted?
de donde es oosteth
Where are you from?

Aquí tiene
akee tyene
Here you are

¿Cuánto tiempo va a estar aquí?
kwanto tyempo ba a estar akee
How long are you going to be here?

¿En qué hotel está?
en ke otel esta
What hotel are you in?

¿Qué clase de hotel quiere?
ke klase de otel kyere
What kind of hotel do you want?

Está en el casco viejo de la ciudad
esta en el kasko byehho de la thyoodad
It's in the old part of town

ACCOMMODATION

• There is a wide range of hotels and guest houses in Spain. Most have a blue plaque at the door with an initial for the type of establishment and the grade.

Hotels (**hotel – H**) are graded from one to five stars according to facilities. Those called **hotel-residencia (HR)** are also graded but do not have a restaurant.

The **hostal (Hs)** and **pensión (P)** are more modest guest houses or boarding houses. An **hostal-residencia (HsR)** generally provides a room only (with no meals, not even breakfast).

Cheaper still are the **fonda (F)** and **casa de huéspedes (CH)**, and you will sometimes see signs in bars or outside houses advertising rooms (**habitaciones**) or beds (**camas**).

Youth hostels are **albergues de juventud**.

For motorists there are also roadside motels (**albergues de carretera**).

• There is a chain of State-run luxury hotels called **paradores**, many of them in restored historical buildings (castles, palaces and monasteries). You can book these from Britain – for details of where they are and how to book, contact the Spanish National Tourist Office (address, page 198).

• If you are travelling along **el Camino de Santiago**, the ancient pilgrim route to Santiago de Compostela, you can stay at monasteries and convents along the route – information from the Spanish National Tourist Office.

• If you're travelling around, you can get lists of hotels from local tourist offices, and they will probably also be able to make a booking for you.

- There are plenty of campsites all over Spain, especially along the coasts. They are graded from one to three stars, and tourist offices have lists.

If you want to camp elsewhere, check the local regulations – for instance, camping may not be allowed in forest areas because of the danger of fire.

- When you book in somewhere you will usually be asked for your passport and to fill in a registration card.

Information requested on a registration card:

Nombre	First name
Apellido	Surname
Domicilio/Calle/Nº	Address/Street/Number
Nacionalidad	Nationality
Profesión	Occupation
Fecha de nacimiento	Date of birth
Lugar (de nacimiento)	Place (of birth)
Nº de pasaporte	Passport number
Expedido en (Exp. en)	Issued at
Fecha	Date
Firma	Signature

You may see

Agua potable	Drinking water
Albergue de carretera	Roadside inn, motel
Albergue de juventud	Youth hostel
Ascensor	Lift
Aseos	Toilets
Baño	Bath(room)
Basuras	Rubbish
Camas	Beds
Camping	Campsite
Casa de huéspedes (CH)	Guest house
Comedor	Dining-room

Completo	Full up, no vacancies
Corriente eléctrica	Electricity
Duchas	Showers
Entrada	Entrance
Fonda (F)	Inn, hotel
Garaje	Garage
Habitaciones (libres)	Rooms (vacant)
Hostal (Hs)	Hotel, guest house
Hostal-Residencia (HsR)	Hotel, guest house (no restaurant)
Hotel (H)	Hotel
Hotel-Residencia (HR)	Hotel (no restaurant)
Lavabos	Toilets
Lavandería	Laundry
Llamar al timbre	Please ring the bell
Media pensión	Half board
No arrojar/tirar basuras	Do not dump rubbish
Parador	State-owned luxury hotel
Pensión (P)	Boarding-house
Pensión completa	Full board
Piscina	Swimming pool
1er piso/2° piso	1st floor/2nd floor
Planta baja	Ground floor
Prohibido acampar	No camping
Prohibido acampar con caravana	No caravans
Prohibido hacer fuego	Do not light fires
Recepción	Reception
Refugio	Mountain shelter
Residuos químicos	Empty chemical toilets here
Restaurante	Restaurant
Sala de televisión	Television room
Salida (de emergencia)	(Emergency) exit
Salón	Lounge
Servicio de habitación	Room service
Servicios	Toilets
Sótano	Basement
Tarifa	Charge, tariff

You may want to say

Booking in and out

I've reserved a room
He reservado una habitación
e reserbado oona abeetathyon

I've reserved two rooms
He reservado dos habitaciones
e reserbado dos abeetathyones

I've reserved a place/space
He reservado una plaza
e reserbado oona platha

My name is . . .
Me llamo . . .
me lyamo . . .

Do you have a room?
¿Tiene una habitación?
tyene oona abeetathyon

A single room
Una habitación individual
oona abeetathyon eendeebeedwal

A double room
Una habitación doble
oona abeetathyon doble

For one night
Para una noche
para oona noche

For two nights
Para dos noches
para dos noches

With bath/shower
Con baño/ducha
kon banyo/doocha

Can I see the room?
¿Puedo ver la habitación?
pwedo ber la abeetathyon

Do you have space for a tent?
¿Tiene sitio para una tienda?
tyene seetyo para oona tyenda

Do you have space for a caravan?
¿Tiene sitio para una caravana?
tyene seetyo para oona karabana

How much is it?
¿Cuánto es?
kwanto es

Per night
Por noche
por noche

Per week
Por semana
por semana

Is there a reduction for children?
¿Hay alguna tarifa reducida para los niños?
iy algoona tareefa redootheeda para los neenyos

Is breakfast included?
¿Está incluido el desayuno?
esta eenkloo-eedo el desiyoono

It's too expensive
Es demasiado caro
es demasyado karo

Do you have anything cheaper?
¿Tiene algo más barato?
tyene algo mas barato

Do you have anything bigger/smaller?
¿Tiene algo más grande/más pequeño?
tyene algo mas grande/mas pekenyo

I'd like to stay another night
Quiero quedarme una noche más
kyero kedarme oona noche mas

I am leaving tomorrow morning
Me voy mañana por la mañana
me boy manyana por la manyana

The bill, please
La cuenta, por favor
la kwenta por fabor

Do you take credit cards?
¿Aceptan tarjetas de crédito?
atheptan tarhhetas de kredeeto

Do you take traveller's cheques?
¿Aceptan cheques de viaje?
atheptan chekes de byahhe

Can you recommend a hotel in Burgos?
¿Puede recomendarme un hotel en Burgos?
pwede rekomendarme oon otel en boorgos

Can you phone them to make a booking, please?
¿Puede llamarles para hacer una reserva, por favor?
pwede lyamarles para ather oona reserba por fabor

In hotels

(*see* Problems and complaints, *page 164;* Time, *page 185*)

Where can I/we park?
¿Dónde se puede aparcar?
donde se pwede aparkar

Do you have a cot for the baby?
¿Tiene una cuna para el bebé?
tyene oona koona para el bebe

Is there room service?
¿Hay servicio de habitación?
iy serbeethyo de abeetathyon

Do you have facilities for
the disabled?
**¿Tiene facilidades para
minusválidos?**
*tyene fatheeleedades para
meenoosbaleedos*

What time is breakfast?
¿A qué hora es el desayuno?
a ke ora es el desiyoono

Can I/we have breakfast in
the room?
**¿Se puede tomar el desayuno
en la habitación?**
*se pwede tomar el desiyoono en
la abeetathyon*

What time is dinner?
¿A qué hora es la cena?
a ke ora es la thena

What time does the hotel close?
¿A qué hora se cierra el hotel?
a ke ora se thyerra el otel

I'll be back very late
Volveré muy tarde
bolbere mwee tarde

(Key) number 42, please
**(La llave) número cuarenta y
dos, por favor**
*(la lyabe) noomero kwarenta
ee dos por fabor*

Are there any messages for me?
¿Hay algún recado para mí?
iy algoon rekado para mee

Where is the bathroom?
¿Dónde está el cuarto de baño?
donde esta el kwarto de banyo

Where is the dining-room?
¿Dónde está el comedor?
donde esta el komedor

Can I leave this in the safe?
**¿Puedo dejar esto en la caja
fuerte?**
*pwedo dehhar esto en la kahha
fwerte*

Can you get my things from
the safe?
**¿Puede sacar mis cosas de la
caja fuerte?**
*pwede sakar mees kosas de la
kahha fwerte*

Can you call me at eight
o'clock?
¿Puede despertarme a las ocho?
pwede despertarme a las ocho

Can you order me a taxi?
¿Puede pedirme un taxi?
pwede pedeerme oon taxee

For right now
Para ahora mismo
para a-ora meezmo

For tomorrow at nine
o'clock
Para mañana a las nueve
para manyana a las nwebe

Can you clean a suit for me?
¿Puede limpiarme un traje?
pwede leempyarme oon trahhe

Can you find me a babysitter?
¿Puede buscarme una niñera?
pwede booskarme oona neenyera

Can you put it on the bill?
¿Puede ponerlo en la cuenta?
pwede ponerlo en la kwenta

Room number 21
Habitación número veintiuno
abeetathyon noomero bayntee-oono

I need another pillow
Necesito otra almohada más
netheseeto otra almo-ada mas

I need a towel
Necesito una toalla
netheseeto oona to-alya

At campsites

Is there a campsite around here?
¿Hay un camping por aquí?
iy oon kampeeng por akee

Can I/we camp here?
¿Se puede acampar aquí?
se pwede akampar akee

Where can I/we park?
¿Dónde se puede aparcar?
donde se pwede aparkar

Where are the showers?
¿Dónde están las duchas?
donde estan las doochas

Where are the toilets?
¿Dónde están los servicios?
donde estan los serbeethyos

Where are the dustbins?
¿Dónde están los cubos de la basura?
donde estan los koobos de la basoora

Is the water drinkable?
¿Es el agua potable?
es el agwa potable

Where is the laundry-room?
¿Dónde está la lavandería?
donde esta la labanderee-a

Where is there an electric point?
¿Dónde hay un enchufe?
donde iy oon enchoofe

Self-catering accommodation

(*see* Directions, *page 22;* Problems and complaints, *page 164*)

I have rented a villa
He alquilado una casa
e alkeelado oona kasa

It's called Casa Pilar
Se llama Casa Pilar
se lyama kasa peelar

I have rented an apartment
He alquilado un apartamento
e alkeelado oon apartamento

We're in number 11
Estamos en el número once
estamos en el noomero onthe

My name is . . .
Me llamo . . .
me lyamo . . .

What is the address?
¿Cuál es la dirección?
kwal es la deerekthyon

How do I/we get there?
¿Cómo se llega allí?
komo se lyega alyee

Can you give me the key?
¿Puede darme la llave?
pwede darme la lyabe

Where is . . .
¿Dónde está . . . ?
donde esta . . .

Where is the stopcock?
¿Dónde está la llave de paso?
donde esta la lyabe de paso

Where is the fusebox?
¿Dónde está la caja de fusibles?
donde esta la kahha de fooseebles

How does the cooker work?
¿Cómo funciona la cocina?
komo foonthyona la kotheena

How does the water-heater
work?
**¿Cómo funciona el
calentador de agua?**
*komo foonthyona el
kalentador de agwa*

Is there air conditioning?
¿Hay aire acondicionado?
iy iyre akondeethyonado

Is there a spare gas bottle?
¿Hay otra bombona de gas?
iy otra bombona de gas

Is there any spare bedding?
¿Hay más ropa de cama?
iy mas ropa de kama

What day do they come to clean?
¿Qué día vienen a limpiar?
ke dee-a byenen a leempyar

Where do I/we put the rubbish?
¿Dónde se tira la basura?
donde se teera la basoora

When do they come to
collect the rubbish?
**¿Cuándo vienen a recoger la
basura?**
*kwando byenen a rekohher la
basoora*

Where can I contact you?
**¿Dónde puedo ponerme en
contacto con usted?**
*donde pwedo ponerme en
kontakto con oosteth*

You may hear

¿En qué puedo ayudarle?
en ke pwedo iyoodarle
Can I help you?

¿Su nombre, por favor?
soo nombre por fabor
Your name, please?

¿Para cuántas noches?
para kwantas noches
For how many nights?

¿Para cuántas personas?
para kwantas personas
For how many people?

¿Con baño o sin baño?
kon banyo o seen banyo
With bath or without bath?

**¿Es una tienda grande o
pequeña?**
*es oona tyenda grande o
pekenya*
Is it a large or a small tent?

Lo siento, está completo
lo syento esta kompleto
I'm sorry, we're full

El pasaporte, por favor
el pasaporte por fabor
Your passport, please

¿Quiere firmar aquí, por favor?
kyere feermar akee por fabor
Would you sign here, please?

Se enciende así
se enthyende asee
You switch it on like this

Se apaga así
se apaga asee
You switch it off like this

Vienen todos los días
byenen todos los dee-as
They come every day

Vienen los viernes
byenen los byernes
They come on Fridays

TELEPHONES

● There are telephone boxes in the streets, and also in many bars. You can telephone abroad from any public telephone. In large towns and cities you can also make long-distance calls from offices of the phone company (**Telefónica**).

● Public telephones take 5-, 25-, 50- and 100-peseta coins. There's a groove on the top of the telephone where you line up coins. Lift the receiver, dial or key in the number, and the coins will drop into the slot when the call is answered.

Telephones operated by phone-cards are expected to spread to the whole of Spain.

● To call abroad, first dial **07**, then the code for the country – for the UK it's **44**. Follow this with the town code minus the **0**, and then the number you want. For example: for a Central London number, dial **07 44 71**, then the number.

● If you want to make a reverse charge call to the UK, dial **900 990 034** and you will get straight through to the UK operator.

● The numbers for directory enquiries are:
003 (for local numbers)
009 (for national numbers)

Instructions you may see in the phone box:

Descuelgue el auricular	Lift the receiver
Espere a oír el tono de marcar	Wait until you hear the dialling tone
Introduzca las monedas	Insert coins
Marque el número	Dial the number

You may see

Guía telefónica	Telephone directory
Internacionales	International calls
Interurbanas nacionales	Long-distance calls
Locutorio	Payphone
No funciona	Out of order
Páginas amarillas	Yellow pages
Prefijo	Code
Telefónica	Spanish telephone company
Teléfono	Telephone
Teléfonos	Central telephone office
Urbanas	Local calls

You may want to say

Is there a telephone?
¿Hay un teléfono?
iy oon telefono

Where is the telephone?
¿Dónde está el teléfono?
donde esta el telefono

Do you have change for the
telephone, please?
**¿Tiene monedas para el
teléfono, por favor?**
*tyene monedas para el telefono
por fabor*

A telephone card, please
**Una tarjeta para el teléfono,
por favor**
*oona tarhheta para el telefono
por fabor*

Do you have a telephone
directory?
¿Tiene una guía telefónica?
tyene oona gee-a telefoneeka

I want to call England
Quiero llamar a Inglaterra
kyero lyamar a eenglaterra

Mr García, please
Señor García, por favor
senyor garthee-a por fabor

Extension number 121, please
**Extensión número ciento
veintiuno, por favor**
*extensyon noomero thyento
bayntee-oono por fabor*

My name is . . .
Me llamo . . .
me lyamo . . .

It's . . . speaking
Soy . . .
soy . . .

When will he/she be back?
¿Cuándo vuelve?
kwando bwelbe

I'll call later
Llamaré más tarde
lyamare mas tarde

Can I hold, please?
¿Puedo esperar, por favor?
pwedo esperar por fabor

Can I leave a message?
¿Puedo dejar un recado?
pwedo dehhar oon rekado

Please tell him/her that . . .
called
Por favor, dígale que ha llamado . . .
por fabor deegale ke ha lyamado . . .

I am at the Hotel Victoria
Estoy en el Hotel Victoria
estoy en el otel beektoree-a

My telephone number is . . .
Mi número de teléfono es . . .
mee noomero de telefono es . . .

Can you ask him/her to call me?
¿Puede decirle que me llame?
pwede detheerle ke me lyame

Can you repeat that, please?
¿Puede repetirlo, por favor?
pwede repeteerlo por fabor

More slowly, please
Más despacio, por favor
mas despathyo por fabor

Sorry, I've got the wrong number
Perdone, tengo el número equivocado
perdone tengo el noomero ekeebokado

We have been cut off/The line went dead
Se ha cortado la línea
se a kortado la leene-a

How much is the call?
¿Cuánto es la llamada?
kwanto es la lyamada

Can you give me a number to call a taxi?
¿Puede darme un número para llamar a un taxi?
pwede darme oon noomero para lyamar a oon taxee

You may hear

¿Diga?/¿Dígame?
deega/deegame
Hello? (*said by person answering phone*)

Al habla/Sí, soy yo
al abla/see soy yo
Speaking

¿De parte de quién?
de parte de kyen
Who's calling?

Un momento, por favor
oon momento por fabor
One moment, please

Espere, por favor
espere por fabor
Please wait

Le pongo
le pongo
I'm putting you through

Comunica/Está comunicando
komooneeka/esta komooneekando
The line's engaged

¿Quiere esperar?
kyere esperar
Do you want to hold on?

No contestan
no kontestan
There's no answer

No está
no esta
He/She is not in

Se ha equivocado de número
see a ekeebokado de noomero
You've got the wrong number

CHANGING MONEY

● The Spanish unit of currency is the **peseta** (abbreviated as **pta.**). There are coins of 1, 5, 10, 25, 50, 100, 200 and 500 pesetas, and banknotes of 500, 1 000, 2 000, 5 000 and 10 000 pesetas.

● You can change money, traveller's cheques or Eurocheques into pesetas at banks, and other places (hotels, travel agencies, etc.) where you see a **cambio** sign.

● Banks are open from 9 a.m. to 2 p.m. Mondays to Fridays, and 9 a.m. to 12.30 p.m. on Saturdays. Savings banks (**caja de ahorros**) may not have exchange facilities.

● In banks you go first to the **cambio** desk where a form is filled in for you to sign. You then get your money from the cashier (**caja**). You may have to give the name of your hotel or the address you're staying at. In Spain, addresses are given with the street name first and the number afterwards, e.g. **Calle de Cervantes, 73**.

● There is an extensive network of cash dispensers outside banks, many of which can be operated with credit cards or Eurocheque cards – check with British banks for details.

You may see the following instructions when using a cash dispenser:

Introduzca su tarjeta	Insert your card
Teclee/Marque su número secreto/personal	Key in your PIN number
Seleccione/Marque la operación (que desea realizar)	Select service you require
Use teclas azules	Use blue buttons

Sacar dinero/Retirada de fondos	Withdraw cash
¿Qué cantidad desea sacar?	How much do you want to withdraw?
Teclee el importe	Key in amount
Cantidad solicitada	Amount requested
Si es correcta pulse la tecla 'Continuar'	If correct, press 'Continuar' ('Continue')
En caso contrario pulse 'Corrección'	If not, press 'Corrección' ('Error')
Su operación se está procesando	Your transaction is being carried out
Espere por favor	Please wait
Cuando termine esta operación ¿desea realizar otra? Sí No	When this transaction is finished, do you want another? Yes No
Retire su tarjeta	Take your card
Retire el recibo y el dinero solicitado	Take your receipt and your cash

You may see

Abierto	Open
Banco	Bank
Caixa (Catalan word)	Bank
Caja	Cashier
Caja de ahorros	Savings bank
Cajero automático	Cash dispenser
Cambio	Exchange, Bureau de change
Cerrado	Closed
Entrada	Entrance
Salida	Exit

You may want to say

I'd like to change some pounds sterling
Quiero cambiar libras esterlinas
kyero kambyar leebras esterleenas

I'd like to change some traveller's cheques
Quiero cambiar cheques de viaje
kyero kambyar chekes de byahhe

I'd like to change a Eurocheque
Quiero cambiar un Eurocheque
kyero kambyar oon e-oorocheke

I'd like to withdraw some money with this credit card
Quiero sacar dinero con esta tarjeta de crédito
kyero sakar deenero kon esta tarhheta de kredeeto

What's the exchange rate today?
¿A cómo está el cambio hoy?
a komo esta el kambyo oy

Can you give me some change, please?
¿Puede darme algo en moneda, por favor?
pwede darme algo en moneda por fabor

Can you give me five 1000-peseta notes?
¿Puede darme cinco billetes de mil pesetas?
pwede darme theenko beelyetes de meel pesetas

I'm at the Hotel Don Quijote
Estoy en el Hotel Don Quijote
estoy en el otel don keehhote

I'm at the Marisol apartments
Estoy en los apartamentos Marisol
estoy en los apartamentos mareesol

I'm staying with friends
Vivo con amigos
beebo kon ameegos

The address is Calle de Santiago, 25
La dirección es Calle de Santiago, veinticinco
la deerekthyon es kalye de santyago baynteetheenko

You may hear

¿Cuánto quiere cambiar?
kwanto kyere kambyar
How much do you want to change?

El pasaporte, por favor
el pasaporte por fabor
Your passport, please

¿Su dirección, por favor?
soo deerekthyon por fabor
Your address, please?

¿El nombre de su hotel, por favor?
el nombre de soo otel por fabor
The name of your hotel, please?

Quiere firmar aquí, por favor
kyere feermar akee por fabor
Sign here, please

Pase a caja, por favor
pase a kahha por fabor
Please go to the cashier

EATING AND DRINKING

● To order something, all you need do is name it, and say 'please', adding 'for me', 'for him' or 'for her' if you're ordering for several people to show who wants what.

If you're ordering more than one of something, add s or **es** to the end of the word to make it plural, e.g. **café – cafés, sopa – sopas, flan – flanes**.

● In bars you often pay for all your drinks and so on when you leave, though in the larger, busy bars you will probably have to pay for each round. It's usual to leave some small change as a tip. It costs more to sit at a table than to stand up at the bar, especially on a terrace or pavement outside a bar or café.

In restaurants the bill will say if service is included (it usually is); otherwise a tip of 10% is normal.

● There is an official classification system for **restaurantes** from one to five forks, which reflects the range and prices of the dishes offered. As well as *à la carte*, there is usually a set-price menu (**menú del día** or **menú turístico**) of three courses plus bread and wine.

● Meal times in Spain are later than in Britain, though restaurants in tourist areas may open earlier. Lunchtime is around 2 p.m., and dinner/supper not before 8.30 p.m. and usually later – around 10 or 10.30 p.m. (later still in places like Barcelona and Madrid). Spaniards often have bar snacks (**tapas**) (see below) earlier in the evening.

● Bars tend to open early in the morning (for breakfast) and stay open till early the following morning. There are no age restrictions.

Bars serve all kinds of drinks – alcohol, soft drinks, coffee and tea etc. Most also serve food, which may be sandwiches or packets of crisps, but are more often **tapas** – snacks or appetisers which can range from a small saucer of olives to a plate of freshly cooked seafood.

Seafood **tapas** are very popular (e.g. prawns, squid rings, mussels, sardines, anchovies – fresh and pickled). Other common **tapas** are **tortilla** (Spanish potato omelette, served cold in wedges), **patatas al alioli** (potatoes in garlic mayonnaise), and **pinchos morunos** (small pork kebabs).

There will often be a menu on the wall, but you may have to ask what's available. If you want a small portion of something, ask for 'some . . .' (**unos/unas . . .**) or **un pincho de . . .** For a larger portion, ask for **una ración de . . .**

● Snack-bars often serve **platos combinados**, which are set dishes of things like ham and eggs or chicken and chips – these are illustrated on the menu and numbered, and you just ask for the number you want. Some snack bars are self-service.

● Coffee is usually the espresso type, served strong and in small cups. You can have **café solo** (black coffee), **café cortado** (with a dash of milk) or **café con leche** (white coffee). If you want a larger cup add the word **doble**.

● Tea (made with tea-bags) comes on its own – you have to ask for milk or lemon. Herbal teas (e.g. camomile or mint) are also available.

● A refreshing Spanish drink you could try is **horchata de chufas**, a milky-looking drink made of groundnuts.

● Sherry comes from the Jerez area of southwest Spain. **Fino** is pale and dry and is the most widely drunk type. **Manzanilla** is similar but comes from the town of Sanlúcar de Barrameda rather than Jerez. A word of warning: **manzanilla** also means camomile tea, so make it clear which drink you want!

Amontillado is matured from **fino** and is richer and a darker colour. **Oloroso** is aged in barrels for several years and is considerably stronger and darker. **Amontillados** and **olorosos** are both dry sherries in Spain – exported versions are generally much sweeter.

Spaniards mostly drink dry sherry rather than sweet. It's served chilled and is often drunk with **tapas**, sometimes with meals. You'll find it drunk most in Madrid and in southern Spain. In fact, in the south, if you order 'wine' without specifying white or red, you may get sherry.

● There are 30 wine-producing areas in Spain, the best-known of which is La Rioja in the north. Others include Penedés (near Barcelona), Ribera del Duero (in Castilla) and Valdepeñas (in La Mancha).

On wine labels, **DO** stands for **denominación de origen**, showing that the wine is from one of the officially registered wine-producing areas. **Reserva** and **Gran Reserva** mean that the wine is good or top quality.

Spain's answer to champagne is called **cava**.

● **Sangría** is a wine-based fruit punch that you can order by the jugful. It also contains brandy so can be stronger than it seems.

● There is a wide range of Spanish brandies and liqueurs. Particularly popular liqueurs are orange-flavoured ones and **anís** (aniseed-flavoured).

● Spanish beer is the light lager type. It comes in bottles or on draught – **una caña** is a glass of draught beer. Dark beer (**cerveza negra**) is sometimes available. You can also get alcohol-free beer (**cerveza sin alcohol**).

● Cider is produced in the north of Spain, in the Asturias region.

• Sandwiches (**bocadillos**) are usually made with rolls or chunks of French bread. **Un sandwich** is a toasted sandwich, made with sliced white bread. Common fillings for **bocadillos** include cheese (**queso**), spicy sausage (**chorizo**), omelette (**tortilla**) and ham (**jamón**). With ham, you'll need to specify whether you want boiled ham (**jamón York**) or Spanish cured ham (**jamón serrano**).

• **Churros** are a popular Spanish snack either for breakfast or at the end of a night out, and they also feature at festivals and carnivals. **Churros** are loops or sticks of deep-fried batter, and they're often eaten with a cup of hot chocolate. You can get them in bars or at stalls or shops called **churrerías**.

• The best-known Spanish dishes are probably **paella**, **gazpacho** and **tortilla**.

Paella valenciana (i.e. from Valencia) is the classic variety and it's generally made of rice coloured with saffron, seafood, red peppers and peas, and may have chicken or other meat. **Paellas** from other regions may have quite different ingredients.

Gazpacho andaluz (from Andalucía) is a cold soup made of tomatoes, green peppers, cucumber, garlic, olive oil and vinegar. Again, there are other varieties of **gazpacho** which have different ingredients.

Tortilla (or **tortilla española**) is the classic Spanish omelette, made with potatoes and a little onion and lots of eggs; in size it looks like a large cake, and is usually served cold cut into wedges. The thin sort of omelette is called **tortilla francesa** (French omelette). Spanish **tortilla** bears no resemblance to the Mexican **tortilla**.

• In the dessert section of Spanish menus you will often see **flan** – this is *not* our type of flan but crème caramel.

You may see

Aceptamos tarjetas de crédito	We accept credit cards
Asador de pollos	Roast chicken take-away
Autoservicio	Self-service
Barbacoa	Barbecue
Bebidas y refrescos	Alcoholic and soft drinks
Bodega	Wine cellar; off licence
Cafetería	Snack-bar
Cervecería	Bar, pub
Cocina	Kitchen
Comedor	Dining-room
Fonda	Inn
Guardarropa	Cloakroom
Hostería	Restaurant
Marisquería	Seafood restaurant
Merendero	Open-air snack bar; picnic area
Mesón	Inn, restaurant
Platos combinados	Set dishes
Restaurante	Restaurant
Salón de té	Tea-room
Servicios	Toilets
Taberna	Tavern, bar
Tasca	Bar, cheap restaurant
Venta	Country inn

General phrases

Are there any inexpensive restaurants around here?
¿Hay algunos restaurantes no muy caros por aquí?
iy algoonos restowrantes no mwee karos por akee

A (one) . . . , please
Un/Una . . . , por favor
oon/oona . . . por fabor

Another . . . , please
Un/Una más . . . , por favor
oon/oona mas . . . por fabor

More . . . , please
Más . . . , por favor
mas . . . por fabor

For me
Para mí
para mee

For him/her/them
Para él/ella/ellos
para el/elya/elyos

This, please
Esto, por favor
esto por fabor

Two of these, please
Dos de éstos, por favor
dos de estos por fabor

Do you have . . . ?
¿Tiene . . . ?
tyene . . .

Is/Are there any . . . ?
¿Hay . . . ?
iy . . .

What is there to eat?
¿Qué hay para comer?
ke iy para komer

What is there for dessert?
¿Qué hay de postre?
ke iy de postre

What do you recommend?
¿Qué me aconseja?
ke me akonsehha

Do you have any typical local dishes?
¿Tiene algunos platos típicos de aquí?
tyene algoonos platos teepeekos de akee

What is this?
¿Qué es esto?
ke e esto

How do you eat this?
¿Cómo se come esto?
komo se kome esto

Cheers!
¡Salud!
salood

Enjoy your meal!
¡Que aproveche!
ke aprobeche

Nothing else, thanks
Nada más, gracias
nada mas grathyas

The bill, please
La cuenta, por favor
la kwenta por fabor

Where are the toilets?
¿Dónde están los servicios?
donde estan los serbeethyos

Bars and cafés

A black coffee, please
Un café solo, por favor
oon kafe solo por fabor

Two white coffees, please
Dos cafés con leche, por favor
dos kafes kon leche por fabor

A tea with milk/lemon
Un té con leche/limón
oon te kon leche/leemon

A camomile tea, please
Una (infusión de) manzanilla, por favor
oona (infoosyon de) manthaneelya por fabor

Mineral water, please
Aqua mineral, por favor
agwa meeneral por fabor

Fizzy/Still
Con gas/Sin gas
kon gas/seen gas

A fizzy orange, please
Una naranjada, por favor
oona naranhhada por fabor

What fruit juices do you have?
¿Qué zumos tiene?
ke thoomos tyene

An orange juice, please
Un zumo de naranja, por favor
oon thoomo de naranhha por fabor

A beer, please
Una cerveza, por favor
oona therbetha por fabor

Two draught beers, please
Dos cañas, por favor
dos kanyas por fabor

A glass of red wine, please
Un (vaso de vino) tinto, por favor
oon (baso de beeno) teento por fabor

A gin and tonic, please
Un gin tonic, por favor
oon jeen toneek por fabor

With ice
Con hielo
kon yelo

What bar snacks do you have?
¿Qué tapas tiene?
ke tapas tyene

Some olives, please
Unas aceitunas, por favor
oonas athaytoonas por fabor

Some crisps, please
Unas patatas fritas, por favor
oonas patatas freetas por fabor

A (large) portion of fried
squid, please
**Una ración de calamares, por
favor**
*oona rathyon de kalamares
por fabor*

What sandwiches do you have?
¿Qué bocadillos tiene?
ke bokadeelyos tyene

A ham sandwich, please
**Un bocadillo de jamón,
por favor**
*oon bokadeelyo de hhamon
por fabor*

Boiled ham/Spanish cured
ham
Jamón York/Jamón serrano
hhamon york/hhamon serrano

Two cheese sandwiches,
please
**Dos bocadillos de queso,
por favor**
*dos bokadeelyos de keso
por fabor*

Do you have ice-creams?
¿Tiene helados?
tyene elados

What flavours do you have?
¿Qué sabores tiene?
ke sabores tyene

A chocolate/vanilla one, please
**Uno de chocolate/vainilla,
por favor**
*oono de chokolate/biyneelya
por fabor*

An (orange) ice-lolly, please
Un polo (de naranja), por favor
oon polo (de naranhha) por fabor

Booking a table

I want to reserve a table for
two people
**Quiero reservar una mesa
para dos personas**
*kyero reserbar oona mesa para
dos personas*

For nine o'clock
Para las neuve
para las nwebe

For tomorrow at half past ten
Para mañana a las diez y media
*para manyana a las dyeth ee
medya*

I have booked a table
He reservado une mesa
e reserbado oona mesa

The name is . . .
A nombre de . . .
a nombre de . . .

In restaurants

A table for four, please
Una mesa para cuatro, por favor
oona mesa para kwatro por fabor

Outside/On the terrace, if
possible
**Fuera/En la terraza, si es
posible**
fwera/en la terratha si es poseeble

Waiter!/Waitress!
¡Camarero!/¡Señorita!
kamarero/senyoreeta

The menu, please
La carta, por favor
la karta por fabor

The wine list, please
La carta de vinos, por favor
la karta de beenos por fabor

Do you have a set menu?
¿Tiene un menú?
tyene oon menoo

Do you have vegetarian dishes?
¿Tiene platos vegetarianos?
tyene platos behhetaryanos

Set dish number three, please
**El plato combinado número
tres, por favor**
*el plato kombeenado noomero
tres por fabor*

The set menu (at 500
pesetas), please
**El menú (de quinientas
pesetas), por favor**
*el menoo (de keenyentas
pesetas) por fabor*

For the first course . . .
De primero . . .
de preemero . . .

Fish soup, please
Sopa de pescado, por favor
sopa de peskado por fabor

Two mixed hors d'œuvres,
  please
**Dos entremeses variados, por
favor**
dos entremeses baryados por fabor

For the second course . . .
De segundo . . .
de segoondo . . .

Pork chop, please
Chuleta de cerdo, por favor
chooleta de therdo por fabor

Swordfish, please
Pez espada, por favor
peth espada por fabor

Are vegetables included?
¿Está incluida la verdura?
esta eenkloo-eeda la berdoora

With chips
Con patatas fritas
kon patatas freetas

And a mixed/green salad
Y una ensalada mixta/verde
*ee oona ensalada meexta/
berde*

For dessert . . .
De postre . . .
de postre . . .

Crème caramel, please
Flan, por favor
flan por fabor

A peach, please
Un melocotón, por favor
oon melokoton por fabor

What cheeses are there?
¿Qué quesos hay?
ke kesos iy

Excuse me, where is my steak?
Perdone, ¿dónde está mi filete?
perdone donde esta mee feelete

More bread, please
Más pan, por favor
mas pan por fabor

More chips, please
Más patatas, por favor
mas patatas por fabor

A glass/A jug of water
Un vaso/Una jarra de agua
oon baso/oona hharra de agwa

A bottle of red house wine
**Una botella de vino tinto de
la casa**
*oona botelya de beeno teento
de la kasa*

Half a bottle of white wine
Media botella de vino blanco
medya botelya de beeno blanko

It's very good
Está muy bueno
esta mwee bweno

It's really delicious
Está muy rico
esta mwee reeko

This is burnt
Esto está quemado
esto esta kemado

This is not cooked
Esto no está hecho
esto no esta echo

No, I ordered the chicken
No, yo pedí el pollo
no yo pedee el polyo

The bill, please
La cuenta, por favor
la kwenta por fabor

Do you accept credit cards?
¿Aceptan tarjetas de crédito?
atheptan tarhhetas de kredeeto

Do you accept traveller's cheques?
¿Aceptan cheques de viaje?
atheptan chekes de byahhe

Excuse me, there is a mistake here
Perdone, hay un error aquí
perdone iy oon error akee

You may hear

Bars and cafés

¿Qué desea(n)?
ke dese-a(n)
What would you like?

¿Qué quiere(n) tomar?
ke kyere(n) tomar
What would you like to have?

¿Quiere hielo?
kyere yelo
Would you like ice?

¿Con gas o sin gas?
kon gas o seen gas
Fizzy or still?

¿Grande o pequeño?
grande o pekenyo
Large or small?

¿Cuál prefiere?
kwal prefyere
Which do you prefer?

Ahora mismo/En seguida
a-ora meezmo/en segeeda
Right away

Tenemos . . .
tenemos . . .
We have . . .

Restaurants

¿Cuántos son?
kwantos son
How many are you?

¿Para cuántas personas?
para kwantas personas
For how many people?

Un momento
oon momento
Just a moment

¿Ha reservado una mesa?
a reserbado oona mesa
Have you booked a table?

Tendrá(n) que esperar diez minutos
tendra(n) ke esperar dyeth meenootos
You will have to wait ten minutes

¿Quiere(n) esperar?
kyere(n) esperar
Would you like to wait?

¿Qué toma(n)?
ke toma(n)?
What would you like?

¿Qué quiere(n) tomar?
ke kyere(n) tomar
What would you like?

¿Quiere(n) tomar un aperitivo?
kyere(n) tomar oon apereeteebo
Would you like an aperitif?

Recomendamos . . .
rekomendamos . . .
We recommend . . .

De primero
de preemero
For the first course

De segundo
de segoondo
For the second course

¿Para beber?
para beber
To drink?

¿Como lo quiere?
komo lo kyere
How would you like it?

¿Para quién es el/la . . . ?
para kyen es el/la . . .
Who is the . . . for?

¿Ha(n) terminado?
a(n) termeenado
Have you finished?

¿Tomará(n) postre, o café?
tomara(n) postre o kafe
Would you like dessert, or coffee?

¿Algo más?
algo mas
anything else?

MENU READER

(NB: The lists below follow the Spanish alphabet – CH, LL and Ñ are separate letters, following C, L and N respectively)

General phrases

Aguas minerales	Mineral waters
Almuerzo	Lunch
Aperitivos	Aperitifs
Aves y caza	Poultry and game
Bebidas (alcohólicas)	(Alcoholic) drinks
Bocadillos	Sandwiches
Cafés e infusiones	Coffees and teas
Carnes	Meat dishes
Carta	Menu
Cena	Dinner
Cervezas	Beers
Cocina casera	Home cooking
Comida	Lunch
Desayuno	Breakfast
Entradas	Starters
Entremeses	Hors d'œuvres
Frutas	Fruit
Gracias por su visita	Thank you for your visit
Huevos	Egg dishes
Insaladas	Salads
IVA incluido	VAT included
Legumbres	Vegetables, pulses
Licores	Spirits; liqueurs
Lista de precios	Price list
Mariscos	Seafood
Masas	Pasta
Menú del día	Menu of the day, set menu

Menú turístico	Tourist menu, set menu
Pan y vino incluidos	Bread and wine included
Pescados	Fish
Plato del día	Dish of the day
Platos combinados	Set dishes
Platos típicos	Typical dishes
Quesos	Cheeses
Raciones	Snacks; portions
Refrescos	Soft drinks
Servicio (no) incluido	Service (not) included
Sopas	Soups
Tapas	Snacks
Verduras	Vegetables
Vinos (blancos/tintos/rosados)	Wines (white/red/rosé)

Drinks

Agua mineral	Mineral water
con gas/sin gas	fizzy/still
Aguardiente	Spirit
Amontillado	Matured dry sherry
Anís	Aniseed liqueur
Batido	Milkshake
Botella	Bottle
Brandy	Brandy
Café	Coffee
cortado	white, with a dash of milk
de importación	imported
descafeinado	decaffeinated
solo o con leche	black or white
Cava	Spanish sparkling wine
Cerveza	Beer
de barril	draught
en botella	bottled
negra	dark
sin alcohol	alcohol-free

Con crianza	Aged
Coñac	Cognac, brandy
Copa	Glass
Cosecha	Vintage
Cubalibre	Rum and coke
Champán	Champagne; Spanish sparkling wine
Chocolate (caliente/fría)	Chocolate (hot/cold)
DO = denominación de origen	From one of the registered wine-producing regions
Dulce	Sweet
Embotellado por	Bottled by
Espumoso	Sparkling
Fino	Light dry sherry
Gaseosa	Lemonade
Gin, Ginebra	Gin
gin tonic	gin and tonic
Granizado	Crushed ice drink
Hielo	Ice
Horchata de chufas	Groundnut milk
Infusión	Herbal tea
de manzanilla	camomile
de menta	mint
Jarra	Jug
Jerez	Sherry
Jugo	Juice
Leche (caliente/fría)	Milk (hot/cold)
Limonada	Lemonade
Manzanilla	Dry sherry; camomile tea
Marca	Brand-name
Mosto	Grape juice
Naranjada	Orangeade
Oloroso	Strong, dark sherry
Oporto	Port
Reserva, Gran Reserva	Good/top quality wine
Ron	Rum

Sangría	Fruit, wine and brandy punch
Seco	Dry
Semiseco	Medium dry
Sidra	Cider
Sifón	Soda (syphon)
Soda	Soda
Sol y sombra	Brandy and aniseed liqueur mixed (literally 'sun and shade')
Té	Tea
con leche/limón	with milk/lemon
helado	iced
Tinto de verano	Red wine and lemonade with ice
Tónica	Tonic
Vaso	Glass
Vendimia	Harvest
Vermút	Vermouth
Vino	Wine
blanco	white
clarete	light red
de Jerez	sherry
de la casa	house wine
de la tierra	superior table wine
del país	local wine
de mesa	table wine
rosado	rosé
tinto	red
Vodka	Vodka
Whisky (con soda)	Whisky (and soda)
Zumo	Juice
de albaricoque/limón/ melocotón	apricot/lemon/peach
de naranja/pera/piña/ tomate	orange/pear/pineapple/ tomato

Aceitunas	Olives
negras/verdes	black/green
Acelgas	Chard
Adobo: al adobo	Pickled, marinated
Agridulce	Sweet and sour
Aguacate	Avocado
Ahumado/a	Smoked
Ajo	Garlic
blanco	garlic and almond soup
al ajo	with garlic
Ajillo: al ajillo	With garlic and oil
Albaricoque	Apricot
Albóndigas	Meatballs
Alcachofas	Artichokes
Alcaparras	Capers
Alioli, Allioli	Garlic mayonnaise
Almejas	Clams
Almendras	Almonds
Almíbar: en almíbar	In syrup (tinned)
Alubias	Beans
blancas	butter beans
pintas	red kidney beans
Ancas de rana	Frogs' legs
Anchoas	Anchovies
Anguila	Eel
Angulas	Elvers, baby eels
Apio	Celery
Arenque	Herring
Arroz	Rice
a la cubana	boiled, with tomato sauce and fried egg
blanco	boiled
con leche	pudding
Asado/a	Roast
Atún	Tuna

Ave(s)	Chicken, fowl
Avellanas	Hazelnuts
Bacalao	Salt cod
a la vizcaina	Basque-style, with peppers, ham, onions, garlic and chilli pepper
Berenjena	Aubergine
Berza	Cabbage
Besugo	Sea-bream
Bistec	Steak
Bizcocho	Sponge cake/finger
Bocadillo	Sandwich
Bogavante	Lobster
Bollo	Roll, bun
Bonito	Tuna
Boquerones	Anchovies (fresh)
Brasa: a la brasa	Barbecued
Brazo de gitano	Kind of Swiss roll
Brocheta	Skewer, kebab
Buey: de buey	Beef
Buñuelo	Light fried pastry (like fritter or doughnut)
Butifarra	Type of white sausage from Catalunya
Caballa	Mackerel
Cabrito	Kid
Cacahuetes	Peanuts
Cacerola: en cacerola	Casseroled
Calabacín	Courgette
Calabaza	Marrow
Calamares	Squid
a la romana	squid rings in batter, deep-fried
Caldereta	Stew
Caldo	Clear soup
gallego	with vegetables, beans and pork

Callos	Tripe
a la madrileña	Madrid-style, in a spicy sausage and tomato sauce
Camarones	Baby prawns, shrimps
Canelones	Cannelloni
Cangrejo (de río)	(River) crab
Caracoles	Snails
Carne	Meat
Casa: de la casa	Of the house, home-made
Castaña	Chestnut
Catalana: a la catalana	Catalan-style, with onion, tomato and herbs
Cazuela: a la cazuela	Casseroled
Cebolla	Onion
Centollo	Spider crab
Cerdo	Pork
Cereza	Cherry
Cigalas	Crayfish
Ciruela	Plum
Ciruela pasa	Prune
Cocido	Stew
madrileño	Madrid speciality: stew served in two courses – soup first, chick-pea, meat and vegetable stew afterwards
Cocido/a	Stewed, boiled
Coco	Coconut
Coctel (de gambas/mariscos)	(Prawn/Seafood) cocktail
Cochinillo asado	Roast sucking pig
Codorniz	Quail
Col	Cabbage
Coles de Bruselas	Brussels sprouts
Coliflor	Cauliflower
Conejo	Rabbit

Consomé	Consommé
al jerez	with sherry
con yema	with egg yolk
de ave/pollo	chicken
Contrafilete	Fillet
Copa helada	Ice-cream sundae/cup
Cordero	Lamb
Costillas	Ribs, cutlets
Crema (de cebolla/espárragos)	Cream (of onion/asparagus) soup
a la crema	creamed, in cream sauce
Crema catalana	Baked custard with caramelised topping
Crocante	Ice-cream with chopped nuts
Croquetas	Croquettes
Cuajada (con miel)	Junket (with honey)
Champiñón, champiñones	Mushrooms
Chanquetes	Fish (like whitebait)
Chilindrón: a la chilindrón	With dried red peppers, tomato and ham
Chipirones	Baby squid
Chirimoya	Custard apple
Chivo	Goat, kid
Chocolate	Chocolate
Chocos	Squid
Chorizo	Spicy sausage
Chuleta	Chop, cutlet
Chuletón	Large chop
Churros	Sticks or rings of batter, deep-fried
Día: del día	Of the day
Dulce de membrillo	Quince jelly
Embutidos	Sausages
Empanada	Meat or fish pasty/pie
Empanado/a	Breaded and fried
Emperador	Type of swordfish

Encebollado/a	With onions, in onion sauce
Endivias	Chicory
Ensaimada	Sweet snail-shaped pastry (from Mallorca)
Ensalada	Salad
mixta/verde	mixed/green
Ensaladilla rusa	Russian salad – diced vegetables in mayonnaise
Entrecot	Entrecôte steak
Entremeses (variados)	(Mixed) hors d'œuvres
Escabechado/a, En escabeche	Pickled, soused, marinated
Escalope (de ternera)	Veal escalope
a la milanesa	breaded veal escalope with cheese
Escarola	Endive
Espadín a la toledana	Kebab
Espaguetis	Spaghetti
Espárragos	Asparagus
Espinacas	Spinach
Estofado/a	Stewed
Fabada (asturiana)	Bean, sausage and black-pudding stew from Asturias
Faisán	Pheasant
Fiambres	Assorted cold meats and sausages
Fideos	Noodles
Filete	Steak, fillet
Flan	Crème caramel
Frambuesa	Raspberry
Fresa, Fresón	Strawberry
Fresco/a	Fresh
Frio/a	Cold
Frito/a	Fried
Fritura de pescado	Mixed fried fish
Fruta del tiempo	Fruit in season
Gallina	Chicken

Gallo	John Dory (fish)
Gambas	Prawns
Ganso	Goose
Garbanzos	Chickpeas
Gazpacho (andaluz)	Cold soup made of tomatoes, green peppers, cucumber, garlic, olive oil and vinegar
Gratinado/a	With cheese topping, au gratin
Guisado/a	Stewed
Guisantes	Peas
con jamón	cooked with cured ham
Gusto: a su gusto	To your choice
Habas	Broad beans
con jamón	cooked with cured ham
Habichuelas	Haricot beans
Helado mantecado	Rich vanilla ice-cream
Helado de nata	Plain ice-cream
Helados (variados)	(Assorted) ice-creams
Hervido/a	Boiled
Hierbas	Herbs
Hígado	Liver
Higo	Fig
Hinojo	Fennel
Horno: al horno	Baked
Huevas	Fish eggs, roe
Huevos	Eggs
a la flamenca	Andalusian-style, baked with spicy sausage, tomato, peas, peppers and asparagus
al plato/fritos	fried
cocidos/duros	hard-boiled
con mayonesa	egg mayonnaise
escalfados	poached
pasados por agua	soft-boiled
revueltos	scrambled

Jabalí	Wild boar
Jamón	Ham
ibérico/de Jabugo/de	types of Spanish cured
Trevélez	ham
serrano	cured
York	cooked
Jerez: al jerez	With sherry, in sherry sauce
Judías	Beans
blancas	haricot
verdes	green/French
Lacón	Type of cooked pork
Langosta	Lobster
Langostino	King prawn
Leche frita	Thick slices of custard fried in breadcrumbs
Leche merengada	Milk and meringue sorbet
Lechón	Sucking pig
Lechuga	Lettuce
Lengua	Tongue
Lenguado	Sole
Lentejas	Lentils
aliñadas	with vinaigrette
guisadas	stewed
Liebre	Hare
Limón	Lemon
Lombarda	Red cabbage
Lomo de cerdo	Loin of pork
Lomo de merluza	Hake steak
Longaniza	Type of spicy sausage
Lubina	Sea bass
Macarrones (gratinados)	Macaroni (cheese)
Macedonia de fruta	Fruit salad
Mahonesa	Mayonnaise
Maíz	Sweet corn
Manos/Manitos de cerdo	Pig's trotters
Mantecada	Small sponge cake
Mantequilla	Butter

Manzana	Apple
asada	baked
Marinera: a la marinera	In fish or seafood and tomato sauce
Mariscada	Mixed shellfish
Mariscos	Seafood
Mayonesa	Mayonnaise
Mazapán	Marzipan
Medallones	Medallions, small steaks
Mejillones	Mussels
Melocotón	Peach
Melón	Melon
con jamón	with cured ham
Membrillo	Quince jelly
Menestra de verduras	Vegetable soup/stew
Merluza	Hake
a la gallega	with paprika and potatoes
Mermelada	Jam
de naranja	marmalade
Mero	Grouper
Miel	Honey
Mixto/a	Mixed
Mollejas	Sweetbreads
Morcilla	Black pudding
Mostaza	Mustard
Nabo	Turnip
Naranja	Orange
Nata	Cream
Natural: al natural	Fresh, raw
Natillas	Egg custard
Nueces	Nuts, walnuts
Ostras	Oysters
Paella (valenciana)	Rice with shellfish, chicken, peppers, peas, saffron, etc. (a **paella** is a large flat pan used to cook this dish)

Paella catalana	Rice with sausage, pork, squid, tomato, peppers, peas
Pa amb tomàquet (Catalan)/ **Pan con tomate**	Bread toasted and rubbed with garlic and fresh tomato
País: del país	Local
Pan	Bread
Panaché de legumbres/verduras	Mixed vegetables
Panceta	Bacon
Parrilla: a la parrilla	Grilled
Parrillada	Mixed grill
Pasas	Raisins
Pastel	Cake; pie
de queso	cheesecake
Patatas	Potatoes
bravas	in spicy tomato sauce
fritas	chips; crisps
guisadas	stewed
Pato	Duck
Pavo	Turkey
Pechuga de pollo	Breast of chicken
Pepinillo	Gherkin
Pepino	Cucumber
Pera	Pear
al vino	in red wine
Percebes	Barnacles
Perdiz	Partridge
Perejil	Parsley
Pescadilla	Whiting
Pescado	Fish
Pescaditos	Sprats
Pestiños (con miel)	**Anís**-flavoured sugared fritters (dipped in honey)
Pez espada	Swordfish
Picadillo	Minced meat or sausage
Pierna (de cordero/chivo)	Leg (of lamb/goat)
Pil-pil: al pil-pil	With chillis, garlic and oil

Pimentón	Chilli pepper
Pimienta	Pepper
Pimientos	Peppers, pimentos
verdes/rojos	green/red
Pinchos	Snacks
Pinchos morunos	Small kebabs
Piña	Pineapple
Piñones	Pine kernels
Pisto	Sautéed mixed vegetables – courgettes, tomatoes, onions, peppers and aubergines
Plancha: a la plancha	Grilled (on a griddle)
Plátano	Banana
Pollo	Chicken
al ajillo	with garlic and oil
a la parrilla	grilled
asado	roast
en pepitoria	in sauce of almonds, saffron, sherry and hard-boiled eggs
Potaje	Thick vegetable soup
Puerro	Leek
Pulpitos	Baby octopus
Pulpo	Octopus
Puntas de espárragos	Asparagus tips
Puré (de patata)	(Potato) purée
Queso	Cheese
de bola	round, mild cheese (like Edam)
de Burgos	soft cream cheese from the Burgos area
de cabra	goat's milk cheese
de Cabrales	strong blue goat's milk cheese from northern Spain
de oveja	sheep's milk cheese

del país	local cheese
fresco	curd cheese
manchego	hard cheese from La Mancha, usually sheep's milk
Quisquillas	Shrimps
Rábano	Radish
Rabo de buey	Oxtail
Rape	Angler fish
Raya	Skate
Rebozado/a	Battered or breaded and fried
Rehogado/a	Sautéed
Relleno/a	Stuffed
Remolacha	Beetroot
Repollo	Cabbage
Requesón	Curd/cream cheese
Revuelto	Scrambled eggs
de espárragos/gambas	with asparagus/prawns
Riñones	Kidneys
Rodaballo	Turbot
Romana: a la romana	Deep-fried in batter
Roscas, rosquillas	Sweet pastries
Sal	Salt
Salchicha	Sausage
Salchichón	Salami-type sausage
Salmón (ahumado)	(Smoked) salmon
Salmonetes	Red mullet
Salpicón de mariscos	Shellfish with vinaigrette
Salsa	Sauce
alioli, allioli	garlic mayonnaise
bechamel	béchamel, white
blanca	white
de tomate	tomato
romesca	dried red peppers, almonds and garlic
verde	green – parsley, onion and garlic

Salteado/a	Sautéed
Samfaina	Mixture of onion, tomato, peppers, aubergine and courgette
Sandía	Water melon
Sardinas	Sardines
Sepia	Cuttlefish
Sesos	Brains
Setas	Mushrooms
Sobrasada	Type of sausage (from Mallorca)
Solomillo	Fillet steak
de cerdo	pork tenderloin
Sopa	Soup
castellana	vegetable
de ajo	garlic and bread
de almendra	almond-based pudding
de arroz	vegetable and rice
de cocido – *see* Cocido	
de picadillo	chicken soup with chopped sausage and egg, and noodles
juliana	vegetable
Sorbete	Sorbet
Tallarines	Tagliatelle, ribbon pasta
Tarta	Cake, gâteau, tart
al whisky	whisky-flavoured ice-cream gâteau
de manzana	apple tart
helada	ice-cream gâteau
Ternera	Veal
Tiempo: del tiempo	In season
Tinta: en su tinta	In its/their own ink (squid, etc.)
Tocin(ill)o de cielo, Tocinitos	Rich crème caramel
Tocino	Bacon

Tomate	Tomato
con tomate	with tomato sauce
Torrijas	Bread sliced, dipped in beaten egg, fried and rolled in sugar and cinnamon
Tortilla	Omelette
a la paisana	with mixed vegetables
española/de patata	Spanish (potato and onion)
francesa	plain (literally 'French')
Tostadas	Toast
Trucha	Trout
Trufas	Truffles
Turrón	Nougat
Uvas	Grapes
Vaca: de vaca	Beef
Vainilla	Vanilla
Vapor: al vapor	Steamed
Variado(s)/a(s)	Assorted
Venado	Venison
Vieiras	Scallops
Vinagreta	Vinaigrette
Vinagre: en vinagre	Pickled
Yemas	Dessert of whipped egg yolks, brandy and sugar
Yogur	Yoghurt
Zanahoria	Carrot
Zarzuela de (pescados y) mariscos	Spicy (fish and) seafood stew

SHOPPING

● Shop opening hours vary a bit, but most shops close for two or three hours in the middle of day. Exceptions are department stores and shops in tourist areas. General opening hours are 9 or 9.30 a.m. to 1 or 1.30 p.m. and 4 or 4.30 p.m. to 8 or 8.30 p.m. Afternoon opening times may be later in summer, especially in the south of Spain.

● There are some chains of department stores with branches mainly in large towns and cities. There are also large self-service supermarkets, especially in tourist areas. On the whole, though, Spanish shops are smaller, individual ones. In villages and small towns it's sometimes hard to tell where shops are – there are often no signs or shop windows, just an open door with a plastic strip curtain.

Many places have markets – some permanent, some only one day a week; some outdoor, some indoor. Some sell only fruit and vegetables, others sell almost anything.

● Chemists (**farmacia**) have a green cross sign outside. They are generally open from 9.30 a.m. to 2 p.m. and 4.30 p.m. to 8 p.m. Lists of duty chemists that are open late are displayed on the shop doors (and are printed in newspapers).

Chemists sell mainly medicines, baby products and health foods. For toiletries and cosmetics go to a **perfumería** or **droguería**.

● Cigarettes and tobacco are sold in State-controlled tobacconists (**estancos**) – they have the sign **Tabacos** (and a yellow symbol on a brown background). Spanish cigarettes are mostly made with strong black tobacco, but the main foreign brands are also available (though they cost a good deal more). **Estancos** also sell stamps.

● Post offices (**Correos**) are generally open from 8 a.m. to 1 or 1.30 p.m. and 4 p.m. to 6 or 7 p.m., Mondays to Fridays and Saturday mornings. Letterboxes (**buzón**) are painted yellow with a red symbol. There may be separate slots for mail within Spain (**España**) and abroad (**extranjero**).

If you only want stamps, you can get them at tobacconists (of which there are far more than post offices), and sometimes at hotels or at newspaper kiosks that sell postcards.

If you want to receive mail at a *poste restante*, have it addressed to **Lista de Correos** at the town or village you're staying in.

● To ask for something in a shop, all you need do is name it and add 'please' – or just point and say 'some of this, please' or 'two of those, please'.

Before you go shopping, try to make a list of what you need – in Spanish. If you're looking for clothes or shoes, work out what size to ask for and other things like colour, material and so on.

Shopkeepers and customers always exchange greetings and goodbyes, so check up on the correct phrases for the time of day (see inside front cover).

You may see

Abierto	Open
Almacenes, Grandes almacenes	Department store
Alimentación	Groceries
Alimentos dietéticos	Health foods
Antigüedades	Antiques
Artículos de cuero/piel	Leather goods
Artículos de deportes	Sports goods
Autoservicio	Self-service
Bodega	Wine cellar; off licence
Bricolage	DIY supplies
Buzón	Postbox

Caja	Cashier
Calzados	Footwear
Carnicería	Butcher's
Centro comercial	Shopping centre
Cerrado	Closed
Comestibles	Groceries
Confecciones	Clothes/Fashions
Confitería	Confectioner's
Correos	Post office
Discos	Records
Droguería	Drugstore
Electrodomésticos	Electrical goods
Entrada	Entrance
Entrada libre	Free admission (no obligation to buy)
Farmacia	Chemist's
Farmacias de guardia	Duty chemists
Ferretería	Ironmonger's/Hardware
Flores, Floristería	Flowers, Florist's
Frutas, Frutería	Fruit, Fruiterer's
Hipermercado	Hypermarket
Joyería	Jeweller's
Juguetes	Toys
Lechería	Dairy
Librería	Bookshop
Liquidación	Sale
Moda	Fashionwear
Muebles	Furniture
Ofertas	Special offers
Óptica	Optician's
Panadería	Baker's
Papelería	Stationer's
Pastelería	Cake shop
Peluquería	Hairdresser's
Perfumería	Drugstore/Perfumery
Pescadería	Fishmonger's

Probadores	Fitting rooms
Productos dietéticos	Health foods
PVP = Precio de Venta al Público	Retail price
Rebajas	Sales/Reductions
Recuerdos	Souvenirs
Regalos	Gifts
Relojería	Watchmaker's
Ropa (de señoras/caballeros/ niños)	Clothes (women's/men's/ children's)
Salida (de emergencia)	(Emergency) exit
Sótano	Basement
Supermercado	Supermarket
Tabacos	Tobacconist's
Tintorería	Dry-cleaner's
Ultramarinos	Groceries
Venta de sellos	Stamps on sale
Verdulería	Greengrocer's
Zapatería	Shoe shop

You may want to say

General phrases

(see also Directions, *page 22;* Problems and complaints, *page 164;* Numbers, *page 200)*

Where is the main shopping area?
¿Dónde está el centro comercial?
donde esta el thentro komerthyal

Where is the chemist's?
¿Dónde está la farmacia?
donde esta la farmathya

Is there a grocer's shop around here?
¿Hay una tienda de comestibles por aquí?
iy oona tyenda de komesteebles por akee

Where can I buy batteries?
¿Dónde se puede comprar pilas?
donde se pwede comprar peelas

What time does the baker's open?

¿A qué hora se abre la panadería?

a ke ora se abre la panaderee-a

What time does the post office close?

¿A qué hora se cierra Correos?

a ke ora se thyerra korreos

What time do you open in the morning?

¿A qué hora abren por la mañana?

a ke ora abren por la manyana

What time do you close this evening?

¿A qué hora cierran esta tarde?

a ke ora thyerran esta tarde

Do you have . . . ?

¿Tiene . . . ?

tyene . . .

Do you have stamps?

¿Tiene sellos?

tyene selyos

Do you have any wholemeal bread?

¿Tiene pan integral?

tyene pan eentegral

How much is it?

¿Cuánto es?

kwanto es

Altogether

En total

en total

How much does this cost?

¿Cuánto cuesta esto?

kwanto kwesta esto

How much do these cost?

¿Cuánto cuestan éstos?

kwanto kwestan estos

I don't understand

No entiendo

no entyendo

Can you write it down, please?

¿Puede escribirlo, por favor?

pwede eskreebeerlo por fabor

It's too espensive

Es demasiado caro

es demasyado karo

Have you got anything cheaper?

¿Tiene algo más barato?

tyene algo mas barato

I don't have enough money

No tengo suficiente dinero

no tengo soofeethyente deenero

Can you keep it for me?

¿Me lo puede guardar?

me lo pwede gwardar

I'm just looking

Estoy sólo mirando

estoy solo meerando

This one, please

Esto, por favor

esto por fabor

That one, please
Eso, por favor
eso por fabor

Three of these, please
Tres de éstos, por favor
tres de estos por fabor

Two of those, please
Dos de ésos, por favor
dos de esos por fabor

Not that one – this one
Eso no – esto
eso no – esto

There's one in the window
Hay uno en el escaparate
iy oono en el eskaparate

That's fine
Está bien
esta byen

Nothing else, thank you
Nada más, gracias
nada mas grathyas

I'll take it
Me lo llevo
me lo lyebo

I'll think about it
Lo pensaré
lo pensare

Do you have a bag, please?
¿Tiene una bolsa, por favor?
tyene oona bolsa por fabor

Can you wrap it, please?
¿Puede envolverlo, por favor?
pwede enbolberlo por fabor

With plenty of paper
Con mucho papel
kon moocho papel

I'm taking it to England
Lo llevo a Inglaterra
lo lyebo a eenglaterra

It's a gift
Es un regalo
es oon regalo

Where do I/we pay?
¿Dónde se paga?
donde se paga

Do you take credit cards?
¿Aceptan tarjetas de crédito?
atheptan tarhhetas de kredeeto

Do you take traveller's cheques?
¿Aceptan cheques de viaje?
atheptan chekes de byahhe

I'm sorry, I don't have any change
Lo siento, no tengo suelto
lo syento no tengo swelto

Can you give me a receipt, please?
¿Puede darme un recibo, por favor?
pwede darme oon retheebo por fabor

Buying food and drink

A kilo of . . .
Un kilo de . . .
oon keelo de . . .

A kilo of grapes, please
Un kilo de uvas, por favor
oon keelo de oobas por fabor

Two kilos of oranges, please
Dos kilos de naranjas, por favor
dos keelos de naranhhas por fabor

Half a kilo of tomatoes, please
Medio kilo de tomates, por favor
medyo keelo de tomates por fabor

A hundred grams of . . .
Cien gramos de . . .
thyen gramos de . . .

A hundred grams of olives, please
Cien gramos de aceitunas, por favor
thyen gramos de athaytoonas por fabor

Two hundred grams of spicy sausage, please
Doscientos gramos de chorizo, por favor
dosthyentos gramos de choreetho por fabor

In a piece
En un trozo
en oon trotho

Sliced
En lonchas
en lonchas

A piece of cheese, please
Un trozo de queso, por favor
oon trotho de keso por fabor

Five slices of ham, please
Cinco lonchas de jamón, por favor
theenko lonchas de hhamon por fabor

Boiled ham/Spanish cured ham
Jamón York/Jamón serrano
hhamon york/hhamon serrano

A bottle of white wine, please
Una botella de vino blanco, por favor
oona botelya de beeno blanko por fabor

A litre of water, please
Un litro de agua, por favor
oon leetro de agwa por fabor

Half a litre of milk, please
Medio litro de leche, por favor
medyo leetro de leche por fabor

Two cans of beer, please
Dos latas de cerveza, por favor
dos latas de therbetha por fabor

A bit of that, please
Un poco de eso, por favor
oon poko de eso por fabor

A bit more
Un poco más
oon poko mas

A bit less
Un poco menos
oon poko menos

What is this?
¿Qué es esto?
ke es esto

What is there in this?
¿Qué hay en esto?
ke iy en esto

Can I try it?
¿Puedo probarlo?
pwedo probarlo

At the chemist's

Aspirins, please
Unas aspirinas, por favor
oonas aspeereenas por fabor

Plasters, please
Unas tiritas, por favor
oonas teereetas por fabor

Do you have something
for . . . ?
¿Tiene algo para . . . ?
tyene algo para . . .

Do you have something for
diarrhoea?
¿Tiene algo para la diarrea?
tyene algo para la dee-arre-a

Do you have something for
insect bites?
**¿Tiene algo para las
picaduras de insectos?**
*tyene algo para las
peekadooras de insektos*

Do you have something for
period pains?
**¿Tiene algo para dolores
menstruales?**
*tyene algo para dolores
menstroo-ales*

Buying clothes and shoes

I want a skirt/a shirt
Quiero una falda/una camisa
kyero oona falda/oona kameesa

I want some sandals
Quiero unas sandalias
kyero oonas sandalyas

My size is 40
Mi talla es la cuarenta
mee talya es la kwarenta

Can you measure me?
¿Puede medirme?
pwede medeerme

Can I try it on?
¿Puedo probármelo?
pwedo probarmelo

Is there a mirror?
¿Hay un espejo?
iy oon espehho

I like it
Me gusta
me goosta

I like them
Me gustan
me goostan

I don't like it
No me gusta
no me goosta

I don't like them
No me gustan
no me goostan

I don't like the colour
No me gusta el color
no me goosta el kolor

Do you have it in other colours?
¿Lo tiene en otros colores?
lo tyene en otros kolores

It's too big
Es demasiado grande
es demasyado grande

They're too big
Son demasiado grandes
son demasyado grandes

It's too small
Es demasiado pequeño
es demasyado pekenyo

They're too small
Son demasiado pequeños
son demasyado pekenyos

Have you got a smaller size?
¿Tiene una talla más pequeña?
tyene oona talya mas pekenya

Have you got a bigger size?
¿Tiene una talla más grande?
tyene oona talya mas grande

Miscellaneous

Five stamps for England, please
Cinco sellos para Inglaterra, por favor
theenko selyos para eenglaterra por fabor

For postcards/letters
Para postales/cartas
para postales/kartas

Three postcards, please
Tres postales, por favor
tres postales por fabor

Matches, please
Unas cerillas, por favor
oonas thereelyas por fabor

A film like this, please
Un rollo así, por favor
oon rolyo asee por fabor

For this camera
Para esta cámara
para esta kamara

Do you have any English newspapers?
¿Tiene periódicos ingleses?
tyene peree-odeekos ingleses

You may hear

¿En qué puedo ayudarle?
en ke pwedo iyoodarle
May I help you?

¿Qué desea?
ke desea
What would you like?

¿Cuánto/Cuánta quiere?
kwanto/kwanta kyere
How much would you like?

¿Cuántos/Cuántas quiere?
kwantos/kwantas kyere
How many would you like?

¿Vale (así)?
bale (asee)
Is that all right?

¿Algo más?
algo mas
Anything else?

Lo siento, se nos ha agotado
lo syento se nos a agotado
I'm sorry, we're sold out

Lo siento, está cerrado ahora
lo syento esta therrado a-ora
I'm sorry, we're closed now

¿Se lo envuelvo?
se lo enbwelbo
Shall I wrap it for you?

Pase a la caja, por favor
pase a la kahha por fabor
Please go to the cashier

¿Tiene suelto?
tyene swelto
Do you have any change?

Hace falta una receta
athe falta oona retheta
You need a prescription

¿Cuál es su talla?
kwal es soo talya
What size are you?

¿Para postal o carta?
para postal o karta
For postcard or letter?

¿Qué tipo de . . . ?
ke teepo de . . .
What sort of . . . ?

¿Qué tipo de cámara tiene?
ke teepo de kamara tyene
What sort of camera do you
   have?

¿Qué tipo de película quiere?
ke teepo de peleekoola kyere
What sort of film do you want?

BUSINESS TRIPS

● You'll probably be doing business with the help of interpreters or in a language everyone speaks, but you may need a few Spanish phrases to cope at a company's reception desk.

● When you arrive for an appointment, all you need do is say who you've come to see and give your name or hand over your business card. However, if you're not expected you may need to make an appointment or leave a message.

You may see

Ascensor	Lift
Cía. = Compañía	Company
Entrada	Entrance
Escalera	Stairs
No fumar	No smoking
No funciona	Out of order
1ᵉʳ piso	1st floor
2º piso	2nd floor
Planta baja	Ground floor
Prohibida la entrada a personas no autorizadas	No entry to unauthorised persons
Prohibido entrar	No entry
Recepción	Reception
Salida (de emergencia)	(Emergency) exit
S.A. = Sociedad Anónima	Limited company

You may want to say

(see also Days, months, dates, page 182, Time, page 185)

Mr García, please
Señor García, por favor
senyor garthee-a por fabor

Mrs Fernández, please
Señora Fernández, por favor
senyora fernandeth por fabor

Miss Rodriguez, please
Señorita Rodríguez, por favor
senyoreeta rodreegeth por fabor

The manager, please
El director, por favor
el deerektor por fabor

My name is . . .
Me llamo . . .
me lyamo . . .

My company is . . .
Mi empresa es . . .
mee empresa es . . .

I have an appointment with
Mr Ramón González
**Tengo una cita con el señor
Ramón González**
*tengo oona theeta kon el
senyor ramon gonthaleth*

I don't have an appointment
No tengo cita
no tengo theeta

I'd like to make an
appointment with Miss
Gómez

Quisiera hacer una cita con
la señorita Gómez
**keesyera ather oona theeta
kon la senyoreeta gometh**

I am free this afternoon at
five o'clock
**Estoy libre esta tarde a las
cinco**
*estoy leebre esta tarde a las
theenko*

I'd like to talk to the export
manager
**Quisiera hablar con el
director de exportaciones**
*keesyera ablar kon el
deerektor de exportathyones*

What is his/her name?
¿Cómo se llama él/ella?
komo se lyama el/elya

When will he/she be back?
¿Cuándo vuelve?
kwando bwelbe

Can I leave a message?
¿Puedo dejar un recado?
pwedo dehhar oon rekado

Can you tell him/her to call
me?
¿Puede decirle que me llame?
pwede detheerle ke me lyame

My telephone number is . . .
Mi número de teléfono es . . .
mee noomero de telefono es . . .

I am staying at the Hotel Reina Isabel
Estoy en el Hotel Reina Isabel
estoy en el otel rayna eesabel

Where is his/her office?
¿Dónde está su oficina?
donde esta soo ofeetheena

I am here for the exhibition
Estoy aquí para la exposición
estoy akee para la exposeethyon

I am here for the trade fair
Estoy aquí para la feria de muestras
estoy akee para la feree-a de mwestras

I am attending the conference
Estoy asistiendo al congreso
estoy aseestyendo al kongreso

I have to make a phone call (to Britain)
Tengo que llamar por teléfono (a Gran Bretaña)
tengo ke lyamar por telefono (a gran bretanya)

I have to send a telex
Tengo que enviar un telex
tengo ke enbyar oon telex

I have to send this by fax
Tengo que enviar esto por fax
tengo ke enbyar esto por fax

I want to send this by post
Quiero enviar esto por Correo
kyero enbyar esto por koree-o

I want to send this by courier
Quiero enviar esto por mensajero especial
kyero enbyar esto por mensahhero espethyal

I need someone to type this for me
Necesito que me pasen esto a máquina
netheseeto ke me pasen esto a makeena

I need a photocopy (of this)
Necesito una fotocopia (de esto)
netheseeto oona fotokopya (de esto)

I need an interpreter
Necesito un intérprete
netheseeto oon eenterprete

You may hear

¿Su nombre, por favor?
soo nombre por fabor
Your name, please?

¿Cómo se llama usted?
komo se lyama oosteth
What is your name?

¿El nombre de su empresa,
    por favor?
*el nombre de soo empresa por
    fabor*
The name of your company,
    please?

¿Tiene usted una cita?
tyene oosteth oona theeta
Do you have an appointment?

¿Tiene una tarjeta?
tyene oona tarhheta
Do you have a card?

¿Le está esperando?
le esta esperando
Is he/she expecting you?

(Espere) un momento, por favor
(espere) oon momento por fabor
(Wait) one moment, please

Le diré que usted está aquí
le deere que oosteth esta akee
I'll tell him/her you're here

Ahora viene
a-ora byene
He/she is just coming

Siéntese usted, por favor
syentese oosteth por fabor
Please sit down

Quiere usted sentarse
kyere oosteth sentarse
Would you sit down

Pase usted, por favor
pase oosteth por fabor
Go in, please

Pase por aquí, por favor
pase por akee por fabor
Come this way, please

El señor García no está
el senyor garthee-a no esta
Mr García is not in

La señorita Gómez está fuera
la senyoreeta gometh esta fwera
Miss Gómez is out

La señora Fernández volverá
    a las once
*la senyora fernandez bolbera a
    las onthe*
Mrs Fernández will be back
    at eleven o'clock

Dentro de media hora/una hora
dentro de medya ora/oona ora
In half an hour/an hour

Coja el ascensor hasta el tercer piso
kohha el asthensor asta el terther peeso
Take the lift to the third floor

Siga por el pasillo
seega por el paseelyo
Go along the corridor

Es la primera/segunda puerta
es la preemera/segoonda pwerta
It's the first/second door

A la izquierda/derecha
a la eethkyerda/derecha
On the left/right

Es el despacho número trescientos veinte
es el despacho noomero tresthyentos baynte
It's room number 320

¡Adelante!
adelante
Come in!

SIGHTSEEING

● You can get information about all the sights worth seeing from the Spanish National Tourist Office (address, page 198) and from local tourist offices. The latter can also tell you about the sightseeing tours by coach that are available in many cities and tourist areas, often with English-speaking guides.

● Opening hours vary for historic buildings, museums, galleries and so on, but most close for several hours in the afternoon. Most are shut on Mondays.

● Spain has a number of national parks and nature reserves. Access to some areas may be allowed only with a local guide.

You may see

Abierto	Open
Cerrado (por restauraciones)	Closed (for restoration)
Horario de visitas	Visiting hours
No pisar el césped	Keep off the grass
No tocar	Do not touch
Prohibida la entrada	No entry
Privado	Private
Visitas con guía	Guided tours

You may want to say

(*see also* At the tourist office, *page 69, for asking for information, brochures, etc.*)

Opening times

(*see* Time, *page 185*)

When is the museum open?
¿Cuándo está abierto el museo?
kwando esta abyerto el moose-o

Is it open on Sundays?
¿Está abierto los domingos?
esta abyerto los domeengos

What time does the castle open?
¿A qué hora se abre el alcázar?
a ke ora se abre el alkathar

Can I/we visit the monastery?
¿Se puede visitar el monasterio?
se pwede beeseetar el monasteree-o

What time does the palace close?
¿A qué hora se cierra el palacio?
a ke ora se thyerra el palathyo

Is it open to the public?
¿Está abierto al público?
esta abyerto al poobleeko

Visiting places

One/Two, please
Uno/Dos, por favor
oono/dos por fabor

For students
Para estudiantes
para estoodyantes

Two adults and child
Dos adultos y un niño
dos adooltos ee oon neenyo

For pensioners
Para jubilados
para hhoobeelados

Are there reductions for children?
¿Hay tarifas reducidas para niños?
iy tareefas redootheedas para neenyos

For the disabled
Para minusválidos
para meenoosbaleedos

For groups
Para grupos
para groopos

Are there guided tours (in English)?
¿Hay visitas con guía (en inglés)?
iy beeseetas kon gee-a (en eengles)

Can I/we take photos?
¿Se puede hacer fotos?
se pwede ather fotos

Would you mind taking a photo of me/us, please?
¿Me hace el favor de hacer una foto de mí/nosotros?
me athe el fabor de ather oona foto de mee/nosotros

When was this built?
¿Cuándo se construyó esto?
kwando se konstrooyo esto

Who painted that picture?
¿Quién pintó ese cuadro?
kyen peento ese kwadro

In what year? (*see* Days, months, dates, page 182)
¿En qué año?
en ke anyo

What time is mass?
¿A qué hora es la misa?
a ke ora es la meesa

Is there a priest who speaks English?
¿Hay un sacerdote que hable inglés?
iy oon satherdote ke able eengles

What is this flower called?
¿Cómo se llama esta flor?
komo se lyama esta flor

What is that bird called?
¿Cómo se llama ese pájaro?
komo se lyama ese pahharo

Is there a picnic area (in the park)?
¿Hay un merendero (en el parque)?
iy oon merendero (en el parke)

Sightseeing excursions

What tourist excursions are there?
¿Qué excursiones turísticas hay?
ke exkoorsyones tooreesteekas iy

Are there any excursions to Toledo?
¿Hay excursiones a Toledo?
iy exkoorsyones a toledo

What time does it leave?	Where does it leave from?
¿A qué hora sale?	**¿De dónde sale?**
a ke ora sale	*de donde sale*

How long does it last?	Does the guide speak English?
¿Cuánto dura?	**¿Habla el guía inglés?**
kwanto doora	*abla el gee-a eengles*

What time does it get back?	How much is it?
¿A qué hora vuelve?	**¿Cuánto es?**
a ke ora bwelbe	*kwanto es*

You may hear

El museo está abierto todos los días excepto los lunes
el moose-o esta abyerto todos los dee-as exthepto los loones
The museum is open every day except Monday

Está cerrado los domingos
esta therrado los domeengos
It is closed on Sundays

El alcázar se construyó en el siglo once
el alkathar se konstrooyo en el seeglo onthe
The castle was built in the eleventh century

Es un cuadro de El Greco
es oon kwadro del greko
It's a painting by El Greco

Hay excursiones los martes y los jueves
iy exkoorsyones los martes ee los hhwebes
There are excursions every Tuesday and Thursday

El autocar sale a las diez de la plaza de Oriente
el owtokar sale a las dyeth de la platha de oree-ente
The coach leaves at ten o'clock from the Plaza de Oriente

ENTERTAINMENTS

● Spain's most popular spectator sports are football and bullfighting. **Pelota** is the national game in the Basque Country. Most professional sports fixtures take place on Sundays.

When buying tickets for a bullfight, there'll be a choice of **sol** or **sombra** – seats in the sun or the shade. **Sombra** seats cost more. You can rent cushions for the hard concrete stands.

● Evening performances at theatres, cinemas, musical events, flamenco shows, etc. often start late – around 10.30 or 11 p.m. It is usual to give a small tip to theatre and cinema ushers.

● Films are categorised as suitable for general viewing (**todos los públicos**), or for people over 13 or over 18 (**mayores de 13/18 años**). Some may be labelled as not recommended for those under 13 or 18 (**no recomendada para menores de 13/18 años**).

Many American and British films are shown in Spanish cinemas, most of them dubbed (**doblada**) but sometimes subtitled (**subtitulada**).

● **Salas rocieras** are bars or restaurants with flamenco or **sevillana** music and dancing. **Sevillanas** are similar to flamenco, but with a set pattern of steps rather than the improvised dancing of pure flamenco. The music in **salas rocieras** may be live or recorded, and customers often join in the dancing of **sevillanas**.

You may see

Agotado	Sold out
Anfiteatro	Balcony, upper tier
Asiento	Seat
Butacas (de patio)	Stalls seats
Cine	Cinema
Cineclub	Film club
Circo	Circus
Discoteca	Discothèque
Entresuelo	Balcony, circle
Estadio	Stadium
Fila	Row
Gradas	Stand, grandstand
Guardarropa	Cloakroom
Hipódromo	Racecourse
Localidades para hoy	Tickets for today's performances
Mayores de 13/18 años	Over-13s/18s only
No hay descanso	There is no interval
No recomendada para menores de 13/18 años	Not recommended for under-13s/18s
No se permite la entrada una vez comenzado el espectáculo	No entry once the performance has begun
Palcos	Boxes
Patio de butacas	Stalls
Principal	Balcony, circle
Prohibido a menores de 18 años	Under-18s not allowed
Puerta	Door
Sala de conciertos	Concert hall
Sala rociera	Bar or restaurant with flamenco music and dancing
Salón de baile	Dance hall
Sesión continua	Continuous performance
Sesión de noche	Evening performance

Sesión de tarde	Matinée
Sesión numerada	Separate performances
Tablao flamenco	Flamenco show
Teatro	Theatre
Teatro de la ópera	Opera house
Todos los públicos	For general viewing
Tribuna	Stand, grandstand
Venta anticipada	Advance booking
Versión original subtitulada (v.o.)	Original language version with subtitles

You may want to say

What's on

(*see* Time, *page 185*)

What is there to do in the evenings?
¿Qué se puede hacer por las noches?
ke se pwede ather por las noches

Is there a disco around here?
¿Hay una discoteca por aquí?
iy oona deeskoteka por akee

Is there any entertainment for children?
¿Hay alguna diversión para niños?
iy algoona deebersyon para neenyos

What's on tonight?
¿Qué ponen esta noche?
ke ponen esta noche

What's on tomorrow?
¿Qué ponen mañana?
ke ponen manyana

At the cinema
En el cine
en el theene

At the theatre
En el teatro
en el te-atro

Who is playing? (*music*)
¿Quién toca?
kyen toka

Who is singing?
¿Quién canta?
kyen kanta

Who is dancing?
¿Quién baila?
kyen biyla

Is the film dubbed or subtitled?
¿La película está doblada o subtitulada?
la peleekoola esta doblada o soobteetoolada

Is there a football match on Sunday?
¿Hay algún partido de fútbol el domingo?
iy algoon parteedo de footbol el domeengo

Who are playing? (*sport*)
¿Quiénes juegan?
kyenes hhwegan

What time does the show start?
¿A qué hora empieza el espectáculo?
a ke ora empyetha el espektakoolo

What time does the concert start?
¿A qué hora empieza el concierto?
a ke ora empyetha el konthyerto

How long does the performance last?
¿Cuánto dura la representación?
kwanto doora la representathyon

When does it end?
¿A qué hora termina?
a ke ora termeena

Tickets

Where can I/we get tickets?
¿Dónde se puede conseguir las entradas?
donde se pwede konsegeer las entradas

Can you get me tickets for the bullfight?
¿Puede conseguirme entradas para la corrida de toros?
pwede konsegeerme entradas para la korreeda de toros

For the football match
Para el partido de fútbol
para el parteedo de footbol

For the theatre
Para el teatro
para el te-atro

Two, please
Dos, por favor
dos por fabor

Two for tonight, please
Dos para esta noche, por favor
dos para esta noche por fabor

Two for the eleven o'clock screening, please
Dos para la sesión de las once, por favor
dos para la sesyon de las onthe por fabor

Are there any seats left for Saturday?
¿Quedan localidades para el sábado?
kedan lokaleedades para el sabado

I want to book a box for four people
Quiero reservar un palco para cuatro personas
kyero reserbar oon palko para kwatro personas

I want to book two seats
Quiero reservar dos localidades
kyero reservar dos lokaleedades

For Friday
Para el viernes
para el byernes

In the stalls
Butacas de patio
bootakas de patyo

In the balcony
De anfiteatro/De entresuelo
de anfeete-atro/de entreswelo

In the shade
De sombra
de sombra

In the sun
De sol
de sol

How much are the seats?
¿Cuánto cuestan las localidades?
kwanto kwestan las lokaleedades

Do you have anything cheaper?
¿Tiene algo más barato?
tyene algo mas barato

That's fine
Está bien/Vale
esta byen/bale

At the show/game

Where is this, please?
(showing your ticket)
¿Dónde está esto, por favor?
donde esta esto por fabor

Where is the cloakroom?
¿Dónde está el guardarropa?
donde esta el gwardarropa

Where is the bar?
¿Dónde está el bar?
donde esta el bar

Where are the toilets?
¿Dónde están los servicios?
donde estan los serbeethyos

A programme, please
Un programa, por favor
oon programa por fabor

Where can I/we get a
programme?
**¿Dónde se puede conseguir
un programa?**
*donde se pwede konsegeer oon
programa*

A cushion, please
Una almohadilla, por favor
oona almo-adeelya por fabor

Is there an interval?
¿Hay descanso?
iy deskanso

You may hear

Se puede conseguir entradas aquí en el hotel
se pwede konsegeer entradas akee en el otel
You can get tickets here in the hotel

En la plaza de toros
en la platha de toros
At the bullring

En el estadio
en el estadyo
At the stadium

Empieza a las siete
empyetha a las syete
It begins at seven o'clock

Dura dos horas y cuarto
doora dos oras ee kwarto
It lasts two and a quarter hours

Termina a las nueve y media
termeena a las nwebe ee medya
It ends at half past nine

Hay un descanso de quince minutos
iy oon deskanso de keenthe meenootos
There is a fifteen-minute interval

¿Para cuándo las quiere?
para kwando las kyere
When would you like them for?

¿De sol o de sombra?
de sol o de sombra
In the sun or in the shade?

¿Butacas de patio, de anfiteatro, de entresuelo?
bootakas de patyo, de anfeete-atro, de entreswelo
In the stalls, in the balcony?

Hay dos aquí, butacas de patio
iy dos akee, bootakas de patyo
There are two here, in the stalls (*indicating on seating plan*)

Lo siento, las localidades están agotadas
lo syento las lokaleedades estan agotadas
I'm sorry, the seats are sold out

¿Puedo ver su entrada?
pwedo ber soo entrada
May I see your ticket?

SPORTS AND ACTIVITIES

● There are good facilities in many parts of Spain for skiing, golf, tennis and watersports – information about locations is obtainable from the Spanish National Tourist Office or travel agents.

● At the beach, a red flag flying means it is dangerous to swim. A yellow flag means swimming is not recommended, and a green flag means it is safe.

● River fishing is the most common sort, but you can also go deep-sea and underwater fishing. In all cases you need a permit, obtainable from an office of the national nature conservation agency ICONA (**Instituto Nacional por la Conservación de la Naturaleza**).

● Spain has plenty of mountain areas for walking and climbing. There are mountain shelters (**refugios**) in many places.

You may see

Alquiler de barcos	Boat hire
Alquiler de esquís	Ski hire
Alquiler de tablas	Sailboards for hire
Campo de fútbol	Football pitch
Campo de golf	Golf course
Coto de caza	Hunting reserve
Coto (privado)	(Private) reserve
Escuela de esquí	Ski school
Peligro	Danger
Peligro de aludes	Danger of avalanches
Piscina (cubierta)	(Indoor) swimming pool
Pista	Ski-run
Pista de tenis	Tennis court

Playa	Beach
Playa particular	Private beach
Polideportivo	Sports centre
Prohibido bañarse	No swimming
Prohibido pescar	No fishing
Teleférico	Cable car
Telesilla	Chair lift
Telesquí	Ski lift

You may want to say

General phrases

Can I/we . . . ?
¿Se puede . . . ?
se pwede . . .

Can I/we hire bikes?
¿Se puede alquilar bicicletas?
*se pwede alkeelar
beetheekletas*

Can I/we go fishing?
¿Se puede pescar?
se pwede peskar

Can I/we go horse-riding?
¿Se puede montar a caballo?
se pwede montar a kabalyo

Where can I/we . . .
¿Dónde se puede . . . ?
donde se pwede . . .

Where can I/we play tennis?
¿Dónde se puede jugar al tenis?
donde se pwede hhoogar al tenis

Where can I/we go climbing?
**¿Dónde se puede hacer
alpinismo?**
*donde se pwede ather
alpeeneezmo*

I don't know how to . . .
No sé . . .
no se . . .

I don't know how to ski
No sé esquiar
no se eskyar

Do you give lessons?
¿Dan clases?
dan klases

I'm a beginner
Soy principiante
soy preentheepyante

I'm quite experienced
Soy bastante experto (*male*)/
experta (*female*)
soy bastante experto/experta

How much is it per hour?
¿Cuánto es por hora?
kwanto es por ora

How much is it for the whole day?
¿Cuánto es por el día entero?
kwanto es por el dee-a entero

How much is it per game?
¿Cuánto es por juego?
kwanto es por hhwego

Is there a reduction for children?
¿Hay algún descuento para niños?
iy algoon deskwento para neenyos

Can I/we hire equipment?
¿Se puede alquilar el equipo?
se pwede alkeelar el ekeepo

Can I/we hire rackets?
¿Se puede alquilar raquetas?
se pwede alkeelar raketas

Can I/we hire clubs?
¿Se puede alquilar los palos?
se pwede alkeelar los palos

Do I/we need a licence?
¿Se requiere un permiso?
se rekyere oon permeeso

Where can I/we get one?
¿Dónde se puede conseguir uno?
donde se pwede konsegeer oono

Is it necessary to be a member?
¿Hace falta ser socio?
athe falta ser sothyo

Beach and pool

Can I/we swim here?
¿Se puede nadar aquí?
se pwede nadar akee

Can I/we swim in the river?
¿Se puede nadar en el río?
se pwede nadar en el ree-o

Is it dangerous?
¿Es peligroso?
es peleegroso

Is it safe for children?
¿Es seguro para los niños?
es segooro para los neenyos

When is high tide?
¿Cuándo hay marea alta?
kwando iy mare-a alta

Skiing

What is the snow like?
¿Cómo está la nieve?
komo esta la nyebe

Is the ski-run wide?
¿Es larga la pista?
es larga la peesta

Is there a ski-run for beginners?
¿Hay una pista para principiantes?
iy oona peesta para preentheepyantes

How much is the lift pass?
¿Cuánto vale un pase para el telesquí?
kwanto bale oon pase para el teleskee

Per day
Por día
por dee-a

Per week
Por semana
por semana

What time is the last ascent?
¿A qué hora es el último ascenso?
a ke ora es el oolteemo asthenso

You may hear

¿Es usted principante?
es oosteth preentheepyante
Are you a beginner?

¿Sabe usted esquiar?
sabe oosteth eskyar
Do you know how to ski?

¿Sabe usted hacer windsurf?
sabe oosteth ather weendsoorf
Do you know how to windsurf?

Son dos mil pesetas por hora
son dos meel pesetas por ora
It's 2 000 pesetas per hour

Hay que pagar un depósito de mil pesetas
iy ke pagar oon deposeeto de meel pesetas
You have to pay a deposit of 1 000 pesetas

Lo siento, está completo
lo syento esta kompleto
I'm sorry, we're booked up

Tendrá que volver más tarde
tendra ke bolber mas tarde
You'll have to come back later

¿Cuál es su talla?
kwal es soo talya
What size are you?

¿Qué tipo de esquís quiere?
ke teepo de eskees kyere
What type of skis do you want?

Hace falta una foto
athe falta oona foto
You need a photo

La nieve está dura/helada
la nyebe esta doora/elada
The snow is heavy/icy

La nieve está blanda
la nyebe esta blanda
The snow is soft

Hay poca nieve
iy poka nyebe
There isn't much snow

HEALTH

Medical details - to show to a doctor

(Tick boxes or fill in details)

	Self Yo		Other members of family/party	
Blood group **Grupo sanguíneo**				
Asthmatic **Asmático/a**				
Blind **Ciego/a**				
Deaf **Sordo/a**				
Diabetic **Diabético/a**				
Epileptic **Epiléptico/a**				
Handicapped **Minusválido/a**				
Heart condition **Cardíaco/a**				
High blood pressure **Tensión alta**				
Pregnant **Embarazada**				

Allergic to **Alérgico/a a:**				
Antibiotics **Antibióticos**				
Penicillin **Penicilina**				
Cortisone **Cortisona**				

Medicines **Medicinas** _____

Self **Yo** _____

Others **Otros** _____

● Your local Department of Health office can provide information about medical care abroad. Within the EC you can obtain the local equivalent of NHS treatment by producing the required form – you will probably have to pay first and reclaim the payment when you return to Britain.

Treatment at first aid posts is free.

● Chemists can often give medical advice and first aid, and provide medicines without a prescription.

● If you need an ambulance, call either the police or the Spanish Red Cross (**la Cruz Roja**).

● To indicate where the pain is you can simply point and say 'it hurts here' (**me duele aquí**). Otherwise you'll need to look up the Spanish for the appropriate part of the body (see page 00).

Notice that in Spanish you refer to 'the head', 'the stomach', etc. rather than '*my* head', '*my* stomach' (**la cabeza, el estómago**).

You may see

Agítese antes de usar	Shake before use
Casa de socorro	First aid post, casualty hospital
Clínica	Clinic, hospital
Consulta	Surgery hours
Dentista	Dentist
Hospital	Hospital
Médico	Doctor
Modo de empleo	Instructions for use
Puesto de socorro	First aid post
Servicio de urgencias	Emergency services
Servicio permanente de ambulancias	Ambulance station
Sólo para uso externo	For external use only
Urgencias	Casualty department
¡Veneno!	Poison!

You may want to say

At the doctor's

I need a doctor
Necesito un médico
netheseeto oon medeeko

Please call a doctor
Por favor, llame a un médico
por fabor lyame a oon medeeko

Quickly
Rápido
rapeedo

Is there someone who
speaks English?
¿Hay alguien que hable inglés?
iy algyen ke able eengles

Can I make an
appointment?
¿Puedo hacer una cita?
pwedo ather oona theeta

It's my husband
Es mi marido
es mee mareedo

It's my wife
Es mi mujer
es mee moohher

It's my friend
Es mi amigo (*male*)/**amiga**
 (*female*)
es mee ameego/ameega

It's my son
Es mi hijo
es mee eehho

It's my daughter
Es mi hija
es mee eehha

How much will it cost?
¿Cuánto costará?
kwanto kostara

Your symptoms	Someone else's symptoms
I feel unwell **Me siento mal** *me syento mal*	He/She feels unwell **Se siente mal** *se syente mal*
	He/She is unconscious **Está inconsciente** *esta eenkonsthyente*
It hurts here **Me duele aquí** *me dwele akee*	It hurts here **Le duele aquí** *le dwele akee*
My ... hurt(s) **Me duele el/la ...** *me dwele el/la ...*	His/Her ... hurt(s) **Le duele ...** *le dwele ...*
My stomach hurts **Me duele el estómago** *me dwele el estomago*	His/Her stomach hurts **Le duele el estómago** *le dwele el estomago*
My back hurts **Me duele la espalda** *me dwele la espalda*	His/Her back hurts **Le duele la espalda** *le dwele la espalda*
My ... hurt **Me duelen los/las ...** *me dwelen los/las ...*	His/Her ... hurt **Le duelen ...** *le dwelen ...*
My eyes hurt **Me duelen los ojos** *me dwelen los ohhos*	His/Her eyes hurt **Le duelen los ojos** *le dwelen los ohhos*
My feet hurt **Me duelen los pies** *me dwelen los pyes*	His/Her feet hurt **Le duelen los pies** *le dwelen los pyes*
I have a sore throat **Tengo dolor de garganta** *tengo dolor de garganta*	He/She has a sore throat **Tiene dolor de garganta** *tyene dolor de garganta*

I have a temperature
Tengo fiebre
tengo fyebre

He/She has a temperature
Tiene fiebre
tyene fyebre

I have diarrhoea
Tengo diarrea
tengo dee-arre-a

He/She has diarrhoea
Tiene diarrea
tyene dee-arre-a

I feel dizzy/sick
Me siento mareado (*male*)/
   mareada (*female*)
me syento mare-ado/mare-ada

He/She feels dizzy/sick
Se siente mareado (*he*)/
   mareada (*she*)
se syente mare-ado/mare-ada

I have been sick
He vomitado
e bomeetado

He/She has been sick
Ha vomitado
a bomeetado

I can't sleep
No puedo dormir
no pwedo dormeer

I can't breathe
No puedo respirar
no pwedo respeerar

I can't move my . . .
No puedo mover el/la . . .
no pwedo mober el/la . . .

My . . . is bleeding
El/La . . . sangra
el/la . . . sangra

He/She is bleeding
Está sangrando
esta sangrando

It's my . . .
Es el/la . . .
es el/la . . .

It's his/her . . .
Es el/la . . .
es el/la . . .

It's my arm
Es el brazo
es el bratho

It's his/her ankle
Es el tobillo
es el tobeelyo

It's my wrist
Es la muñeca
es la moonyeka

It's his/her leg
Es la pierna
es la pyerna

I think that . . .
Creo que . . .
kre-o ke . . .

It's broken
Es roto/rota
esta roto/rota

It's sprained
Está torcido/torcida
esta tortheedo/tortheeda

I have cut myself
Me he cortado
me e kortado

He/She has cut himself/
herself
Se ha cortado
se a kortado

I have burnt myself
Me he quemado
me e kemado

He/She has burnt himself/
herself
Se ha quemado
se a kemado

I have been stung by an insect
Me ha picado un insecto
me a peekado oon eensekto

He/She has been stung by
an insect
Le ha picado un insecto
le a peekado oon eensekto

I have been bitten by a dog
Me ha mordido un perro
me a mordeedo oon perro

He/She has been bitten by a
dog
Le ha mordido un perro
le a mordeedo oon perro

You may hear

¿Qué le pasa?
ke le pasa
What is the matter?

¿Dónde le duele?
donde le dwele
Where does it hurt?

¿Le duele aquí?
le dwele akee
Does it hurt here?

¿Mucho? ¿Poco?
moocho poko
A lot? A little?

¿Cuánto tiempo hace que se siente así?
kwanto tyempo athe ke se syente asee
How long have you been feeling like this?

¿Cuántos años tiene?
kwantos anyos tyene
How old are you?/How old is he/she?

Abra la boca, por favor
abra la boka por fabor
Open your mouth, please

Desvístase, por favor
desbeestase por fabor
Get undressed, please

Acuéstese ahí, por favor
akwestese a-ee por fabor
Lie down over there, please

¿Está tomando algún medicamento?
esta tomando algoon medeekamento
Are you taking any medicines?

¿Está alérgico/alérgica a algún medicamento?
esta alerhheeko/alerhheeka a algoon medeekamento
Are you allergic to any medicines?

¿Está vacunado/a contra el tétano?
esta bakoonado/a kontra el tetano
Have you been vaccinated against tetanus?

¿Qué ha comido (hoy)?
ke a komeedo (oy)
What have you eaten (today)?

Hay una infección/Está infectado
iy oona eenfekthyon/esta eenfektado
There's an infection/It's infected

Tiene una intoxicación
tyene oona eentoxeekathyon
You have food poisoning

Es un infarto
es oon eenfarto
It's a heart attack

Tengo que ponerle una inyección
tengo ke ponerle oona eenyekthyon
I have to give you an injection

Tengo que darle unos puntos
tengo ke darle oonos poontos
I have to give you some stitches

Hay que hacer una radiografía
iy ke ather oona radyografee-a
It is necessary to do an X-ray

Necesito una muestra de sangre/orina
netheseeto oona mwestra de sangre/oreena
I need a blood/urine sample

158

Le voy a dar una receta
le boy a dar oona retheta
I am going to give you a prescription

Tome una píldora tres veces al día
tome oona peeldora tres bethes al dee-a
Take one tablet three times a day

Antes/Despúes de las comidas
antes/despwes de las komeedas
Before/After meals

Al acostarse
al akostarse
At bedtime

Tiene que descansar
tyene ke deskansar
You must rest

Tiene que estar tres días en la cama
tyene ke estar tres dee-as en la kama
You must stay in bed for three days

Tiene que volver dentro de cinco días
tyene ke bolber dentro de theenko dee-as
You must come back in five days' time

Tiene que beber muchos líquidos
tyene ke beber moochos leekeedos
You must drink plenty of liquids

No debe comer nada
no debe komer nada
You should eat nothing

Tendrá que ir al hospital
tendra ke eer al ospeetal
You will have to go to hospital

No es nada grave
no es nada grabe
It is nothing serious

No le pasa nada
no le pasa nada
There is nothing wrong with you

Puede vestirse
pwede besteerse
You can get dressed

You may want to say

At the dentist's

I need a dentist
Necesito un dentista
netheseeto oon denteesta

I have toothache
Tengo dolor de muelas
tengo dolor de mwelas

This tooth hurts
Me duele este diente
me dwele este dyente

I have broken a tooth
Me he roto un diente
me e roto oon dyente

I have lost a filling
He perdido un empaste
e perdeedo oon empaste

I have lost a crown/cap
He perdido una corona/funda
e perdeedo oona korona/foonda

He/She has toothache
Tiene dolor de muclas
tyene dolor de mwelas

He/She has broken a tooth
Se ha roto un diente
se a roto oon dyente

He/She has lost a filling
Ha perdido un empaste
a perdeedo oon empaste

He/She has lost a crown/cap
Ha perdido una corona/funda
a perdeedo oona korona/foonda

Can you fix it temporarily?
¿Puede arreglarlo temporalmente?
pwede arreglarlo temporalmente

Can you give me an injection?
¿Puede ponerme una inyección?
pwede ponerme oona eenyekthyon

Can you give him/her an
   injection?
¿Puede ponerle una inyección?
pwede ponerle oona eenyekthyon

This denture is broken
Esta dentadura está rota
esta dentadoora esta rota

Can you repair it?
¿Puede repararla?
pwede repararla

How much will it cost?
¿Cuánto costará?
kwanto kostara

You may hear

Abra la boca, por favor
abra la boka por fabor
Open your mouth, please

Necesita un empaste
netheseeta oon empaste
You need a filling

Tengo que sacarlo
tengo ke sakarlo
I have to extract it

Voy a ponerle una inyección
*boy a ponerle oona
   eenyekthyon*
I'm going to give you an
   injection

Parts of the body

English	Spanish	Pronunciation
ankle	**el tobillo**	*tobeelyo*
appendix	**el apéndice**	*apendeethe*
arm	**el brazo**	*bratho*
back	**la espalda**	*espalda*
bladder	**la vejiga**	*behheega*
blood	**la sangre**	*sangre*
body	**el cuerpo**	*kwerpo*
bone	**el hueso**	*weso*
bottom	**el trasero**	*trasero*
bowels	**los intestinos**	*eentesteenos*
breast	**el seno**	*seno*
buttock	**la nalga**	*nalga*
cartilage	**el cartílago**	*karteelago*
chest	**el pecho**	*pecho*
chin	**la barbilla**	*barbeelya*
ear	**la oreja**	*orehha*
elbow	**el codo**	*kodo*
eye	**el ojo**	*ohho*
face	**la cara**	*kara*
finger	**el dedo**	*dedo*
foot	**el pie**	*pye*
genitals	**los órganos genitales**	*organos hheneetales*
gland	**la glándula**	*glandoola*
hair	**el pelo**	*pelo*
hand	**la mano**	*mano*
head	**la cabeza**	*kabetha*
heart	**el corazón**	*korathon*
heel	**el talón**	*talon*
hip	**la cadera**	*kadera*
jaw	**la mandíbula**	*mandeeboola*
joint	**la articulación**	*arteekoolathyon*
kidney	**el riñón**	*reenyon*
knee	**la rodilla**	*rodeelya*
leg	**la pierna**	*pyerna*

ligament	**el ligamento**	*leegamento*
lip	**el labio**	*labyo*
liver	**el hígado**	*eegado*
lung	**el pulmón**	*poolmon*
mouth	**la boca**	*boka*
muscle	**el músculo**	*mooskoolo*
nail	**la uña**	*oonya*
neck	**el cuello**	*kwelyo*
nerve	**el nervio**	*nerbyo*
nose	**la nariz**	*nareeth*
penis	**el pene**	*pene*
private parts	**las partes pudendas**	*partes poodendas*
rectum	**el recto**	*rekto*
rib	**la costilla**	*kosteelya*
shoulder	**el hombro**	*ombro*
skin	**la piel**	*pyel*
spine	**la espina dorsal**	*espeena dorsal*
stomach	**el estómago**	*estomago*
tendon	**el tendón**	*tendon*
testicles	**los testículos**	*testeekoolos*
thigh	**el muslo**	*mooslo*
throat	**la garganta**	*garganta*
thumb	**el pulgar**	*poolgar*
toe	**el dedo del pie**	*dedo del pye*
tongue	**la lengua**	*lengwa*
tonsils	**las amígdalas**	*ameegdalas*
tooth	**el diente**	*dyente*
vagina	**la vagina**	*bahheena*
wrist	**la muñeca**	*moonyeka*

PROBLEMS AND COMPLAINTS

(*For car breakdowns, see page 36; see also* Emergencies, *page 272*)

● There are three types of police in Spain, all of them armed. They are:

La Policía Municipal (Municipal Police) – they come under the local authority at the town hall (**el ayuntamiento**). They are responsible for law and order in the local authority area, and also for traffic control. They wear blue uniforms.

La Policía Nacional (National Police) – they are responsible for law and order at national level. They wear dark blue uniforms.

La Guardia Civil (Civil Guard) – they are responsible for law and order in rural areas, and also for traffic control on main roads and in cities. They wear green uniforms.

● If your car is towed away, contact the **Policía Municipal**, who will tell you where to go to collect it.

● In a hotel, if all else fails and you can't get a complaint sorted out to your satisfaction, you can ask for the complaints book (**el libro de reclamaciones**). Hotels are required by law to have one – you write down your complaint and it is forwarded to the Spanish Ministry of Tourism.

You may see

Comisaría	Police station
No funciona	Out of order
Libro de reclamaciones	Complaints book
Servicio al cliente	Customer services

You may want to say

General phrases

Can you help me?
¿Puede ayudarme?
pwede iyoodarme

Can you fix it (immediately)?
¿Puede arreglarlo (inmediatamente)?
pwede arreglarlo (inmedyatamente)

When can you fix it?
¿Cuándo puede arreglarlo?
kwando pwede arreglarlo

Can I speak to the manager?
¿Puedo hablar con el gerente?
pwedo ablar kon el hherente

There's a problem with . . .
Hay un problema con . . .
iy oon problema kon . . .

There isn't/aren't any . . .
No hay . . .
no iy . . .

I need . . .
Necesito . . .
netheseeto . . .

The . . . doesn't work
El/La . . . no funciona
el/la . . . no foonthyona

The . . . is broken
El . . . está roto/La . . . está rota
el . . . esta roto/la . . . esta rota

I can't . . .
No puedo . . .
no pwedo . . .

It wasn't my fault
No ha sido mi culpa
no a seedo mee koolpa

I have forgotten my . . .
He olvidado el/la . . .
e olbeedado el/la . . .

I have lost my . . .
He perdido el/la . . .
e perdeedo el/la . . .

We have lost our . . .
Hemos perdido los/las . . .
emos perdeedo los/las . . .

Someone has stolen my . . .
Me han robado el/la . . .
me an robado el/la . . .

My . . . has disappeared
Mi . . . ha desaparecido
mee . . . a desaparetheedo

My . . . isn't here
Mi . . . no está
mee . . . no esta

Something is missing
Falta algo
falta algo

The . . . is missing
Falta el/la . . .
falta el/la . . .

This isn't mine
Esto no es mío
esto no es mee-o

Where you're staying

There isn't any (hot) water
No hay agua (caliente)
no iy agwa (kalyente)

There isn't any toilet paper
No hay papel higiénico
no iy papel eehhyeneeko

There isn't any electricity
No hay luz
no iy looth

There aren't any towels
No hay toallas
no iy to-alyas

I need another pillow
Necesito otra almohada
netheseeto otra almo-ada

I need another blanket
Necesito otra manta
netheseeto otra manta

I need a light bulb
Necesito una bombilla
netheseeto oona bombeelya

The light doesn't work
La luz no funciona
la looth no foonthyona

The shower doesn't work
La ducha no funciona
la doocha no foonthyona

The lock is broken
La cerradura está rota
la therradoora esta rota

The switch on the lamp is broken
El interruptor de la lámpara está roto
el eenterrooptor de la lampara esta roto

I can't open the window
No puedo abrir la ventana
no pwedo abreer la bentana

I can't turn the tap off
No puedo cerrar el grifo
no pwedo therrar el greefo

The toilet doesn't flush
La cisterna no funciona
la theesterna no foonthyona

The wash-basin is blocked
El lavabo está atascado
el labado esta ataskado

The wash-basin is dirty
El lavabo está sucio
el lababo esta soothyo

The room is . . .
La habitación es . . .
la abeetathyon es . . .

The room is too dark
La habitación es demasiado oscura
la abeetathyon es demasyado oskoora

The room is too small
La habitación es demasiado pequeña
la abeetathyon es demasyado pekenya

It's too hot in the room
Hace demasiado calor en la habitación
athe demasyado kalor en la abeetathyon

The bed is very uncomfortable
La cama es muy incómoda
la kama es mwee eenkomoda

There's a lot of noise
Hay mucho ruido
iy moocho roo-eedo

There's a smell of gas
Huele a gas
wele a gas

In bars and restaurants

This isn't cooked
Esto no está hecho
esto no esta echo

This is burnt
Esto está quemado
esto esta kemado

This is cold
Esto está frío
esto esta free-o

I didn't order this,
I ordered . . .
No pedí esto, pedí . . .
no pedee esto pedee . . .

This glass is cracked
Este vaso está roto
este baso esta roto

This is dirty
Esto está sucio
esto esta soothyo

This smells bad
Esto huele mal
esto wele mal

This tastes strange
Esto tiene un sabor raro
esto tyene oon sabor raro

There is a mistake on the bill
Hay un error en la cuenta
iy oon error en la kwenta

In shops

I bought this here (yesterday)
Compré esto aquí (ayer)
kompre esto akee (iyer)

Can you change this for me?
¿Puede cambiarme esto?
pwede kambyarme esto

I want to return this
Quiero devolver esto
kyero debolber esto

Can you refund me the money?
¿Puede devolverme el dinero?
pwede debolberme el deenero

Here is the receipt
Aquí está el recibo
akee esta el retheebo

It has a flaw
Tiene un defecto
tyene oon defekto

It has a hole
Tiene un agujero
tyene oon a-oohhero

There is a stain/mark
Hay una mancha
iy oona mancha

This is off/rotten
Esto está pasado
esto esta pasado

This isn't fresh
Esto no está fresco
esto no esta fresko

The lid is missing
Falta la tapa
falta la tapa

Forgetting and losing things and theft

I have forgotten my ticket
He olvidado el billete
e olbeedado el beelyete

I have forgotten the key
He olvidado la llave
e olbeedado la lyabe

I have lost my wallet
He perdido la cartera
e perdeedo la kartera

I have lost my driving licence
He perdido el carné de conducir
e perdeedo el karne de kondootheer

We have lost our rucksacks
Hemos perdido las mochilas
emos perdeedo las mocheelas

Where is the lost property office?

¿Dónde está la oficina de objetos perdidos?

donde esta la ofeetheena de obhhetos perdeedos

Where is the police station?

¿Dónde está la comisaría?

donde esta la komeesaree-a

Someone has stolen my bag

Me han robado el bolso

me an robado el bolso

Someone has stolen the car

Me han robado el coche

me an robado el koche

Someone has stolen my money

Me han robado el dinero

me an robado el deenero

If someone is bothering you

Please leave me alone

Por favor, déjeme en paz

por fabor dehheme en path

Go away, or I'll call the police

Váyase, o llamo a la policía

biyase o lyamo a la poleethee-a

There is someone bothering me

Hay alguien que me está molestando

iy algyen ke me esta molestando

There is someone following me

Hay alguien que me está siguiendo

iy algyen ke me esta seegyendo

You may hear

Helpful and unhelpful replies

Un momento, por favor

oon momento por fabor

Just a moment, please

Por supuesto

por soopwesto

Of course

Aquí tiene

akee tyene

Here you are

Le traeré otro/otra

le triy-ere otro/otra

I'll bring you another one

Le traeré uno/una inmediatamente
le triy-ere oono/oona inmedyatamente
I'll bring you one immediately

Ahora mismo/En seguida
a-ora meezmo/en segeeda
Right away

Se lo arreglaré mañana
se lo arreglare manyana
I'll fix it for you tomorrow

Lo siento, no es posible
lo syento no es poseeble
I'm sorry, it's not possible

Lo siento, no puedo hacer nada
lo syento no pwedo ather nada
I'm sorry, there's nothing I can do

Yo no soy el responsable
yo no soy el responsable
I am not the person responsible

No somos responsables
no somos responsables
We are not responsible

Debería usted denunciarlo en la comisaría
debereé-a oosteth denoonthyarlo en la komeesaree-a
You should report it to the police

Lo mejor sería . . .
lo mehhor seree-a . . .
The best thing would be . . .

Questions you may be asked

¿Cuándo lo compró?
kwando lo kompro
When did you buy it?

¿Tiene usted el recibo?
tyene oosteth el retheebo
Do you have the receipt?

¿Cuándo ocurrió?
kwando okoorree-o
When did it happen?

¿Dónde lo/la ha perdido?
donde lo/la a perdeedo
Where did you lose it?

¿Dónde lo/la han robado?
donde lo/la an robado
Where was it stolen?

¿Cómo es su bolso?
komo es soo bolso
What does your bag look like?

¿Cómo es su coche?
komo es soo koche
What does your car look like?

¿Qué marca es?
ke marka es
What make is it?

¿Cuál es la matrícula de su coche?
kwal es la matreekoola de soo koche
What is the registration number of your car?

¿Cómo se llama usted?
komo se lyama oosteth
What's your name?

¿Dónde se aloja usted?
donde se alohha oosteth
Where are you staying?

¿Cuál es su dirección?
kwal es soo deerekthyon
What is your address?

¿Cuál es el número de su habitación?
kwal es el noomero de soo abeetathyon
What is your room number?

¿Cuál es el número de su apartamento?
kwal es el noomero de soo apartamento
What is the number of your apartment?

¿En qué chalé/casa está usted?
en ke chale/kasa esta oosteth
What villa are you in?

¿Cuál es el número de su pasaporte?
kwal es el noomero de soo pasaporte
What is your passport number?

¿Tiene seguro?
tyene segooro
Are you insured?

Haga el favor de rellenar esta hoja
aga el fabor de relyenar esta ohha
Please fill in this form

BASIC GRAMMAR

Nouns

All Spanish nouns have a gender – masculine or feminine. You can often tell the gender from the word ending.

Most nouns ending in **-o** are masculine. The few exceptions include **mano** (hand), **radio** (radio) and **foto** (photo). Nouns ending in **-or** are also generally masculine.

Most nouns ending in **-a** are feminine. Exceptions include **día** (day), **mapa** (map), and words ending in **-ma** like **telegrama** (telegram) and **clima** (climate). Nouns ending in **-dad** and **-ión** are also generally feminine.

Words with other endings can be either gender – the Dictionary indicates which.

A masculine plural noun can refer to a mixture of masculine and feminine, e.g.:

hermanos	(brothers *or* brothers and sisters)
hijos	(sons *or* children, i.e. sons and daughters)
los españoles	(Spanish men *or* the Spanish)

Plurals

Nouns are generally made plural by adding **s** if they end in a vowel, or **es** if they end in a consonant, e.g.:

libro – libros   coche – coches   hotel – hoteles

The same applies to adjectives, e.g.:

blanco – blancos   azul – azules

Articles ('a'/'an', 'the')

The Spanish indefinite article (the equivalent of 'a' or 'an') has different forms: **un** is used with masculine nouns, **una** with feminine ones, e.g.:

un coche   una camisa

The definite article ('the') has different forms for masculine and feminine, and also for singular and plural:

	masculine	*feminine*
singular	**el**	**la**
plural	**los**	**las**

e.g.:

	el coche	**la camisa**
	los coches	**las camisas**

In the Dictionary, nouns are given with the definite article to show their gender.

'A' and 'de'

When **a** (at, to) and **de** (of) are followed by the article **el**, they become **al** and **del**, e.g.:

al centro   antes del puente

Adjectives

Adjectives 'agree' with the nouns they are describing – they have different endings for masculine and feminine, singular and plural.

Many adjectives end in **-o** for masculine and **-a** for feminine, with an added **s** for the plural of both, e.g.:

un coche blanco   una camisa blanca
coches blancos   camisas blancas

Some adjectives have only one ending for the singular, both
masculine and feminine, and add s or es for the plural. They
include those ending in -e and those ending in a consonant,
e.g.:

un coche verde	una camisa verde
coches verdes	camisas verdes
un coche azul	una camisa azul
coches azules	camisas azules

Note that adjectives denoting a person's nationality, even if
they end in a consonant, have different endings for masculine
and feminine singular, e.g.:

	masculine	*feminine*	
singular	inglés	inglesa	(English)
plural	ingleses	inglesas	
singular	español	española	(Spanish)
plural	españoles	españolas	

174 Position of adjectives

Most adjectives come after the noun, e.g.:

vino blanco   excursiones turísticas   una camisa azul

Some common adjectives always come *before* the noun,
including:

bueno (good)	**malo** (bad)
mucho (much, many)	**poco** (not much, few)
bastante (quite a lot)	**demasiado** (too much/many)
alguno (any, some)	**otro** (other)
todo (every, all)	**cada** (each)
primero (first)	**último** (last)

e.g.:
una buena idea (a good idea)
todos los días (every day)
la primera vez (the first time)

Comparatives and superlatives ('more', 'the most')

'More' is **más** and comes before the adjective – it also gives the equivalent of 'bigger', 'smaller', e.g.:
más interesante (more interesting)
más grande (bigger)
más viejo (older)

'Less' is **menos**:
menos importante (less important)
menos complicado (less complicated)

The comparatives of 'good' and 'bad' are **mejor** (better) and **peor** (worse).

'Than', as in 'more than' and 'less than', is **que**, e.g.:
este coche es más grande que el otro (this car is bigger than the other)

To say 'the most' or 'the least', put the definite article **el** or **la** before **más** or **menos**, e.g.:
la región más interesante (the most interesting region)
el/la más grande del mundo (the biggest in the world)

Possessives ('my', 'your', 'his', 'her', etc.)

Like other adjectives, possessive adjectives 'agree' with the nouns they are describing. The forms are:

	singular	*plural*
	masculine, feminine	*masculine, feminine*
my	**mi**	**mis**
your	**tu**	**tus**
his/her/your*	**su**	**sus**
our	**nuestro, nuestra**	**nuestros, nuestras**
your	**vuestro, vuestra**	**vuestros, vuestras**
their/your*	**su**	**sus**

(* 'Your' when addressing someone as **usted** – see '**You**' below)

e.g.:
mi hermano (my brother)
nuestra casa (our house)

There is no Spanish equivalent of the English apostrophe s as in 'John's brother', 'John and Susan's house', etc. Instead, the word **de** ('of') is used:
el hermano de John (John's brother)
la casa de John y Susan (John and Susan's house)

Demonstratives ('this', 'that')

There is one way of saying 'this' and two of saying 'that' – one for things that are fairly close, one for things 'over there':

	singular		*plural*	
	masculine	*feminine*	*masculine*	*feminine*
this, these	**este**	**esta**	**estos**	**estas**
that, those	**ese**	**esa**	**esos**	**esas**
that, those (over there)	**aquel**	**aquella**	**aquellos**	**aquellas**

All of these words are also used as demonstrative pronouns ('this one', 'that one', etc.). In this case they're written with an accent: **éste, ésos, aquél**, etc.

There are also 'neuter' forms: **esto, eso, aquello**. They are used when no specific noun is being referred to, e.g.:
esto es imposible (this is impossible)

Subject pronouns ('I', 'you', 'he', 'she', etc.)

I	**yo**
you (informal)*	**tú**
you (formal)*	**usted**
he	**él**
she	**ella**
we	**nosotros** (*masculine*), **nosotras** (*feminine*)
you (informal)*	**vosotros** (*masculine*), **vosotras** (*feminine*)
you (formal)*	**ustedes**
they	**ellos** (*masculine*), **ellas** (*feminine*)

(* see **'You'** below)

These pronouns are not used much – Spanish verbs have different endings which show what the subject is (see **Verbs** below). **Usted** and **ustedes** tend to be used more than the others, to show politeness, but in general the subject pronouns are used mainly for emphasis or to avoid confusion, e.g.:
él es inglés, ella es escocesa (he is English, she is Scottish)

'You'

In English there is only one way of addressing people using the word 'you'. In Spanish, there are two ways – one is more polite/formal, the other more casual/informal.

The informal way is used between friends and relatives, between people of the same age group, and to children. The part of the verb used is the second person (singular or plural as appropriate). The word for 'you' is **tú** (**vosotros/vosotras** in the plural).

The formal way uses the third person of the verb (singular or plural). The word for 'you' is **usted** (**ustedes** in the plural). Most of the phrases in this book use the formal way of saying 'you'.

Object pronouns

These are the equivalent of 'me', 'him', 'it', 'us' etc. Spanish has both direct object and indirect object pronouns. (Indirect objects are the equivalent of 'to/for me', 'to/for us' etc.)

The same words are used for both types, except in the third person. The full list is:

	me	nos
	te	os
direct	lo, la	los, las
indirect	le	les

They generally come before the verb, e.g.:
lo hablo bien (I speak it well)
¿**le** está esperando? (is he/she expecting you?)

But they can be added to the end of an infinitive of a verb, e.g.:
¿puede decir**le** que me **llame**? (can you tell him/her to call me?)

Verbs

Spanish verbs have different endings according to (i) the subject of the verb, (ii) the tense. There are three main groups of verbs, with different sets of endings for each group.

In dictionaries, verbs are listed in the infinitive form which ends in **-ar**, **-er** or **-ir** (these are the three groups).

Below are the endings for the present tense of these three groups:

	-ar	-er	-ir
	hablar	comer	vivir
yo	hablo	como	vivo
tú	hablas	comes	vives
él, ella, usted	habla	come	vive
nosotros/as	hablamos	comemos	vivimos
vosotros/as	habláis	coméis	vivís
ellos/as, ustedes	hablan	comen	viven

The Spanish present tense translates both the English 'I . . .' and 'I am . . .-ing' forms, e.g. **hablo** means both 'I speak' and 'I am speaking'.

Reflexives

Reflexive verbs are listed in dictionaries with the reflexive pronoun **se** on the end, e.g. **llamarse** (to be called), **quedarse** (to stay).

The reflexive pronouns are:

me	nos
te	os
se	se

e.g. **me llamo, te llamas, se llama,** etc.

'To be'

There are two Spanish verbs meaning 'to be': **ser** and **estar**.

Estar is used for temporary states and for locations, e.g.:
estoy de vacaciones (I am on holiday)
está enfermo (he is ill)
el banco está en la plaza mayor (the bank is in the main square)

Otherwise **ser** is used, e.g.:
soy inglés (I am English)
España es un país muy bonito (Spain is a very beautiful country)

Ser and **estar** are both irregular:

	ser	estar
yo	soy	estoy
tú	eres	estás
él, ella, usted	es	está
nosotros/as	somos	estamos
vosotros/as	sois	estáis
ellos/as, ustedes	scn	están

Other irregular verbs

Other common verbs that are also irregular include:

tener (to have)	ir (to go)	poder (to be able)	querer (to want; to love)	venir (to come)
tengo	voy	puedo	quiero	vengo
tienes	vas	puedes	quieres	vienes
tiene	va	puede	quiere	viene
tenemos	vamos	podemos	queremos	venimos
tenéis	vais	podéis	queréis	venís
tienen	van	pueden	quieren	vienen

Parts of other irregular verbs are given in the Dictionary.

Other verb tenses

A few verbs in other tenses that you may find useful:

ir (to go)	I went	fui
	we went	fuimos
	I used to go	iba
	we used to go	íbamos
ser (to be)	I was/used to be	era
	we were/used to be	éramos
estar (to be)	I was	estuve
	we were	estuvimos
	I have been	he estado
	we have been	hemos estado
tener (to have)	I had/used to have	tenía
	we had/used to have	teníamos
venir (to come)	I came	vine
	we came	vinimos
	I used to come	venía
	we used to come	veníamos

For talking about the future, you can often use the present tense, e.g.:

mañana juego al tenis (tomorrow I am playing tennis)

In a similar way to English, you can also say 'I am going to …', using the verb **ir**, followed by **a** and an infinitive, e.g.:

mañana voy a jugar al tenis (tomorrow I am going to play tennis)
vamos a ir a Granada (we are going to go to Granada)

Negatives

To make a verb negative, put **no** before it, e.g.:

no tengo hijos (I don't have any children)
no entiendo (I don't understand)
el señor García no está (Mr García isn't in)

Spanish has double negatives, e.g.:

no tengo nada (I don't have anything) (**nada** literally means 'nothing')

Questions

When a question does not begin with a question word ('where?', 'how?', 'why?', etc.), the word order is generally the same as it would be in an ordinary statement. The intonation of the voice changes to make it a question, e.g.:

hay un bar en la plaza   there is a bar in the square
¿hay un bar en la plaza?   is there a bar in the square?

Note that, in writing, questions begin with an upside-down question mark. The same happens with exclamations: **¡Viva España!**

DAYS, MONTHS, DATES

Names of days and months are not written with capital letters.

Days

Monday	**lunes**	*loones*
Tuesday	**martes**	*martes*
Wednesday	**miércoles**	*myerkoles*
Thursday	**jueves**	*hhwebes*
Friday	**viernes**	*byernes*
Saturday	**sábado**	*sabado*
Sunday	**domingo**	*domeengo*

Months

January	**enero**	*enero*
February	**febrero**	*febrero*
March	**marzo**	*martho*
April	**abril**	*abreel*
May	**mayo**	*miyo*
June	**junio**	*hhoonyo*
July	**julio**	*hhoolyo*
August	**agosto**	*agosto*
September	**septiembre**	*septyembre*
October	**octubre**	*oktoobre*
November	**noviembre**	*nobyembre*
December	**diciembre**	*deethyembre*

Seasons

spring	**la primavera**	*la preemabera*
summer	**el verano**	*el berano*
autumn	**el otoño**	*el otonyo*
winter	**el invierno**	*el eenbyerno*

General phrases

day	el día	el *dee-a*
week	la semana	la semana
fortnight	quince días	*keen*the *dee-as*
month	el mes	el mes
year	el año	el *anyo*
today	hoy	*oy*
tomorrow	mañana	*manyana*
yesterday	ayer	*iyer*
(in) the morning	(por) la mañana	*(por)* la *manyana*
(in) the afternoon/ evening	(por) la tarde	*(por)* la *tarde*
(at) night	(por) la noche	*(por)* la *noche*
this morning	esta mañana	*esta manyana*
this afternoon/ evening	esta tarde	*esta tarde*
tonight	esta noche	*esta noche*
tomorrow morning	mañana por la mañana	*manyana por la manyana*
yesterday afternoon/ evening	ayer por la tarde	*iyer por la tarde*
last night	anoche	*anoche*
on Monday	el lunes	el *loones*
on Tuesdays	los martes	los *martes*
every Wednesday	todos los miércoles	*todos los myerkoles*
in August/spring	en agosto/primavera	*en ...*
at the beginning of March	a principios de marzo	*a preentheepyos de ...*
in the middle of June	a mediados de junio	*a medyados de ...*
at the end of September	a finales de septiembre	*a feenales de ...*

183

in six months time	**dentro de seis meses**	*dentro de . . .*
during the summer	**durante el verano**	*doorante . . .*
two years ago	**hace dos años**	*athe . . .*
(in) the '90s	**(en) los años noventa**	*(en) los anyos . . .*
last . . .	**. . . pasado/a**	*. . . pasado/pasada*
last Monday	**el lunes pasado**	*el loones pasado*
last week	**la semana pasada**	*la semana pasada*
last month	**el mes pasado**	*el mes pasado*
last year	**el año pasado**	*el anyo pasado*
next . . .	**. . . próximo/a**	*. . . proxeemo/proxeema*
or	**. . . que viene**	*ke byene*
next Tuesday	**el martes próximo**	*el martes proxeemo*
next week	**la semana próxima**	*la semana proxeema*
next month	**el mes que viene**	*el mes ke byene*
next year	**el año que viene**	*el anyo ke byene*

184

What day is it today?	**¿Qué día es hoy?**
	ke dee-a es oy
What is the date today?	**¿Qué fecha es hoy?**
	ke fecha es oy
When is your birthday?	**¿Cuándo es su cumpleaños?**
	kwando es soo koomple-anyos
When is your saint's day?*	**¿Cuándo es su santo?**
	kwando es soo santo
It's (on) the first of January	**Es el primero de enero**
	el preemero de enero
(on) Tuesday 10th May	**martes el diez de mayo**
	martes el dyeth de miyo
1990	**mil novecientos noventa**
	meel nobethyentos nobenta
the 15th century	**el siglo XV (quince)**
	el seeglo keenthe

* Spaniards celebrate the saint's day corresponding to their Christian name

TIME

one o'clock	la una	la *oona*
two o'clock	las dos	las *dos*
twelve o'clock, etc.	las doce	las *dothe*
quarter past...	...y cuarto	...ee *kwarto*
half past...	...y media	...ee *medya*
five past...	...y cinco	...ee *theenko*
twenty-five past...	...y vienticinco	...ee *baynteetheenko*
quarter to...	...menos cuarto	...menos *kwarto*
ten to...	...menos diez	...menos *dyeth*
twenty to...	...menos veinte	...menos *baynte*
in the morning (a.m.)	de la mañana	de la *manyana*
in the afternoon/ evening (p.m.)	de la tarde	de la *tarde*
at night	de la noche	de la *noche*
in the early morning	de la madrugada	de la *madroogada*
noon/midday	mediodía	medyo*dee-a*
midnight	medianoche	medya*noche*
a quarter of an hour	un cuarto de hora	oon *kwarto* de ora
three quarters of an hour	tres cuartos de hora	tres *kwartos* de ora
half an hour	media hora	medya ora

185

24-hour clock

0000	las cero (horas)	las *thero* (oras)
0900	las nueve (horas)	las *nwebe* (oras)
1300	las trece (horas)	las *trethe* (oras)
1430	las catorce treinta	las *katorthe traynta*
2149	las veintiuna cuarenta y nueve	las *bayntee-oona kwarenta ee nwebe*

at...	**a la .../a las ...**	*a la .../a las ...*
exactly/precisely...	**las ... en punto**	*las ... en poonto*
just after...	**las ... y pico**	*las ... ee peeko*
about...	**sobre las ...**	*sobre las ...*
approximately...	**aproximadamente ...**	*aproxeemadamente ...*
nearly...	**casi las ...**	*kasee las ...*
soon	**pronto**	*pronto*
early	**temprano**	*temprano*
late	**tarde**	*tarde*
on time	**a tiempo**	*a tyempo*
earlier on	**antes**	*antes*
later on	**más tarde**	*mas tarde*
half an hour ago	**hace media hora**	*athe ...*
in ten minutes' time	**en diez minutos**	*en ...*
or	**dentro de ...**	*dentro de ...*

What time is it?	**¿Qué hora es?**	
	ke ora es	
It's...	**Es .../Son ...**	
	es .../son ...	
It's one o'clock	**Es la una**	
	es la oona	
It's six o'clock	**Son las seis**	
	son las says	
It's quarter past eight	**Son las ocho y cuarto**	
	son las ocho ee kwarto	
(At) what time ...?	**¿A qué hora ...?**	
	a ke ora ...	
At...	**A la .../A las ...**	
	a la .../a las ...	
At half past one	**A la una y media**	
	a la oona ee medya	
At quarter to seven	**A las siete menos cuarto**	
	a las syete menos kwarto	
At 2055	**A las veinte cincuenta y cinco**	
	a las baynte theenkwenta ee theenko	

186

COUNTRIES AND NATIONALITIES

Languages are the same as the masculine adjective. Nationalities are written with a small letter.

Country	Nationality (masculine, feminine)
Africa **África**	**africano, africana**
Algeria **Argelia**	**argeliano, argeliana**
Asia **Asia**	**asiático, asiática**
Australia **Australia**	**australiano, australiana**
Austria **Austria**	**austríaco, austríaca**
Basque Country **el País Vasco** **Euskadi** (*in Basque*)	**vasco, vasca**
Belgium **Bélgica**	**belga, belga**
Canada **el Canadá**	**canadiense, canadiense**
Catalonia **Cataluña** **Catalunya** (*in Catalan*)	**catalán, catalana**
Central America **América Central**	**centroamericano, centroamericana**
China **China**	**chino, china**
Czechoslovakia **Checoslovaquia**	**checoslovaco, checoslovaca**
Denmark **Dinamarca**	**danés, danesa**

England	**Inglaterra**	**inglés, inglesa**
Europe	**Europa**	**europeo, europea**
France	**Francia**	**francés, francesa**
Germany	**Alemaña**	**alemán, alemana**
Great Britain	**Gran Bretaña**	**británico, británica**
Greece	**Grecia**	**griego, griega**
Hungary	**Hungría**	**húngaro, húngara**
India	**la India**	**indio, india**
Ireland	**Irlanda**	**irlandés, irlandesa**
Italy	**Italia**	**italiano, italiana**
Japan	**Japón**	**japonés, japonesa**
Mexico	**Méjico**	**mejicano, mejicana**
Morocco	**Marruecos**	**marroquí, marroquí**
Netherlands **los Países Bajos, Holanda**		**holandés, holandesa**
New Zealand	**Nueva Zelanda**	**neozelandés, neozelandesa**
North America **América del Norte**		**norteamericano, norteamericana**
Northern Ireland **Irlanda del Norte**		
Norway	**Noruega**	**noruego, noruega**
Poland	**Polonia**	**polaco, polaca**
Portugal	**Portugal**	**portugués, portuguesa**
Russia	**Rusia**	**ruso, rusa**
Scotland	**Escocia**	**escocés, escocesa**

South America	América del Sur	sudamericano, sudamericana
Soviet Union	la Unión Soviética	
Spain	España	español, española
Sweden	Suecia	sueco, sueca
Switzerland	Suiza	suizo, suiza
Turkey	Turquía	turco, turca
United Kingdom	el Reino Unido	
United States	Estados Unidos	estadounidense, estadounidense norteamericano, norteamericana
Wales	País de Gales	galés, galesa
West Indies	las Antillas	antillano, antillana
Yugoslavia	Yugoslavia	yugoslavo, yugoslava

GENERAL SIGNS AND NOTICES

Abierto	Open
Agua potable	Drinking water
Ascensor	Lift
Aseos	Toilets
Atención	Caution/Beware
Averiado	Out of order
Aviso	Notice
Buzón	Postbox
Caballeros	Gentlemen
Caja	Cash desk
Caliente	Hot
Cerrado (por vacaciones)	Closed (for holidays)
Completo	Full, No vacancies
Consérvese en sitio fresco	Keep in a cool place
Consúmase antes de	Consume before
Cuidado	Caution/Take care
Cuidado con el escalón	Mind the step
Cuidado con el perro	Beware of the dog
Damas	Ladies
Demora	Delay
Despacho de billetes	Ticket office
Empujar	Push
Entrada	Entrance
Entrada libre	Free admission
Entre sin llamar	Enter without knocking
Fecha de caducidad	Expiry date
Frío	Cold
Fumadores	Smokers
Horario/Horas de visita	Visiting hours
Horas de oficina	Office hours
Huelga	Strike
Lavabos	Toilets

Lavar a mano	Hand-wash
Lavar en seco	Dry-clean
Libre	Free, Vacant
Liquidación	Sale
Llame al timbre	Ring the bell
Llegadas	Arrivals
Mirador	Viewing point
Modo de empleo	Instructions for use
No fumadores	Non-smokers
No fumar	No smoking
No funciona	Out of order
No obstruya la entrada	Do not obstruct entrance
No se admiten ...	... not admitted
No tocar	Do not touch
Ocupado	Occupied, Engaged
Ojo al tren	Beware of the train
Oportunidades	Bargains
Peligro (de muerte)	Danger (of death)
Peligro de incendio	Fire hazard
Pintura fresca	Wet paint
Piso	Floor
Planta baja	Ground floor
Privado	Private
Prohibido arrojar/tirar basuras	No litter
Prohibido asomarse	Do not lean out
Prohibido el paso/Prohibido entrar	No entry
Prohibido fumar	No smoking
Prohibido hablar con el conductor	Do not talk to the driver
Prohibida la entrada (a personas no autorizadas)	No entry (to unauthorised persons)
Prohibido pisar el césped/ la hierba	Keep off the grass
Rebajas	Sales, Reductions
Recién pintado	Wet paint

191

Reservado	Reserved
Reservado el derecho de admisión	The management reserves the right of admission
Retraso	Delay
Sala de espera	Waiting room
Salida (de emergencia)	(Emergency) exit
Se alquila	To let
Se ruega (no)...	Please (do not)...
Se vende	For sale
Señoras	Ladies
Servicios	Toilets
Silencio	Silence
Sótano	Basement
Tirar	Pull
Toque el timbre	Ring the bell
Venta de sellos	Stamps sold
Zona monumental	Historical area

CONVERSION TABLES
(approximate equivalents)

Linear measurements

centimetres   **centímetros (cm)**
metres   **metros (m)**
kilometres   **kilómetros (km)**

10 cm = 4 inches   1 inch = 2.54 cm
50 cm = 19.6 inches   1 foot = 30 cm
1 metre = 39.37 inches   1 yard = 0.91 m
(just over 1 yard)
100 metres = 110 yards
1 km = 0.62 miles

1 mile = 1.61 km

To convert
km to miles: divide by 8 and multiply by 5
miles to km: divide by 5 and multiply by 8

Miles		Kilometres
0.6	1	1.6
1.2	2	3.2
1.9	3	4.8
2.5	4	6.4
3	5	8
6	10	16
12	20	32
19	30	48
25	40	64
31	50	80
62	100	161
68	110	177
75	120	193
81	130	209

Liquid measures

litre   **litro (l)**

1 litre = 1.8 pints   1 pint = 0.57 litre
5 litres = 1.1 gallons   1 gallon = 4.55 litres
'A litre of water's a pint and three quarters'

Gallons		Litres
0.2	1	4.5
0.4	2	9
0.7	3	13.6
0.9	4	18
1.1	5	23
2.2	10	45.5

Weights

gram   **gramo (g)**
100 grams   **cien gramos**
200 grams   **doscientos gramos**
kilo   **kilo (kg)**

100 g = 3.5 oz   1 oz = 28 g
200 g = 7 oz   ¼ lb = 113 g
½ kilo = 1.1 lb   ½ lb = 227 g
1 kilo = 2.2 lb   1 lb = 454 g

Pounds		Kilos (Grams)
2.2	1	0.45 (450)
4.4	2	0.9 (900)
6.6	3	1.4 (1400)
8.8	4	1.8 (1800)
11	5	2.3 (2300)
22	10	4.5 (4500)

Area

hectare | **hectárea (ha)**

1 hectare = 2.5 acres   1 acre = 0.4 hectares

To convert
hectares to acres: divide by 2 and multiply by 5
acres to hectares: divide by 5 and multiply by 2

Hectares		Acres
0.4	1	2.5
2.0	5	12
4	10	25
10	25	62
20	50	124
40.5	100	247

Clothing and shoe sizes

Women's dresses and suits

UK	10	12	14	16	18	20
Continent	36	38	40	42	44	46

Men's suits and coats

UK	36	38	40	42	44	46
Continent	46	48	50	52	54	56

Men's shirts

UK	14	14½	15	15½	16	16½	17
Continent	36	37	38	39	41	42	43

Shoes

UK	2	3	4	5	6	7	8	9	10	11
Continent	35	36	37	38	39	41	42	43	44	45

Waist and chest measurements

inches	28	30	32	34	36	38	40	42	44	46	48	50
centimetres	71	76	81	87	91	97	102	107	112	117	122	127

Tyre pressures

lb/sq in	15	18	20	22	24	26	28	30	33	35
kg/sq cm	1.1	1.3	1.4	1.5	1.7	1.8	2.0	2.1	2.3	2.5

NATIONAL HOLIDAYS

Año Nuevo	New Year's Day	1 January
Epifanía/Día de los Reyes	Epiphany	6 January
San José	St Joseph's Day	19 March
Viernes Santo	Good Friday	
Lunes de Pascua	Easter Monday	
Día del Trabajo	Labour Day	1 May
Corpus Christi	Corpus Christi Day	
Santiago Apóstol	St James's Day	25 July
Asunción	Assumption	15 August
Día de la Hispanidad	Columbus Day	12 October
Todos los Santos	All Saints Day	1 November
Inmaculada Concepción	Immaculate Conception	8 December
Navidad	Christmas Day	25 December

USEFUL ADDRESSES

In the UK and Ireland

Spanish National Tourist Office
57 St James's Street
London SW1A 1LD
Tel: 071-499 0901

Spanish Embassy
24 Belgrave Square
London SW1X 8QA
Tel: 071-235 5555

Spanish Embassy
17A Merlyn Park
Dublin 4
Tel: Dublin 69 16 40

Spanish Chamber of Commerce
5 Cavendish Square
London W1M 0DP
Tel: 071-637 9061

Spanish Institute (Instituto de España)
(for cultural information)
102 Eaton Square
London SW1W 9AN
Tel: 071-235 1484/5

In Spain

British Embassy
Calle Fernando el Santo, 16
28010 Madrid
Tel: 419 0200

British Consulate
Centro Colón
Marqués de la Ensenada 16
28004 Madrid
Tel: 532 5217

There are British consulates in: Algeciras, Alicante, Barcelona,
Bilbao, Málaga, Santander, Sevilla, Tarragona, Vigo; and, in
the islands, Ibiza, Menorca, Palma de Mallorca, Lanzarote,
Las Palmas and Santa Cruz de Tenerife.

Irish Embassy
Calle Claudio Coello, 73
28001 Madrid
Tel: 276 3500

NUMBERS

0	**cero**	*thero*
1	**uno**	*oono*
2	**dos**	*dos*
3	**tres**	*tres*
4	**cuatro**	*kwatro*
5	**cinco**	*theenko*
6	**seis**	*says*
7	**siete**	*syete*
8	**ocho**	*ocho*
9	**nueve**	*nwebe*
10	**diez**	*dyeth*
11	**once**	*onthe*
12	**doce**	*dothe*
13	**trece**	*trethe*
14	**catorce**	*katorthe*
15	**quince**	*keenthe*
16	**dieciséis**	*dyetheesays*
17	**diecisiete**	*dyetheesyete*
18	**dieciocho**	*dyetheeocho*
19	**diecinueve**	*dyetheenwebe*
20	**veinte**	*baynte*
21	**veintiuno**	*bayntee-oono*
22	**veintidós**	*baynteedos*
23 etc.	**veintitrés**	*baynteetres*
30	**treinta**	*traynta*
31	**treinta y uno**	*traynta ee oono*
32 etc.	**treinta y dos**	*traynta ee dos*
40	**cuarenta**	*kwarenta*
50	**cincuenta**	*theenkwenta*
60	**sesenta**	*sesenta*
70	**setenta**	*setenta*
80	**ochenta**	*ochenta*
90	**noventa**	*nobenta*

100	**cien**	*thyen*
101 etc.	**ciento uno**	*thyento oono*
200	**doscientos**	*dosthyentos*
300	**trescientos**	*tresthyentos*
400	**cuatrocientos**	*kwatrothyentos*
500	**quinientos**	*keenyentos*
600	**seiscientos**	*saysthyentos*
700	**setecientos**	*setethyentos*
800	**ochocientos**	*ochothyentos*
900	**novecientos**	*nobethyentos*
1,000	**mil**	*meel*
2,000 etc.	**dos mil**	*dos meel*
1,000,000	**un millón**	*oon meelyon*
2,000,000 etc.	**dos millones**	*dos meelyones*

● Words for hundreds (like other adjectives) have different endings for masculine and feminine, e.g. **doscientos gramos** (200 grams), **doscientas pesetas** (200 ptas).

● For talking about millions of something, add **de**, e.g. **dos millones de habitantes** (2,000,000 inhabitants).

● Years
1990 **mil novecientos noventa**
1492 **mil cuatrocientos noventa y dos**

DICTIONARY

In the Spanish alphabet, **ch**, **ll** and **ñ** are separate letters, following **c**, **l** and **n** respectively.

Spanish nouns are given with the definite article ('the') to show their gender: **el** for masculine, **la** for feminine (**los** or **las** in the plural). Where the gender is not clear, the abbreviations (*m*) or (*f*) are added.

Adjectives which have different endings for masculine and feminine are shown like this: **blanco/a** (i.e. **blanco** for masculine, **blanca** for feminine). See Basic grammar, page 172, for notes on gender, plurals, etc.

Other abbreviations: (*pl*) = plural.

Spanish-English

Words for food and drink are given in the Menu reader, page 101.

See also General signs and notices, page 190, and the 'You may see' lists in the individual sections.

A

a to; at
  a . . . kilómetros/minutos
    . . . kilometres/minutes away
  a las . . . at . . . o'clock
abajo down, downstairs, below
  de abajo lower, bottom
abierto/a open
el abogado lawyer
el abono season ticket

el abrazo hug
  un (fuerte) abrazo, abrazos best wishes, regards
el abrebotellas bottle opener
el abrelatas tin/can opener
el abrigo coat
  abrir to open
  absoluto: en absoluto absolutely not, not at all
la abuela grandmother
el abuelo grandfather

aburrido/a bored, boring
AC=año de Cristo AD
acabar to finish
acampar to camp
acaso perhaps
el **accidente** accident
el **aceite** oil
aceptar to accept
la **acera** pavement
el **acero** steel
el **acondicionador (de pelo)** (hair) conditioner
aconsejar to advise, recommend
la **actividad** activity
acto: en el acto while you wait
acuerdo: de acuerdo agreed, fine, very well
adecuado/a suitable
a de JC=antes de Jesucristo BC
adelantado: por adelantado in advance
adelante forward; come in!
además besides, as well
adentro indoors
admiten: no se admiten . . . . . . not allowed
la **aduana** customs
adulto/a adult
advertir to warn
aéreo/a (of) air
el **aerodeslizador** hovercraft, hydrofoil
el **aeropuerto** airport
la **afeitadora** shaver
afeitar to shave
afilado/a sharp
afuera outside
las **afueras** outskirts

la **agencia** agency
la **agenda** diary
agitado/a rough
agotado/a exhausted, worn out; sold out
agradable pleasant
agradecido/a grateful
agridulce sweet and sour
agrio/a sour
el **agua** (f) water
agudo/a sharp, acute
la **aguja** needle
el **agujero** hole
ahí there
ahora now
ahumado/a smoked
el **aire** air
    al aire libre outdoors, open-air
el **aire acondicionado** air conditioning
el **ajo** garlic
ajustado/a tight
al=a+el to the
el **albergue** hotel, hostel
el **alcalde** mayor
el **alcázar** castle, fortress
el **alcornoque** cork oak
alegre happy
el **alfiler** pin
la **alfombra** carpet
algo anything, something
    ¿algo más? anything else?
el **algodón** cotton
    el algodón hidrófilo cotton wool
alguien someone
alguno/a any, some
los **alimentos** food
la **almohada** pillow
el **almuerzo** lunch

el **alojamiento** accommodation
la **alpargata** espadrille
alquilar to rent, hire
alrededor (de) around
los **alrededores** surrounding area, outskirts
alto/a high; tall
la **alumna, el alumno** pupil
allá there
allí there
el **ama** (f) **de casa** housewife
amable kind
amargo/a bitter
amarillo/a yellow
el **ambiente** atmosphere
ambos/as both
la **amiga** friend, girlfriend
el **amigo** friend, boyfriend
amueblado/a furnished
anciano/a old
ancho/a broad, wide
andando on foot, walking
el **andén** platform
el **anfiteatro** amphitheatre; (*theatre*) circle
el **anfitrión, la anfitriona** host, hostess
el **anillo** ring
el **aniversario** anniversary
anoche last night
el **ante** suede
la **antena** aerial
antes (de) before
antiadherente non-stick
el **anticonceptivo** contraceptive
el **anticongelante** antifreeze
las **antigüedades** antiques
el **anuncio** notice; advertisement
el **año** year
apagar to switch/turn off

el **aparato** appliance, machine
el **aparcamiento** parking, car park
aparcar to park
el **apartamento** apartment, fla
aparte (de) apart (from); extra
el **apeadero** halt (*railway*)
el **apellido** surname
apenas hardly, scarcely
apetece: ¿le/te apetece . . . ? do you feel like . . . ?
apoyarse to lean
aprender to learn
apretar to push, press
aproveche: ¡que aproveche! enjoy your meal!, bon appétit!
aproximadamente approximately
aquel, aquella that
aquél, aquélla that one
aquellos/as those
aquéllos/as those ones
aquí here
árabe Arab
la **araña** spider
el **arañazo** scratch
el **árbitro** referee
el **árbol** tree
la **arena** sand
el **armario** cupboard
arrancar to switch on
arreglar to arrange; to fix
arriba up, upstairs, above
de arriba upper, top
el **arroyo** stream
el **arte** (f) art
la **articulación** joint (*body*)
asado/a roast
el **ascensor** lift

los **aseos** toilets
así thus, like this/that
el **asiento** seat
áspero/a rough
el **asunto** matter, subject, topic
atacar to attack
atar to tie
atascado/a blocked, jammed
atención beware, take care
atestado/a crowded
atrás behind
  hacia atrás backwards
aumentar to increase
aun even
aún still, yet
aunque although
el **autobús** bus
el **autocar** coach
la **autopista** motorway
el **autostop** hitch-hiking
Av, Avda=avenida
la **avenida** avenue
averiado/a broken down, out
  of order
el **avión** aeroplane
el **aviso** notice; warning
ayer yesterday
ayudar to help
el **ayuntamiento** town hall
la **azafata** air stewardess
la **azúcar** sugar
  el **azúcar terciado** brown
  sugar
azul blue
azul marino navy blue

B

la **baca** roof rack
la **bacinica** (child's) potty
la **bahía** bay

bailar to dance
bajar to come/go down; to
  get off (bus, etc.); to take
  down; to turn down
  (volume)
bajo below; under(neath)
bajo/a low; short
el **balón** ball, football
el **baloncesto** basketball
el **banco** bank
la **bandeja** tray
la **bañera** bath(tub)
el **baño** bath
barato/a cheap
la **barba** beard
la **barca** (rowing) boat
el **barco** boat
el **barquillo** ice-cream cone
la **barra** bar, counter; loaf of
  bread
la **barra de labios** lipstick
el **barrio** district, quarter
basta that's enough
bastante quite, fairly;
  enough; quite a lot
el **bastón** walking stick
la **basura** rubbish
la **batería** car battery
el **baúl** trunk
el/la **bebé** baby
beber to drink
la **bebida** drink
la **belleza** beauty
el **beso** kiss
el **betún** shoe polish
el **biberón** baby's bottle
la **biblioteca** library
la **bicicleta** bicycle
bien well; fine
el **bigote** moustache
el **billete** ticket; banknote

blanco/a white
    en blanco blank
blando/a soft
el **bloc** notepad, writing pad
la **blusa** blouse
la **boca** mouth
el **bocadillo** sandwich
la **boda** wedding
la **bodega** wine cellar, wine shop
la **boite** nightclub
el **bolígrafo** ballpoint pen
la **bolsa** bag; stock exchange
el **bolsillo** pocket
el **bolso** handbag
el **bollo** roll
la **bomba** bomb; pump
los **bomberos** fire brigade
la **bombilla** (light)bulb
los **bombones** chocolates
    bonito/a pretty, nice, lovely
    bordo: a bordo aboard
    borracho/a drunk
el **bosque** wood, forest
la **bota** boot
la **botella** bottle
el **botijo** jar
el **botón** button
el **botones** bellboy
las **bragas** panties (*women's*)
    bravo/a brave; rugged, rough
el **brazo** arm
    brillante shiny
el **brillante** diamond
la **broma** joke
    bronceado/a (sun-)tanned
    buenas (*short for* buenos días,
    **buenas tardes, buenas
    noches**) good morning/
    afternoon/evening/night
    bueno/a, buen good
el **bulto** bulky object,

    package; lump
el **burro** donkey
    buscar to look for, to
    search
la **butaca** armchair; stalls
    (*theatre*)
el **buzón** letterbox, postbox

C

C/ = calle street
el **caballero** gentleman
el **caballo** horse
    cabe: no cabe it doesn't fit,
    it won't go in
el **cabello** hair
la **cabeza** head
la **cabra** goat
la **cacerola** saucepan
    cada each, every
la **cadena** chain
el **café** café; coffee
la **cafetera** coffee pot
la **caja** box; cash desk
la **caja de ahorros** savings
    bank
el **cajón** drawer
los **calcetines** socks
la **calefacción** heating
el **calentador** heater
la **calidad** quality
    caliente hot
el **calor** heat
    hace calor it's hot
    tener calor to be hot
la **calzada** roadway, road
    surface
los **calzoncillos** underpants
    (*men's*)
    callado/a quiet
la **calle** street
    ¡cállese!/¡cállate! be quiet!,
    shut up!

la **cama** bed
la **cámara** camera
la **camarera** waitress
el **camarero** waiter; steward
el **camarote** cabin
cambiar to change
el **camino** track, path; way, route
el **camión** lorry
la **camisa** blouse, shirt
la **camiseta** T-shirt
el **camisón** nightdress
la **campana** bell
el **campo** field; country(side)
el **canal** canal; channel (*TV*)
la **canción** song
la **cancha** court (*tennis, pelota etc.*)
el **canguro** kangaroo; babysitter
cansado/a tired
cantar to sing
la **cantina** station buffet
la **caña** cane; glass of draught beer
la **cara** face
los **caramelos** sweets
el **carbón** coal
la **cárcel** prison
el **cardenal** bruise
el **cargo** charge
cariñoso/a affectionate
la **carne** meat
el **carné/carnet de conducir** driving licence
caro/a expensive; dear
la **carpeta** file (*document*)
la **carrera** career; university course; race
la **carretera** (main) road
el **carril** lane (*on road*)
el **carrito** trolley

la **carta** letter; menu
la **cartelera** noticeboard; entertainments listings
la **cartera** wallet; briefcase
el **carterista** pickpocket
el **cartón** cardboard; carton
la **casa** house; home
casado/a married
la **cascada** waterfall
la **cáscara** shell; rind, peel
casi almost, nearly
las **castañuelas** castanets
el **castillo** castle
causa: a causa de because of
la **CE** EC, European Community
la **cena** dinner
cenar to have dinner
el **cenicero** ashtray
el **centro** centre; middle
el **cepillo** brush
la **cerámica** pottery
el **cerdo** pig; pork
las **cerillas** matches
cerca (de) close (to), near
cerrado/a closed; blocked
la **cerradura** lock
cerrar to close
el **césped** lawn
la **cesta** basket
la **cicatriz** scar
ciego/a blind
el **cielo** sky; heaven
el **cierre** fastener; buckle
la **cifra** figure, number
el **cigarrillo** cigarette
el **cine** cinema
la **cinta** ribbon; tape; cassette
la **cintura** waist
el **cinturón** belt
la **circulación** traffic

la **cita** appointment, date
la **ciudad** town, city
claro/a clear; light (coloured), pale
 ¡claro! of course!
la **clase** class; lesson; type, sort
el **clavel** carnation
el **clavo** nail
el/la **cliente** customer; client
el **clima** climate
 climatizado/a air-conditioned
cobrar to charge; to cash (*cheque*)
la **cocina** cooking; kitchen
cocinar to cook
el **coche** car
el **coche de línea** coach, long-distance bus
el **cochecito (de niño)** pram

el **código** code
coger to take, catch, get
la **cola** tail; queue; glue
el **colchón** mattress
colgar to hang up
la **colilla** cigarette end
la **colina** hill
el **color** colour
la **combinación** combination; connection; plan; petticoat, slip
el **comedor** dining-room
comer to eat
los **comestibles** food, groceries
la **comida** food; meal; lunch
la **comisaría** police station
como as, like
¿cómo? pardon?
¿cómo . . . ? how . . . ?
cómodo/a comfortable; convenient

la **compañía** company
completamente completely
completo/a complete; full (up)
comprar to buy
las **compras** shopping
las **compresas** sanitary towels
comprobar to check
el **compromiso** obligation; appointment; engagement
común common
con with
concurrido/a busy, crowded
el **concurso** competition
conducir to drive
el **conductor** driver
congelado/a (deep) frozen
el **congreso** conference, congress
el **conjunto** group
conmigo with me
conocer to know, be acquainted with
 conozco I know
la **conocida, el conocido** acquaintance
conseguir to obtain, get
conservar to keep
las **conservas** tinned food
constipado/a: estar constipado/a to have a cold
el **contador** meter
la **contaminación** pollution
el **contenido** contents
contento/a pleased
contestar to answer
contigo with you
contra against
conviene: no me conviene it doesn't suit me, it's not convenient

la **copa** cup; glass; drink
el **corazón** heart
la **corbata** tie
el **cordero** lamb
la **corona** crown
el **corcho** cork
Correos post office
correr to run
la **correspondencia** connection
la **corriente** (electrical) power, current; draught (*air*)
cortar to cut, to cut off
cortés polite
las **Cortes** Spanish parliament
la **cortina** curtain
corto/a short
la **cosa** thing
la **cosecha** harvest; vintage
la **costa** coast
costar to cost
la **costura** sewing
el **coto** (hunting) preserve, reserve
creer to think, believe
creo que sí/no I think so/I don't think so
la **crema** cream; lotion
la **cremallera** zip
el **crimen** crime
el **cruce** crossroads; junction
el **crucero** cruise
crudo/a raw
la **cruz** cross
cruzar to cross
el **cuaderno** exercise book
el **cuadro** picture, painting; square, check
¿**cuál**?, ¿**cuáles**? which?
cualquier(a) any, whichever
¿**cuándo**? when?
¿**cuánto/a**? how much?

¿**cuántos/as**? how many?
¿**cuántas veces**? how often?, how many times?
¿**cuántos años tiene**? how old is he/she?, how old are you?
¿**cuánto tiempo**? how long? (*time*)
el **cuarto** quarter; room
la **cubierta** cover; deck
cubierto/a covered; overcast (*weather*)
los **cubiertos** cutlery
el **cubo** bucket; bin
cubrir to cover
la **cuchara** spoon
el **cuchillo** knife
el **cuello** neck; collar
la **cuenta** bill; account
el **cuento** story
la **cuerda** rope; string
el **cuero** leather
el **cuerpo** body
cuesta, cuestan it costs, they cost
la **cueva** cave
cuidado: tener cuidado to take care
cuidar to look after
la **culpa** fault
el **cumpleaños** birthday
la **cuñada** sister-in-law
el **cuñado** brother-in-law
el **cura** priest
cuyo/a whose

CH

el **chal** shawl
el **chaleco** waistcoat
el **champú** shampoo
el **chándal** tracksuit
la **chaqueta** jacket
charlar to chat, talk
la **chica** girl
el **chicle** chewing gum
el **chico** boy
chiquito/a, chiquitín/ina very
small, tiny
el **chiste** joke
el **chófer** driver
el **choque** collision, crash
el **chupete** dummy (*baby's*)

D

D=don courtesy title for
man, Mr
Da=doña courtesy title for
woman, Mrs
el **daño** damage
dar to give
de of; from; about
debajo (de) under;
underneath
débil weak
decidir to decide
décimo/a tenth
decir to say, to tell
es decir that's to say, in
other words
el **declive** slope
el **dedo** finger
el **dedo del pie** toe
la **degustación** tasting,
sampling
dejar to leave

del=de+el of the
delante (de) in front (of)
delantero/a front
delgado/a slim
demás rest
demasiado/a too (much)
la **demora** delay
el **dentífrico** toothpaste
dentro (de) in, inside
denunciar to report
el **deporte** sport
la **derecha** right
los **derechos (de aduana)**
(customs) duty
desagradable unpleasant
el **desayuno** breakfast
descalzo/a barefoot
el **descanso** rest; interval, half-
time
desconocido/a unknown,
strange
descortés rude
describir to describe
descubrir to discover
el **descuento** discount
desear to want
desde from
desde luego of course
la **desgracia** misfortune,
accident
desgraciadamente
unfortunately
desnudo/a naked, nude
despacio slowly
el **despacho** office
después after(wards), later on
después de after
el **destino** destination
el **destornillador** screwdriver
la **desventaja** disadvantage
detrás (de) behind

devolver to give back, return
el día day
el día festivo (public) holiday
el día laboral weekday, working day
la diapositiva slide (*photo*)
diario/a daily
el dibujo drawing
los dibujos animados cartoon film
el diente tooth
difícil difficult
¿diga?, ¿dígame? hello (*on phone*); can I help you? (*in shops etc.*)
digamos let's say
el dinero money
la dirección direction; address
el disco disc; record
discrecional optional
la discusión discussion, argument
el diseño drawing; design, pattern
distinto/a different
divertido/a funny, amusing
doblar to turn
doble double
los dodotis disposable nappies
el dolor pain, ache
¿dónde? where?
dormir to sleep
el dormitorio bedroom
dos two
  los/las dos both
doy I give
la ducha shower
duele (it) hurts
la dueña, el dueño owner
duermo; duerme I sleep; he/she sleeps, you sleep

dulce sweet
durante during
duro/a hard

E

echar to throw (away); to put in
echarse to lie down
la edad age
el edificio building
EE UU=Estados Unidos United States
efectivamente really, in fact; exactly
eficaz effective
el ejemplo example
el the
él he; him
ella she; her
ellas they; them
ello it
ellos they; them
la embajada embassy
el embalse reservoir
embarazada pregnant
el embarcadero pier, jetty
el embarque boarding, embarcation
el embotellamiento traffic jam; bottleneck
los embutidos sausages, sausage products
la emisora radio station
emocionante exciting
empezar to begin
  empiezo I begin
  empieza he/she/it begins; you begin
emplear to use, employ
la empresa firm, business

empujar to push
en in; on
encantado/a delighted
el **encendedor** (cigarette) lighter
encender to light, switch/turn on
encima (de) on top (of)
encontrar to find; to meet
el **enchufe** plug; socket
la **energía** energy, power
enfadado/a angry, annoyed
enfermo/a ill
enfrente (de) opposite
¡enhorabuena! congratulations!
enorme enormous
la **enseñanza** teaching, education
enseñar to teach; to show
entender to understand
entero/a whole
entiendo I understand
entonces then
la **entrada** entrance, way in; admission; ticket
entrar (en) to enter, go in
entre among; between
la **entrega** delivery
el **entresuelo** (theatre) circle
el **envase** container
enviar to send
el **equipaje** luggage, baggage
el **equipo** team; equipment
equivocado/a mistaken, wrong
es he/she/it is; you are
la **escalera** stairs, staircase
el **escaparate** shop window
escarpado/a steep
la **escoba** broom
esconder to hide

escribir to write
escuchar to listen (to)
la **escuela** school
escupir to spit
ese/a that
ése/a that one
eso that (one)
esos/as those
ésos/as those ones
el **esmalte** varnish, enamel
el **espacio** space
espantoso/a awful, dreadful
España Spain
español/ola Spanish
el **esparadrapo** sticking plaster
la **especia** spice
especial special; peculiar
la **especie** type, kind
el **espectáculo** show, spectacle
el **espejo** mirror
esperar to wait (for); to expect; to hope (for)
la **esposa** wife
el **esposo** husband
la **espuma** foam
el **esquí** ski; skiing
esquiar to ski
la **esquina** corner
está he/she/it is; you are
la **estación** station; season
el **estacionamiento** parking
el **estadio** stadium
el **estado** state
la **estancia** stay
el **estanco** tobacconist's
estar to be
el **este** east
este/a this
éste/a this one
esto this (one)
el **estómago** stomach

estos/as these
éstos/as these ones
estoy I am
estrecho/a narrow; tight
la **estrella** star
el **estreno** première, first
  performance
estropeado/a broken down,
  out of order
la **estufa** stove
el **éxito** success
explicar to explain
la **exposición** exhibition
el **extranjero** abroad
extranjero/a foreign
extraño/a strange, odd

F

la **fábrica** factory
fácil easy
la **facturación** check-in
la **falda** skirt
falso/a false, fake
la **falta** lack
  hace falta . . . . . . is
    needed
la **familia** family
el **farol** street lamp
FC=el ferrocarril railway
la **fecha** date
feliz happy
feo/a ugly
la **feria** fair
los **fiambres** cold meats
la **fiebre** fever; (high)
  temperature
la **fiesta** festival, holiday
la **fila** row, tier
la **filial** branch

el **fin** end
el **fin de semana** weekend
la **finca** (country) estate
firmar to sign
flaco/a thin
flojo/a slack, loose; flabby
la **flor** flower
el **folleto** leaflet, brochure
el **fontanero** plumber
la **forastera, el forastero**
  stranger
la **forma** form, shape
  de todas formas anyway
los **fósforos** matches
la **frase** phrase; sentence
fregar los platos to do the
  washing up
frente a facing; faced with
fresco/a fresh; cool
el **frigorífico** refrigerator
frío/a cold
  hace frío it's cold
    (*weather*)
  tener frío to be cold
frito/a fried
la **frontera** border, frontier
el **fuego** fire; light (*for cigarette*)
la **fuente** fountain
fuera (de) outside
fuerte strong; loud
la **fuerza** strength, power
fumar to smoke
funcionar to work, function
la **funda** pillowcase
fundamentalmente basically
la **furgoneta** van

213

G

las **gafas** glasses, spectacles
la **galleta** biscuit
ganar to earn; to win
la **garganta** throat
la **gaseosa** lemonade
la **gasolina** petrol
gastar to spend
el **gato** cat
GC= la Guardia Civil Civil
   Guard
la **gente** people
el **gerente** manager
la **gitana, el gitano** gypsy
el **gobierno** government
el **golpe** knock, blow
la **goma** rubber
la **gomita** rubber band
gordo/a fat
la **gota** drop
grabar to record
gracias thank you
gracioso/a funny
el **grado** degree (*temperature*)
gran, grande big, large; great
Gran Bretaña Great Britain
los **grandes almacenes**
   department store
la **granja** farm
gratis free
grave serious
el **grifo** tap
la **gripe** flu
gris grey; dull
el **grito** shout, cry
grosero/a rude
la **grúa** tow truck
grueso/a thick
el **guante** glove
guapo/a good-looking;
   handsome; pretty

guardar to keep
el **guardarropa** cloakroom
guardia: de guardia on duty
la **guerra** war
el/la **guía** guide; guidebook
gusta: me gusta/gustan I like
   le gusta/gustan he/she/it
   likes; you like
gusto: mucho gusto it's a
   pleasure (to meet you)

H

la **habitación** room
hablar to speak, to talk
hace he/she/it does/make;
   you do/make
   hace . . . (años) . . . (years)
   ago
hacer to do, to make
hacia towards
hago I do/make
la **hamaca** deckchair
la **hambre** hunger
   tener hambre to be hungry
hasta until; as far as; even,
   including
hasta luego/pronto see you
   soon, so long
hay there is/are
   ¿qué hay? how are things?
hay que you have to, you
   must, it is necessary to
el **hecho** fact
hecho/a done, made;
   cooked; ripe (*cheese*)
el **helado** ice-cream
herido/a injured, wounded
la **hermana** sister
el **hermano** brother
hermoso/a beautiful

hervido/a boiled
el hielo ice
la hierba grass; herb
el hierro iron
la hija daughter
el hijo son
el hilo thread
el hogar home; house, household
hola hello
el hombre man
la hoja leaf; sheet of paper; form, document; blade (*razor*)
la hora hour
el horario timetable
las horas punta rush hour
el horno oven
hoy today
huele it smells
la huelga strike
la huerta kitchen garden, vegetable garden
el huésped guest; host
el hueso bone
el huevo egg
húmedo/a damp
el humo smoke

I

ida (solamente) single, one-way (*ticket*)
ida y vuelta return
el idioma language
la iglesia church
igual equal; the same
me da igual it's all the same to me, I don't care
impermeable waterproof
el impermeable raincoat

importa: no importa it doesn't matter
el importe amount
imprescindible essential
impresionante impressive
imprevisto/a unexpected
el incendio fire
incluido/a included
incluso/a included; including
incómodo/a uncomfortable; inconvenient
el inconveniente problem
el infierno hell
la informática computer science/studies, information technology
el informe report
inglés, inglesa English
la inquilina, el inquilino tenant
la insolación sunstroke
insólito/a unusual
instantáneo/a instant
el interruptor switch
la intervista interview
introducir to introduce; to insert
inútil useless
el invierno winter
ir to go
la isla island
el IVA VAT
la izquierda left

J

el jabón soap
jamás never
el jamón ham
el jarabe syrup
el jardín garden

la **jarra** jug
el **jefe** boss, head, chief
el **jerez** sherry
la **jornada** day
joven young
jubilado/a retired
la **judía** bean
el **juego** game; gambling; set, collection
jugar to play
el **juguete** toy
junto/a together
¡**justo**! that's right!
justo/a fair; just; correct
la **juventud** youth

L

la **the**; her; it
el **lado** side
   al lado de beside, next to
el **lago** lake
la **lámpara** lamp
la **lana** wool
lanzar to throw
el **lápiz** pencil
largo/a long
las the; them
lástima: ¡**qué lástima**! what a pity!
la **lata** tin, can
el **lavabo** wash-basin; toilet
la **lavandería** laundry
lavar to wash
le him; (to) him/her/it; (to) you
la **lectura** reading
la **leche** milk
leer to read
lejos far (away)

la **lengua** tongue; language
la **lente** lens
lento/a slow
les (to) them; (to) you
levantar to lift, raise
la **ley** law
la **libra (esterlina)** pound (sterling)
libre free, unoccupied, vacant; for hire
la **librería** bookshop
el **libro** book
ligero/a light
la **lima** file; lime
limpiar to clean
   limpiar en seco to dry-clean
limpio/a clean
la **línea** line
liso/a smooth
listo/a ready
la **litera** berth, couchette
el **litoral** coast
lo it; him
la **localidad** place; seat; ticket
la **loción** lotion
loco/a crazy, mad
Londres London
la **lonja** slice
los the; them
la **lotería** lottery
luego then
el **lugar** place
lujo: **de lujo** de luxe, luxury
la **luna** moon
la **luz** light; electricity

LL

la llamada call
llamar to call
  ¿cómo se llama (usted)?
    what is your name?
la llave key
la llave inglesa spanner
la llegada arrival
llegar (a) to arrive (at), reach
lleno/a full (up)
llevar to carry; to take
  (away); to wear
llorar to cry
lloviendo: está lloviendo it's
  raining
la lluvia rain

M

la madera wood
la madre mother
maduro/a mature, ripe
la maestra, el maestro (primary
  school) teacher
mal badly
la maleta suitcase
malo/a, mal bad
la mancha stain
mandar to send
la manera way, manner
la manga sleeve
la manifestación demonstration
  (*protest*)
la mano hand
la manta blanket
la manzanilla camomile tea;
  type of dry sherry
mañana tomorrow
la mañana morning
el maquillaje make-up
la máquina machine

la máquina de escribir
  typewriter
el mar sea
la marca make, brand
marchar to go
marcharse to go (away), to
  leave
  me marcho I'm going/
    leaving
el marido husband
los mariscos shellfish
marrón brown
el martillo hammer
más more; plus
matar to kill
la matrícula registration
  number
el matrimonio marriage;
  married couple
mayor elder; bigger; main
la mayor parte, la mayoría
  most, majority
me (to) me
el mechero (cigarette) lighter
medianoche midnight
mediante using, by means of
las medias stockings
el médico doctor
la medida measurement; size
medio/a half
el medio ambiente environment
mediodía midday
los medios means
mejor better; best
menor smaller; smallest;
  least
menos less; minus
  por lo menos at least
menudo: a menudo often
el mercado market
la merienda snack, picnic; tea

la **mermelada** jam
el **mes** month
la **mesa** table
meter to put
la **mezcla** mixture
mi my
mí me
el **microondas** microwave (oven)
miedo: tener miedo to be afraid
el **miembro** member
mientras while
mientras tanto meanwhile
minusválido/a disabled, handicapped
mío/a mine
mirar to look (at), to watch
mis my (*pl*)
la **misa** mass
mismo/a same; self
la **mitad** half
mixto/a mixed
la **mochila** rucksack
la **moda** fashion
el **modo** way, manner
mojado/a wet
molestar to bother, annoy
el **molino** mill
la **moneda** currency; coin
el **monedero** purse
la **montaña** mountain(s)
montar to ride
el **monte** mountain
montón: un montón (de), montones a lot (of), lots (of)
morado/a purple
moreno/a dark (*hair/skin*)
la **mosca** fly
mostrar to show
la **moto(cicleta)** motorbike

mover to move
la **muchacha** girl
el **muchacho** boy
mucho very (much), a lot
mucho/a a lot (of)
muchos/as many, lots (of)
los **muebles** furniture
el **muelle** quay, pier
muerto/a dead
la **muestra** sample
la **mujer** woman; wife
la **multa** fine
el **mundo** world
la **muñeca** wrist; doll
el **muro** wall
muy very

N

nada nothing
de nada not at all, don't mention it
nada más nothing else
nadar to swim
nadie no-one, nobody
los **naipes** playing cards
la **naranja** orange
la **nariz** nose
Na Sra=Nuestra Señora Our Lady
la **natación** swimming
Navidad Christmas
necesitar to need
los **negocios** business
negro/a black
la **nevera** refrigerator
ni nor
ni . . . ni neither . . . nor
ni siquiera not even
la **niebla** fog

la **nieta** granddaughter
el **nieto** grandson
la **nieve** snow
ninguno/a, ningún no, not any
  en ninguna parte nowhere
la **niña** girl
el **niño** boy
no no; not
la **noche** night
el **nombre** name
el **norte** north
nos us
nosotros/as we; us
las **noticias** news
la **novia** girlfriend, fiancée
el **novio** boyfriend, fiancé
nublado/a cloudy
nudo/a naked, nude
la **nuera** daughter-in-law
nuestro/a our, ours
nuevo: de nuevo again
nuevo/a new
el **número** number; size (*shoe*)
nunca never

O

o or
  o ... o ... either ... or ...
la **obra** work; play (*theatre*)
ocupado/a occupied, taken; engaged; busy
el **oeste** west
la **oferta** offer
la **oficina** office
el **oído** hearing; ear
  ¡oiga!, ¡oye! listen!; hello!
el **ojo** eye
el **olor** smell
la **onda** wave

ordenado/a tidy
el **ordenador** computer
la **oreja** ear
el **oro** gold
os you, to you
el **otoño** autumn
otra vez again
otro/a another, other
la **oveja** sheep
oxidado/a rusty
¡oye! listen! hello!

P

el **padre** father
los **padres** parents
pagar to pay (for)
la **página** page
el **país** country
el **paisaje** countryside, scenery
el **pájaro** bird
la **palabra** word
pálido/a pale
el **palo** stick, pole; (golf) club
el **pan** bread
el **pantalón, los pantalones** trousers
la **pantalla** screen
el **panty, los pantys** tights
los **pañales** nappies
el **paño** cloth
el **pañuelo** handkerchief
el **papel** paper
para for; in order to
la **parada** stop; (*taxi*) rank
el **paraguas** umbrella
parar to stop
parecer to seem
la **pared** wall
la **pareja** couple

el **pariente**, la **parienta** relation/ relative
el **paro** unemployment
el **parque** park
la **parte** part
el **partido** (*political*) party; game, match
pasado/a past; last
el **pasajero** passenger
pasar to pass; to spend (*time*); to happen
el **pasatiempo** pastime, hobby
Pascua Easter
el **paseo** walk; ride
el **pasillo** corridor, aisle
el **paso a nivel** level crossing
el **paso de peatones** pedestrian crossing
la **pasta de dientes** toothpaste
el **pastel** cake, pastry
los **patines** skates
la **paz** peace
el **peaje** toll
el **peatón** pedestrian
el **pedazo** piece
pedir to ask (for)
el **peine** comb
la **película** film
el **peligro** danger
el **pelo** hair
la **pelota** ball; Basque national ball-game
la **peluquería** hairdresser's, barber's
pena: ¡qué pena! what a pity!
pensar to think
la **pensión** pension; boarding house
peor worse; worst
pequeño/a small, little
perder to lose; to miss

perdone, perdón pardon me/ excuse me
perezoso/a lazy
el **periódico** newspaper
el/la **periodista** journalist
el **permiso** licence, permit
permitido/a allowed
pero but
el **perro** dog
la **persiana** (Venetian) blind
la **persona** person
pesado/a heavy; boring, tedious
el **pescado** fish
el **peso** weight
la **pez** fish
picante hot, spicy
picar to sting, bite
el **pie** foot
la **piedra** stone
la **piel** skin; fur; leather
la **pierna** leg
la **pila** battery
la **píldora** pill
la **pimienta** pepper
pintar to paint
la **pintura** paint, painting
la **piscina** swimming pool
el **piso** floor, storey; flat
la **pista** track, course; (ski-)run (tennis) court
la **plancha** iron; sailboard
la **planta** plant; floor, storey
la **plata** silver
el **platillo** saucer
el **plato** dish; course
la **playa** beach
la **plaza** square
la **plaza de toros** bullring
el **plomo** lead
pobre poor

un poco a bit, a little
poco/a little, not much
pocos/as few, not many
poder to be able
podrido/a rotten
la policía police
la política politics
el polvo dust; powder
el pollo chicken
poner to put; to place; to put down
por by; for; per; through; via
por ejemplo (p.ej.) for example
por favor please
¿por qué? why?
porque because
la postal postcard
el postre dessert
potente powerful
el precio price
precioso/a lovely
preciso/a precise, exact; necessary
preferir to prefer
preguntar to ask
el premio prize
la prenda garment
preocupado/a worried
preparar to prepare, get ready
presentar to introduce
la prima cousin
la primavera spring
primero/a, primer first
el primo cousin
el/la principiante beginner
el principio beginning
prisa: tener prisa to be in a hurry
privado/a private

el problema problem
la procedencia point of departure
el profesor, la profesora teacher; lecturer; professor
profundo/a deep
prohibido/a prohibited, forbidden
pronto soon
la propietaria, el propietario owner; landlady, landlord
la propina tip
próximo/a next
público/a public
el pueblo people; village
puede he/she/it can; you can
puedo I can
el puente bridge
la puerta door; gate
el puerto port, harbour, docks
el pulgar thumb
pulsar to press, push
la pulsera bracelet
el puño fist; handful, fistful; cuff
el puro cigar

221

Q

que that, which; than
¿qué? what?; which?
¿qué tal? how are things?
quemar to burn
querer to want; to love
el queso cheese
¿quién?, ¿quiénes? who?
quiere decir it means
quiero I want; I love
la quiniela football pools
quisiera I would like; you would like; he/she would like

quitar to remove, take away
quizá/quizás perhaps, maybe

R

la **rama** branch
raro/a rare, odd
rasgado/a torn
rayado/a striped
la **razón** reason
  tiene(s) razón you are right
real royal
realidad: en realidad in fact
la **rebaja** reduction
el **recado** message
la **receta** recipe; prescription
el **recibo** receipt
la **reclamación** complaint
la **recogida** collection
  recto, todo recto straight on
el **recuerdo** memory; souvenir
la **red** net; network
redondo/a round
el **reembolso** refund
el **refresco** cold drink
el **regalo** gift, present
el **régimen** diet
la **región** region, area
la **regla** ruler
la **reina** queen
el **reloj** clock; watch
rellenar to fill (in)
el **remedio** remedy, cure
remolcar to tow
la **RENFE** Spanish Railways
reparar to repair
repente: de repente suddenly
repetir to repeat
el **reportaje** report
la **representación** performance

el **repuesto** spare part; refill;
  replacement
resbaladizo/a slippery
la **reserva** reservation, booking
reservar to reserve, book
el **resfriado** cold (*illness*)
la **respuesta** answer, reply
el **resultado** result
el **retraso** delay
el **retrete** toilet
revelar to show; to develop
  (*film*)
revés: al revés the wrong way
  round, upside down, inside
  out
revisar to check
la **revista** magazine
el **rey** king
rico/a rich; delicious
rígido/a stiff
el **rincón** corner
el **río** river
la **risa** laugh
rizado/a curly
**RNE = Radio Nacional de
  España** Spanish National
  Radio
robar to rob, to steal
rodeado/a (de) surrounded
  (by)
rojo/a red
el **rollo** (roll of) film
romper to break
la **ropa** clothes, clothing
la **ropa interior** underwear
rosa pink
la **rosa** rose
roto/a broken
rubio/a fair, blond(e)
la **rueda** wheel
el **ruido** noise
la **ruina** ruin

222

S

S=San Saint
SA=Sociedad Anónima Limited, PLC
la sábana sheet
saber to know (how to)
el sabor taste; flavour
el sacacorchos corkscrew
sacar to get/take out, to remove
el sacerdote priest
la sal salt
la sala room, lounge; (concert) hall
salado/a salty; savoury
salgo I go out/am going out
la salida exit, way out; departure
salir to come/go out; to leave, depart
el salón lounge, living-room
saltar to jump
la salud health
¡salud! cheers!
salvaje wild
salvar to rescue, save
la sangre blood
sano/a healthy
san, santo, santa saint
la sartén frying pan
el sastre tailor
se him/her/itself; yourself; themselves
sé, no sé I know, I don't know
secar to dry
seco/a dry
secundario/a secondary
la sed thirst
tener sed to be thirsty

la seda silk
seguida: en seguida immediately, right away
seguido/a continuous
según according to, depending on
segundo/a second
el seguro insurance
seguro/a sure, certain; safe
el sello stamp
el semáforo traffic lights
la semana week
sencillo/a simple
el sendero path
sensato/a sensible
sentado/a sitting (down)
el sentido sense; feeling
sentir to feel
la señal sign; signal
las señas address
el señor gentleman; Mr
la señora lady; Mrs
la señorita young lady; Miss
ser to be
serio/a serious
el servicio service; service charge
los servicios (public) toilets
la servilleta napkin, serviette
servir to serve
la sesión session; (cinema) performance, screening
si if; whether
sí yes
el SIDA AIDS
siempre always
siento: lo siento I'm sorry
la sierra saw; mountain range
el siglo century
el significado meaning
siguiente following, next

silencioso/a silent
la silla chair
la silla de ruedas wheelchair
la sillita de ruedas push-chair
simpático/a nice, charming, pleasant
sin without
sin embargo however
sino but (rather)
el/la sinvergüenza rascal, scoundrel
el sitio place
sobre on; upon; about
el sobre envelope
sobre todo above all, especially
la sobrina niece
el sobrino nephew
el socio member; partner
el sol sun; sunshine
224 **solamente** only
solicitar to apply for
sólo only
solo/a alone; lonely
soltero/a single, unmarried
la sombra shade; shadow
la sonrisa smile
la sopa soup
sordo/a deaf
la sorpresa surprise
el sostén bra
el sótano basement
soy I am
Sr=señor Mr
Sra=señora Mrs
Sres=señores Mr and Mrs
Srta=señorita Miss
Sta=Santa Saint
Sto=Santo Saint
su, sus his/her/its; their; your
suave smooth; mild; gentle

subir to come/go up; to lift up, take up; to increase
subterráneo/a underground
sucio/a dirty
la sucursal branch (of bank etc.)
la suegra mother-in-law
el suegro father-in-law
el sueldo wage
el suelo floor; ground
el suelto (small) change
el sueño sleep; dream
    tener sueño to be sleepy
la suerte luck
    tener suerte to be lucky
    ¡buena suerte! good luck!
el supositorio suppository
supuesto: por supuesto of course
el sur south
el susto fright, scare
suyo/a his/her/its; theirs; yours

T

el tabaco tobacco
tal such
la talla size
el taller workshop; garage
el tamaño size
también also, as well, too
tampoco neither
tan so
tanto/a so much
tantos/as so many
la tapa lid; snack, appetiser
el tapón plug
la taquilla booking office, box office
tardar to take (time)

tarde late
la tarde afternoon, evening
la tarjeta card
el tarro pot; jar
la tarta cake, gâteau; tart; pie
la taza cup
el teatro theatre
la tecla key (*on keyboard*)
el techo ceiling; roof
el tejado roof
el tejido textile
la tela fabric, material
el teleférico cable car
la tempestad storm
la temporada season
temprano early
el tenedor fork
tener to have
tengo I have
   tengo que I must, I have to
el tentempié snack
tercero/a, tercer third
la terraza terrace
el terrón sugar lump
el testigo witness
la tía aunt
el tiempo time; weather
la tienda shop; tent
   tiene he/she/it has; you have
   tiene que he/she/it must, has to; you must, you have to
la tierra earth; land; ground
las tijeras scissors
el timbre bell
tinto/a red (*wine*)
el tío uncle; bloke, guy
el tipo type, sort, kind; chap
tirar to throw; to throw away; to pull
las tiritas sticking plasters

la toalla towel
el tocadiscos record player
el tocador dressing table; powder room
tocar to touch; to play (*instrument*)
todavía yet; still
todo everything
todo/a, todos/as all, every
todo el mundo everyone
tomar to take; to have (to drink)
la tonelada ton
torcido/a twisted, sprained
la tormenta (thunder)storm
el tornillo screw
el toro bull
la torre tower
la tos cough
trabajar to work
el trabajo work, job
la traducción translation
traducir to translate
el traje dress; suit; outfit
el traje de baño bathing costume, swimsuit
el trampolín diving board
tranquilo/a calm, quiet
el transbordo transfer
el trapo rag
tras after; behind
trasero/a rear, back
tratar to treat; to deal with
   se trata de . . . it's to do with . . .
través: a través de through; across
el tren train
la tripulación crew
triste sad, unhappy
el trozo piece, bit

tu, tus your
tú you
la tumbona deckchair
el turno turn
tuyo/a yours
TVE=Televisión Española
Spanish Television

U

Ud, Uds=usted, ustedes you
últimamente lately
último/a last; latest
un a/an; one
una a/an; one
único/a unique; only
la universidad university
uno one
unos/as some
la uña nail
la urbanización urban
development; housing
estate
el uso use; usage; custom
usted, ustedes you
útil useful
utilizar to use

V

va he/she/it goes/is going;
you go/are going
la vaca cow
las vacaciones holiday(s)
vacilar to hesitate
vacío/a empty
el vagón carriage (*train*)
la vajilla crockery; dishes
vale fine, OK
vale la pena it's worth it

valiente brave
el valle valley
el vapor steam
los vaqueros jeans
varios/as several, some
el vaso glass
vaya, váyase go, go away
Vd, Vds=usted, ustedes you
veces (*pl of* vez) times
a veces sometimes
muchas veces often
la vecina, el vecino neighbour
la vecindad neighbourhood
la vela candle; sail, sailing
la velocidad speed
veloz fast
vencer to defeat, beat
el vendedor, la vendedora
salesman, saleswoman
vender to sell
el veneno poison
vengo I come/am coming
venir to come
la venta sale; country inn
la ventaja advantage
la ventana window
ver to see
el/la veraneante holidaymaker
el verano summer
veras: ¿de veras? really?
la verbena verbena; local
open-air festival
la verdad truth
¿verdad? right?, true?, isn't
that so?
verde green
la verdura green vegetables;
greenery
verificar to check
el vestido dress

la vez time
    a la vez at the same time
    de vez en cuando from time to time, occasionally
    en vez de instead of
    otra vez again
    una vez más again, one more time
viajar to travel
el viaje journey, trip
la vida life
el vidrio glass
    viejo/a old
viene he/she/it comes/is coming; you come/are coming
    . . . que viene next . . .
el viento wind
el vino wine
la viña vineyard
    violar to rape
el viraje bend, curve
    visitar to visit
la vista (eye)sight; look; view
la viuda widow
el viudo widower
    ¡viva . . . ! long live . . .!, up with . . .!
la vivienda housing
    vivir to live
    vivo/a live, alive; vivid, bright
el volumen volume
    volver to return
    vosotros/as you
    voy I go/am going
la voz voice
el vuelo flight
la vuelta turn; return
    vuestro/a your; yours

W

el wáter toilet

Y

    y and
    ya already; now
    ¡ya! of course!
el yerno son-in-law
    yo I

Z

las zapatillas trainers, sports shoes
el zapato shoe
la zarzuela Spanish light opera
el zumo juice

English-Spanish

There is a list of car parts on page 39, and parts of the body on page 162. See also the lists on pages 182–189.

A

a/an **un, una**
abbey **la abadía**
about (*on the subject of*) **sobre, de**
  (*approximately*) **más o menos**
above (*upstairs etc.*) **arriba**
  (*on top of*) **encima de**
abroad **en el extranjero**
  to go abroad **ir al extranjero**
abscess **el absceso**
to accept **aceptar**
accident **el accidente**
accommodation **el alojamiento**
according to **según**
account (*bank*) **la cuenta**
accountant **el contable**
ache **el dolor**
acid **el ácido**
across (*on the other side of*) **al otro lado de**
acrylic **el acrílico**
to act **actuar**
activity **la actividad**
actor **el actor**
actress **la actriz**
adaptor (*voltage*) **el adaptador**
  (*multiple plug*) **el enchufe múltiple**
adhesive tape **la cinta adhesiva**
address **la dirección**
admission **la entrada**
  admission charge **el precio de entrada**
adopted **adoptivo/a**
adult **el adulto, la adulta**
advance: in advance **por adelantado**
advanced (*level*) **avanzado/a**
advertisement **el anuncio**
advertising **la publicidad**
aerial **la antena**
aeroplane **el avión**
afford: I can't afford it **no tengo suficiente dinero**
afraid: to be afraid **tener miedo** (tener, *see page 180*)
after **después de**
  afterwards **después**
afternoon **la tarde**
aftershave **la loción para después del afeitado, el aftershave**
again **otra vez**
against **contra**
age **la edad**
agency **la agencia**
ago: ... ago **hace ...**
to agree **estar de acuerdo** (estar, *see page 179*)
AIDS **el SIDA**
air **el aire**
  by air **por avión**
air conditioning **el aire acondicionado**
air force **la aviación**
airline **la línea aérea**
air mattress **el colchón neumático**
airport **el aeropuerto**
aisle **el pasillo**
  (*church*) **la nave**

alarm la **alarma**
alarm clock el **despertador**
alcohol el **alcohol**
alcoholic **alcohólico/a**
alive **vivo/a**
all **todo/a, todos/as**
allergic to **alérgico/a a**
to allow **permitir**
  allowed **permitido/a**
all right (*agreed*) **de acuerdo**
almond la **almendra**
alone **solo/a**
along **por**
  along (*the river etc.*) **a lo largo de**
already **ya**
also **también**
although **aunque**
always **siempre**
am (*see* to be)
ambition la **ambición**
ambulance la **ambulancia**
among **entre**
amount la **cantidad**
amusement park el **parque de atracciones**
anaesthetic el **anestésico**
and **y**
angry **enfadado/a**
animal el **animal**
anniversary el **aniversario**
annoyed **enfadado/a**
anorak el **anorak**
another (one) **otro/a**
answer la **respuesta**
to answer **contestar**
antibiotic el **antibiótico**
antifreeze el **anticongelante**
antique la **antigüedad**
antiseptic el **antiséptico**
any **alguno/a**

anyone **alguien**
anything (*something*) **algo**
  anything else? ¿**algo más?**
anyway **de todas formas**
anywhere **en cualquier parte**
apart (from) **aparte (de)**
aperitif el **aperitivo**
apartment el **apartamento**
appendicitis la **apendicitis**
apple la **manzana**
appointment la **cita**
approximately **aproximadamente, más o menos**
apricot el **albaricoque**
arch el **arco**
archaeology la **arqueología**
architect el **arquitecto**
architecture la **arquitectura**
are (*see* to be)
area (*surface*) el **área** (*f*)
  (*region*) la **región**
argument la **discusión**
arm el **brazo**
armband (*swimming*) el **flotador**
army el **ejército**
around **alrededor (de)**
  around the corner **a la vuelta de la esquina**
to arrange **organizar**
arrest: under arrest **detenido/a**
arrival la **llegada**
to arrive **llegar**
art el **arte** (*f*)
  fine arts **las bellas artes**
art gallery la **galería de arte**
arthritis la **artritis**
artichoke la **alcachofa**
article el **artículo**
artificial **artificial**
artist el **artista**

as **como**
as far as **hasta**
ash **la ceniza**
ashtray **el cenicero**
to ask **preguntar**
to ask for **pedir**
asparagus **los espárragos**
aspirin **la aspirina**
assistant **el/la ayudante**
asthma **el asma** (*f*)
at **a, en**
athletics **el atletismo**
atmosphere **el ambiente**
to attack **atacar**
attractive **atractivo/a**
aubergine **la berenjena**
auction **la subasta**
aunt **la tía**
author **el autor, la autora**
automatic **automático/a**
autumn **el otoño**
avalanche **el alud**
avocado **el aguacate**
to avoid **evitar**
away: . . . . (kilometres) away **a . . .**
(**kilómetros**)
awful **espantoso/a**

B

baby **el/la bebé**
baby cereal **la papilla**
baby food **la comida para bebés**
baby's bottle **el biberón**
baby wipes **las toallitas**
limpiadoras
babysitter **el canguro**
back: at the back **de atrás**
(*reverse side*) **el dorso**
backwards **hacia atrás**
bacon **el beicon, el tocino**
bad **malo/a**

badly **mal**
bag **la bolsa**
baggage **el equipaje**
baker **el panadero**
baker's **la panadería**
balcony **el balcón**
(*theatre etc.*) **el anfiteatro,**
el entresuelo
bald **calvo/a**
ball (*tennis etc.*) **la pelota**
(*football*) **el balón**
ballet **el ballet**
ballpoint pen **el bolígrafo**
banana **el plátano**
band (*music*) **la banda**
bandage **la venda**
bank **el banco**
barber's **la peluquería**
basement **el sótano**
basket **la cesta**
basketball **el baloncesto**
bath **el baño**
to have a bath **tomar**
un baño
bathing costume **el traje**
de baño
bathroom **el cuarto de baño**
battery **la pila**
(*car*) **la batería**
bay **la bahía**
to be **ser; estar** (*see page 179*)
I am **soy; estoy**
we are **somos; estamos**
he/she/it is. you are **es;**
está
beach **la playa**
bean **la judía**
French/green **la judía**
verde
beard **la barba**
beautiful **hermoso/a**
because **porque**
bed **la cama**

bedroom **el dormitorio**
bee **la abeja**
beef **la carne de vaca**
beer **la cerveza**
beetroot **la remolacha**
before **antes (de)**
to begin **empezar**
   I begin **empiezo**
   he/she/it begins; you begin
     empieza
beginner **el/la principiante**
beginning **el principio**
behind **detrás (de)**
beige **beige**
to believe **creer**
   I believe so/not **creo que sí/no**
bell **la campana**
   (doorbell) **el timbre**
to belong to **pertenecer a**
   (to be a member of) **ser socio**
   de (ser, see page 179)
below **abajo**
   (beneath) **debajo de**
belt **el cinturón**
bend **la curva**
bent **torcido/a**
berry **la baya**
berth **la litera**
beside (next to) **al lado de**
besides **además**
best **(el/la/lo) mejor**
better **mejor**
between **entre**
beyond **más allá (de)**
bib **el babero**
Bible **la Biblia**
bicycle **la bicicleta**
big **grande**
bigger **más grande**
bill **la cuenta**
bin **el cubo**

bindings (ski) **las fijaciones**
bin liner **la bolsa de basura**
binoculars **los prismáticos**
biology **la biología**
bird **el pájaro**
birthday **el cumpleaños**
biscuit **la galleta**
bishop **el obispo**
a bit **un poco**
to bite **morder**
bitter **amargo/a**
black **negro/a**
   black and white (film)
   blanco y negro
blackberry **la zarzamora**
black coffee **el café solo**
blackcurrant **la grosella negra**
blanket **la manta**
bleach **la lejía**
to bleed **sangrar**
blind **ciego/a**
blind (Venetian) **la persiana**
blister **la ampolla**
blocked **obstruido/a**
   (road) **cerrado/a**
blond(e) **rubio/a**
blood **la sangre**
blouse **la blusa**
to blow **soplar**
blow-dry **el secado a mano**
blue **azul**
blusher **el colorete**
boarding **el embarque**
boarding card **la tarjeta de**
   embarque
boat **el barco**
   by boat **en barco**
body **el cuerpo**
boiled **hervido/a**
boiled egg **el huevo pasado**
   por agua

boiler la caldera
bomb la bomba
bone el hueso
book el libro
to book reservar
booking la reserva
booking office (*railway etc.*)
  el despacho de billetes
  (*theatre*) la taquilla
bookshop la librería
boot la bota
  (*car*) el maletero
border (*edge*) el borde
  (*frontier*) la frontera
bored, boring aburrido/a
both ambos/as, los/las dos
bottle la botella
bottle opener el abrebotellas
bottom el fondo
  (*body*) el trasero
bow (*ship*) la proa
bow (*knot*) el lazo
bowl el tazón
bowls (*game*) las bochas
box la caja
  (*theatre*) el palco
box office la taquilla
boy el chico
boyfriend el amigo, el novio
bra el sostén
bracelet la pulsera
braces los tirantes
brain el cerebro
branch la rama
  (*bank etc.*) la sucursal
brand la marca
brandy el coñac
brass el latón
brave valiente
bread el pan
to break romper

I have broken he roto
breakdown truck la grúa
breakfast el desayuno
to breathe respirar
bricklayer el albañil
bride la novia
bridegroom el novio
bridge el puente
briefcase la cartera
bright (*colour*) vivo/a
  (*light*) fuerte
bring: can you bring
  me . . .? ¿me trae . . .?
British británico/a
broad ancho/a
broad bean la haba
brochure el folleto
broken roto/a
broken down estropeado/a
bronchitis la bronquitis
bronze el bronce
brooch el broche
broom la escoba
brother el hermano
brother-in-law el cuñado
brown marrón
  (*hair*) castaño/a
brown sugar el azúcar
  terciado
bruise el cardenal
brush el cepillo
bucket el cubo
budgerigar el periquito
buffet la cafetería
to build construir
building el edificio
bulb (*electric*) la bombilla
bull el toro
bullfight la corrida de toros
bullfighter el torero
bullring la plaza de toros

bumper el parachoques
burn la quemadura
to burn quemar
   burnt quemado/a
bus el autobús
   by bus en autobús
bush el arbusto
business los negocios
business trip el viaje de negocios
businessman el hombre de negocios
businesswoman la mujer de negocios
business studies las ciencias empresariales
bus station la estación de autobuses
bus stop la parada de autobús
busy ocupado/a
but pero
butane gas el gas butano
butcher's la carnicería
butter la mantequilla
butterfly la mariposa
button el botón
to buy comprar
by por

C

cabbage la col, la berza
cabin la cabina
cable car el teleférico
café el café
cake el pastel
cake shop la pastelería
calculator la calculadora
call (phone) la llamada
to call llamar

to be called llamarse
   I am called me llamo
   he/she/it is called se llama
   what is he/she/it called?
   ¿cómo se llama?
calm tranquilo/a
camera la cámara
camomile tea la manzanilla
to camp acampar
   camped la cama de camping/campaña
camping el camping
campsite el camping
can (to be able) poder
   (see page 180)
   I can puedo
   can you . . .? ¿puede . . .?
   (to know how to) saber
   I (don't) know how to . . .
   (no) sé . . .
can (tin) la lata
can opener el abrelatas
to cancel cancelar
cancer el cáncer
candle la vela
canoe la canoa
capital (city) la capital
captain el capitano
car el coche
   by car en coche
carafe la garrafa
caravan la caravana
caravan site el camping
cardigan la rebeca
care: to take care tener cuidado
   (tener, see page 180)
   I don't care no me importa
careful cuidadoso/a
careless descuidado/a
car park el aparcamiento
carpenter el carpintero

carpet la alfombra
carriage (*railway*) el vagón
carrier bag la bolsa (de plástico)
carrot la zanahoria
to carry llevar
to carry on continuar
car wash el lavado automático
case: just in case por si acaso
cash: to pay cash pagar al contado
to cash (*cheque*) cobrar
cash desk la caja
cassette la cinta, la cassette
cassette player el cassette
castanets las castañuelas
castle el castillo
cat el gato
catalogue el catálogo
to catch (*train/bus*) coger
cathedral la catedral
Catholic católico/a
cauliflower la coliflor
to cause causar
cave la cueva
ceiling el techo
celery el apio
cellar el sótano
(*wine*) la bodega
cemetery el cementerio
centimetre el centímetro
central central
central heating la calefacción central
centre el centro
century el siglo
cereal los cereales
certain seguro/a
certainly (*why not?*) ¿cómo no?
certificate el certificado
chain la cadena
chair la silla

chair lift la telesilla
chalet el chalet
champagne el champán
(*Spanish*) la cava
change (*small coins*) el suelto
to change cambiar
(*clothes*) cambiarse
I have to change tengo que cambiarme
changing room el probador
channel el canal
English Channel el Canal de la Mancha
chapel la capilla
charcoal el carbón
charge el precio
charter flight el vuelo chárter
cheap barato/a
check (*pattern*) a cuadros
to check controlar
check-in (desk) el mostrador de facturación
to check in hacer la facturación
cheek la mejilla
cheeky descarado/a
cheers! ¡salud!
cheese el queso
cheesecake la tarta de queso
chef el cocinero
chemist's la farmacia
chemistry la química
cheque el cheque
cherry la cereza
chess el ajedrez
chestnut la castaña
chewing gum el chicle
chicken el pollo
chickenpox la varicela
child el niño, la niña
children los niños
(*sons and daughters*) los hijos

chimney **la chimenea**
china **la porcelana**
chips **las patatas fritas**
chocolate **el chocolate**
chocolates **los bombones**
to choose **escoger**
chop (*meat*) **la chuleta**
Christian **cristiano/a**
Christian name **el nombre de pila**
Christmas **la Navidad**
Christmas Eve **la Nochebuena**
church **iglesia**
cigar **el puro**
cigarette **el cigarrillo**
cigarette lighter **el encendedor**
cinema **el cine**
cinnamon **la canela**
circle **el círculo**
  (*theatre*) **el anfiteatro, el
    entresuelo**
circus **el circo**
city **la ciudad**
civil servant **el funcionario, la
  funcionaria**
class **la clase**
classical music **la música clásica**
clean **limpio/a**
to clean **limpiar**
cleansing cream **la crema
  limpiadora**
clear **claro/a**
clerk **el/la oficinista**
clever **inteligente**
cliff **el acantilado**
climate **el clima**
to climb (up) **subir**
climber **el/la alpinista**
climbing **el alpinismo**
clinic **la clínica**
cloakroom **el guardarropa**

clock **el reloj**
close (by) **cerca**
close to **cerca de**
to close **cerrar**
  I close **cierro**
  he/she/it closes; you close
    cierra
closed **cerrado/a**
cloth (*for cleaning*) **el paño**
clothes **la ropa**
clothes peg **la pinza**
cloud **la nube**
cloudy **nublado/a**
club **el club**
  (*golf*) **el palo**
coach **el autocar**
  (*railway*) **el vagón**
coal **el carbón**
coarse (*texture*) **burdo/a**
  (*skin etc.*) **áspero/a**
coast **la costa**
coat **el abrigo**
coat-hanger **la percha**
cocktail **el cóctel**
coffee **el café**
coin **la moneda**
cold **frío/a**
  I'm cold **tengo frío**
  it's cold (weather) **hace frío**
cold: to have a cold **estar
  resfriado/a (estar,** *see page 179*),
  tener resfriado (tener, *see page*
  180)
collar **el cuello**
  (*dog's etc.*) **el collar**
colleague **el/la colega**
to collect **coleccionar**
collection (*stamps etc.*) **la
  colección**
  (*postal/rubbish*) **la recogida**
college **el colegio**

colour **el color**
  (*in colour*) **en color**
colour-blind **daltoniano/a**
comb **el peine**
to come **venir** (*see page 180*)
  are you coming? **¿viene?**
to come back **volver**
  I come/am coming back
  vuelvo
to come down **bajar**
comedy **la comedia**
to come in **entrar**
  come in! **¡adelante!**
to come out **salir**
comfortable **cómodo/a**
comic (*magazine*) **el tebeo**
commercial **comercial**
common **común**
communion **la comunión**
communism **el comunismo**
communist **comunista**
compact disc **el disco compacto,
el compact disc**
company **la compañía**
compared with **comparado/a con**
compartment **el compartimento**
compass **la brújula**
to complain (*make a complaint*)
reclamar
complaint **la reclamación**
completely **completamente**
complicated **complicado/a**
compulsory **obligatorio/a**
composer **el compositor**
computer **el ordenador**
computer science/studies **la
informática**
concert **el concierto**
concert hall **la sala de conciertos**
concussion **la conmoción cerebral**
condition **la condición**
conditioner (*hair*) **el**

condicionador
condom **el anticonceptivo**
conference **el congreso**
to confirm **confirmar**
connection (*travel*) **la
correspondencia**
conscious **consciente**
conservation **la conservación**
conservative **conservador/ora**
constipation **el estreñimiento**
consulate **el consulado**
to contact **comunicarse con**
  I want to contact . . . **quiero
comunicarme con . . .**
contact lens **la lente de
contacto**
contact lens cleaner **la
solución limpiadora para
lentes de contacto**
continent **el continente**
contraceptive **el
anticonceptivo**
contract **el contrato**
convenient **práctico/a**
  it's not convenient for me
  no me conviene
convent **el convento**
cook **el cocinero, la cocinera**
to cook **cocinar**
cooker **la cocina**
cool **fresco/a**
cool box **la nevera portátil**
copper **el cobre**
copy **la copia**
  (*book*) **el ejemplar**
cork **el corcho**
corkscrew **el sacacorchos**
corner (*street*) **la esquina**
  (*room*) **el rincón**
correct **correcto/a**
corridor **el pasillo**
cosmetics **los cosméticos**

cost el precio
o cost **costar**
   how much does it cost?
   ¿cuánto cuesta?
cot **la cuna**
cottage **la casita de campo**
cotton (*material*) **el algodón**
   (*thread*) **el hilo**
cotton wool **el algodón**
   (**hidrófilo/en rama**)
couchette **la litera**
cough **la tos**
cough medicine **el jarabe para la**
   tos
o count **contar**
counter (*shop*) **el mostrador**
country (*nation*) **el país**
country(side) **el campo**
couple (*things*) **un par**
   (*people*) **la pareja**
courgette **el calabacín**
course (*lessons*) **el curso**
   (*food*) **el plato**
court (*law*) **el tribunal**
   (*sport*) **la pista**
cousin **el primo, la prima**
cover **la cubierta**
cover charge **el cubierto**
cow **la vaca**
cramp (*medical*) **el calambre**
crash (*car*) **el choque**
crayon **el lápiz de color**
crazy **loco/a**
cream (*food*) **la nata**
   (*lotion*) **la crema**
credit card **la tarjeta de crédito**
crisps **las patatas fritas**
cross **la cruz**
   Red Cross **la Cruz Roja**
o cross (*road etc.*) **cruzar**

cross-country skiing **el esquí**
   nórdico
crossing (*sea*) **la travesía**
crossroads **el cruce**
crowded **atestado/a**
crown **la corona**
cruise **el crucero**
crutch **la muleta**
to cry **llorar**
crystal **el cristal**
cucumber **el pepino**
cuff **el puño**
cup **la taza**
cupboard **el armario**
cure (*remedy*) **el remedio**
to cure **curar**
curling tongs **las pinzas**
   eléctricas
curly **rizado/a**
current (*electrical*) **la corriente**
curtain **la cortina**
curve **la curva**
cushion **el cojín**
custard **las natillas**
customs **la aduana**
cut **el corte**
to cut, to cut off **cortar**
cutlery **los cubiertos**
cycling **el ciclismo**
cyclist **el/la ciclista**
cystitis **la cistitis**

D

daily **diario/a**
damaged **dañado/a**
damp **húmedo/a**
dance **el baile**
to dance **bailar**
danger **el peligro**
dangerous **peligroso/a**

dark **oscuro/a**
(*hair/skin*) **moreno/a**
darling **querido/a**
darts **los dardos**
data (*information*) **los datos**
date (*day*) **la fecha**
(*fruit*) **el dátil**
daughter **la hija**
daughter-in-law **la nuera**
day **el día**
day after tomorrow **pasado mañana**
day before yesterday **anteayer**
day after/before **el día siguiente/anterior**
dead **muerto/a**
deaf **sordo/a**
dealer **el comerciante**
dear (*loved*) **querido/a**
(*expensive*) **caro/a**

death **la muerte**
debt **la deuda**
decaffeinated **descafeinado/a**
deck **la cubierta**
deckchair **la tumbona, la hamaca**
to decide **decidir**
to declare **declarar**
deep **profundo/a**
deep freeze **el congelador**
deer **el ciervo**
defect **el defecto**
definitely! **sí, desde luego**
to defrost **deshelar**
degree (*temperature*) **el grado**
(*university*) **el título**
delay **la demora, el retraso**
delicate **delicado/a**
delicious **delicioso/a, rico/a**
demonstration **la demostración**
(*protest*) **la manifestación**
dentist **el dentista**
dentures **la dentadura postiza**

deodorant **el desodorante**
to depart **salir**
department **el departamento**
department store **los grandes almacenes**
departure **la salida**
departure lounge **la sala de embarque**
deposit **el depósito**
to describe **describir**
description **la descripción**
desert **el desierto**
design **el diseño**
to design **diseñar**
designer **el diseñador, la diseñadora**
dessert **el postre**
destination **el destino**
detail **el detalle**
detergent **el detergente**
to develop (*film*) **revelar**
diabetes **la diabetes**
to dial **marcar**
dialling code **el prefijo**
dialling tone **el tono de marcar**
diamond **el brillante**
diarrhoea **la diarrea**
diary **la agenda**
dice **el dado, los dados**
dictionary **el diccionario**
to die **morir**
... died ... **murió**
diesel **el gasóleo, el gas-oil**
diet **el régimen**
to be on a diet **estar a régimen** (estar, *see p. 179*)
different **distinto/a**
difficult **difícil**
dining-room **el comedor**
dinner **la cena**

dinner jacket **el smoking**
diplomat **el diplomático**
direct **directo/a**
direction **la dirección**
director **el director**
directory (*telephone*) **la guía telefónica**
dirty **sucio/a**
disabled **minusválido/a**
disappointed **decepcionado/a**
disc **el disco**
disco **la discoteca**
discount **el descuento**
dish **el plato**
dishwasher **el lavavajillas, el lavaplatos**
disinfectant **el desinfectante**
dislocated **dislocado/a**
disposable nappies **los dodotis, los pañales**
distance **la distancia**
distilled water **el agua destilada**
district **la zona**
to dive **saltar al agua**
diversion (*road*) **la desviación**
diving-board **el trampolín**
divorced **divorciado/a**
dizzy **mareado/a**
to do **hacer**
    I do **hago**
    he/she/it does; you do **hace**
    we do **hacemos**
docks **el puerto**
doctor **el médico**
document **el documento**
dog **el perro**
doll **la muñeca**
dollar **el dólar**
dome **la cúpula**
dominoes **el dominó**
donkey **el burro**

door **la puerta**
double **doble**
double bed **la cama de matrimonio**
dough **la masa**
down **abajo**
downstairs **abajo**
drain **el desaguadero**
drama **el drama**
draught (*air*) **la corriente**
draught beer **la cerveza de barril**
    glass of draught beer **una caña**
to draw **dibujar**
drawer **el cajón**
drawing **el dibujo**
drawing-pin **la chinche**
dreadful **espantoso/a**
dress **el vestido**
dressing (*medical*) **el vendaje** (*salad*) **el aliño**
drink **la bebida**
    to have a drink **tomar una copa**
to drink **beber**
to drip **gotear**
to drive **conducir**
    I drive **conduzco**
driver **el conductor**
driving licence **el carné de conducir**
drowned **ahogado/a**
drug **la droga**
drug addict **el/la toxicómano/a; el/la drogadicto/a**
drum **el tambor**
drunk **borracho/a**
dry **seco/a**
dry-cleaner's **la tintorería**
dubbed **doblado/a**
duck **el pato**
dull (*weather*) **gris**

dumb **mudo/a**
dummy (*baby's*) **el chupete**
during **durante**
dust **el polvo**
dustbin **el cubo de la basura**
dusty **polvoriento/a**
duty (*customs*) **los derechos**
duty-free **libre de derechos**
duvet **el edredón**

E

each **cada**
ear **la oreja**
earache **el dolor de oídos**
earlier (*before*) **antes**
early **temprano**
to earn **ganar**
earring **el pendiente**
earth **la tierra**
earthquake **el terremoto**
east **el este**
eastern **del este, oriental**
Easter **Pascua**
easy **fácil**
to eat **comer**
economical **económico/a**
economy, economics
  la economía
egg **el huevo**
either . . . or **o . . . o**
elastic band **la gomita**
election **la elección**
electric **eléctrico/a**
electrician **el electricista**
electricity **la electricidad, la luz**
electronic **electrónico/a**
else: everything else **todo lo
  demás**
embarrassing **embarazoso/a**
embassy **la embajada**
emergency **la emergencia**

empty **vacío/a**
  (*house etc.*) **desocupado/a**
to empty **vaciar**
enamel **el esmalte**
end **el fin**
to end **terminar**
energetic **enérgico/a**
energy **la energía**
engaged (*to be married*)
  prometido/a
  (*occupied*) **ocupado/a**
engine **el motor**
engineer **el ingeniero**
engineering **la ingeniería**
England **Inglaterra**
English **inglés, inglesa**
enough **bastante**
to enter **entrar (en)**
entertainment **la diversión**
enthusiastic **entusiasta**
entrance **la entrada**
envelope **el sobre**
environment **el medio
  ambiente**
equal **igual**
equipment **el equipo**
-er (e.g. bigger, cheaper)
  más . . .
escalator **la escalera mecánic**
espadrille **la alpargata**
especially **especialmente,
  sobre todo**
essential **imprescindible**
estate (*country*) **la finca**
estate agent **el agente
  inmobiliario**
evaporated milk **la leche
  evaporada**
even (*including*) **hasta**
  (*not odd*) **par**
evening **la tarde**
evening dress **el traje de
  noche**

every (*each*) **cada**
   (*all*) **todos/as**
everyone **todo el mundo**
everything **todo**
everywhere **en todas partes**
exactly **exactamente, exacto**
examination (*school etc.*) **el examen**
example **el ejemplo**
   for example **por ejemplo**
excellent **excelente**
except **excepto**
excess luggage **el exceso de equipaje**
exchange **cambiar**
exchange rate **el cambio**
excited **emocionado/a**
exciting **emocionante**
excursion **la excursión**
excuse me **perdone, ¡perdón!**
executive **el ejecutivo, la ejecutiva**
exercise **el ejercicio**
exhibition **la exposición**
exit **la salida**
expect **esperar**
expensive **caro/a**
experience **la experiencia**
expert **el experto, la experta**
explain **explicar**
explosion **la explosión**
export **la exportación**
export **exportar**
extension (*telephone*) **la extensión**
external **externo/a**
extra (*in addition*) **aparte**
eye **el ojo**
eyebrow **la ceja**
eyebrow pencil **el lápiz de cejas**
eyelash **la pestaña**
eyeliner **el lápiz de ojos**
eyeshadow **la sombra de ojos**

F

fabric **la tela**
face **la cara**
face cream **la crema de belleza**
face powder **los polvos de la cara**
facilities **las facilidades**
fact **el hecho**
   in fact **en realidad**
factory **la fábrica**
to fail (*exam/test*) **no aprobar**
failure **el fracaso**
faint: fainted, in a faint **desmayado/a**
fair (*hair*) **rubio/a**
fair **la feria**
   trade fair **la feria de muestras**
fairly (*quite*) **bastante**
faith **la fe**
faithful **fiel**
fake **falso/a**
fall: he/she fell down **se cayó**
false **falso/a**
   (*teeth/eye etc.*) **postizo/a**
family **la familia**
famous **famoso/a**
fan **el abanico**
   (*electric*) **el ventilador**
   (*supporter*) **el hincha**
fantastic **fantástico/a**
far (*away*) **lejos**
   is it far? **¿está lejos?**
fare **el precio del billete**
farm **la granja**
farmer **el agricultor, la agricultora**
fashion **la moda**
fashionable/in fashion **de moda**
fast **rápido/a**
fat **la grasa**
fat (*large*) **gordo/a**

father **el padre**
father-in-law **el suegro**
fault (*defect*) **el defecto**
faulty **defectuoso/a**
favourite **favorito/a**
feather **la pluma**
fed up **harto/a**
to feed **dar de comer a**
  (*baby*) **dar el pecho a**
to feel **sentir**
  I feel well/unwell **me siento
    bien/mal**
  he/she feels; you feel
    se siente
felt-tip pen **el rotulador**
female, feminine **femenino/a**
feminist **femenista**
fence **la cerca**
ferry **el ferry**
festival (*village etc.*) **la fiesta**
  (*film etc.*) **el festival**

fever **la fiebre**
few **pocos/as**
  a few (*some*) **algunos/as**
fiancé(e) **el novio, la novia**
fibre **la fibra**
field **el campo**
fig **el higo**
fight **la pelea**
file (*inc. computer*) **la carpeta**
  (*nail, DIY*) **la lima**
to fill (in/up) **llenar**
filling (*dental*) **el empaste**
film (*cinema*) **la película**
  (*for camera*) **el rollo**
film star **la estrella (de cine)**
filter **el filtro**
finance **las finanzas**
to find **encontrar**
fine (*weather*) **bueno/a**
  (*OK*) **vale**
fine (*penalty*) **la multa**

to finish **acabar**
fire **el fuego**
fire brigade **los bomberos**
fire extinguisher **el extintor**
firewood **la leña**
fireworks **los fuegos
  artificiales**
firm (*company*) **la empresa**
first **primero/a**
first aid **los primeros auxilios**
first aid box/kit **el botiquín**
fish **la pez**
  (*for eating*) **el pescado**
to fish/go fishing **pescar**
fishing **la pesca**
fishing rod **la caña de pescar**
fishmonger's **la pescadería**
fit (*healthy*) **en forma**
to fit **ir bien (ir,** *see page 180***)**
fitting room **el probador**
to fix **arreglar**
fizzy **con gas**
flag **la bandera**
flat (*apartment*) **el
  apartamento**
flat (*level*) **llano/a**
  (*battery*) **descargado/a**
flavour **el sabor**
flaw **el defecto**
flea **la pulga**
flight **el vuelo**
flight bag **la bolsa de viaje**
flippers **las aletas**
flood **la inundación**
floor **el suelo**
  (*storey*) **el piso**
  ground floor **la planta
    baja**
flour **la harina**
flower **la flor**
flu **la gripe**
fluid **el líquido**

fly la mosca
fly sheet el doble techo
foam la espuma
fog la niebla
foggy: it's foggy hay niebla
foil el papel de estaño
folding (*chair etc.*) plegable
following (*next*) siguiente
food la comida
food poisoning la intoxicación
  (por alimentos)
foot el pie
  on foot andando
football el fútbol
footpath el sendero
for para; por
forbidden prohibido/a
foreign extranjero/a
forest el bosque
to forget olvidar
to forgive perdonar
fork el tenedor
form (*document*) la hoja
fortnight quince días
forward (hacia) adelante
foundation (*make-up*) la crema
  base
fountain la fuente
foyer el vestíbulo
fracture la fractura
fragile frágil
frankly francamente
freckle la peca
free gratis
  (*available, unoccupied*) libre
freedom la libertad
to freeze congelar
freezer el congelador
frequent frecuente
fresh fresco/a
fridge el frigorífico

fried frito/a
friend el amigo, la amiga
frightened asustado/a
fringe el flequillo
frog la rana
from de, desde
front: in front (of) delante (de)
front door la puerta principal
frontier la frontera
frost la helada
frozen congelado/a
fruit la fruta
fruit shop la frutería
frying pan la sartén
fuel el carburante
full lleno/a
full board la pensión completa
full up completo/a
funeral el entierro
funfair el parque de
  atracciones
funny (*amusing*) divertido/a
  (*peculiar*) raro/a
fur la piel
furniture los muebles
further on más adelante
fuse el fusible

G

gallery la galería
gambling el juego
game el juego
  (*match*) el partido
  (*hunting*) la caza
garage el garaje
garden el jardín
gardener el jardinero
garlic el ajo
gas el gas

gas bottle/cylinder **la bombona de gas**
gas refill **el cargador de gas**
gastritis **la gastritis**
gate **la puerta**
general **general**
generous **generoso/a**
gentle **suave**
gentleman **el señor**
genuine **auténtico/a**
geography **la geografía**
to get (*obtain*) **obtener**
to get off (*bus etc.*) **bajar**
to get on (*bus etc.*) **subir**
gift **el regalo**
gin **la ginebra**
gin and tonic **el gin tonic**
girl **la chica**
girlfriend **la amiga, la novia**
to give **dar**
    I give **doy**
    can you give me . . . ? **¿me da . . . ?**
glass (*container*) **el vaso**
    (*material*) **el vidrio**
glasses **las gafas**
glove **el guante**
glue **la cola**
to go **ir** (*see page 180*)
    I go/am going (to) **voy (a)**
    let's go **vamos**
to go down **bajar**
to go in **entrar (en)**
to go out **salir**
    I go/am going out **salgo**
to go up **subir**
goal (*sport*) **el gol**
goat **la cabra**
God **Dios**
goggles (*diving*) **las gafas de bucear**
gold **el oro**

(made of) gold **de oro**
golf **el golf**
golf clubs **los palos de golf**
golf course **el campo de golf**
good **bueno/a**
good afternoon/evening **buenas tardes**
good morning **buenos días**
goodnight **buenas noches**
goodbye **adiós**
government **el gobierno**
gram **el gramo**
grammar **la gramática**
grandchildren **los nietos**
granddaughter **la nieta**
grandfather **el abuelo**
grandmother **la abuela**
grandparents **los abuelos**
grandson **el nieto**
grandstand **las gradas**
grape **la uva**
grapefruit **el pomelo**
grass **la hierba**
grateful **agradecido/a**
greasy **grasiento/a**
great **grande**
great! **¡estupendo!**
Great Britain **la Gran Bretaña**
green **verde**
green card **la carta verde**
greengrocer's **la verdulería**
to greet **saludar**
grey **gris**
grilled **a la parrilla**
grocer's **la tienda de comestibles**
ground **el suelo**
ground floor **la planta baja**
groundsheet **la tela impermeable**
group **el grupo**

to grow (*cultivate*) cultivar
guarantee la garantía
guest el invitado, la invitada
  (*hotel*) el huésped
guest house la pensión
guide el/la guía
guidebook la guía (turística)
guided tour la visita con guía
guilty culpable
guitar la guitarra
gun el fusil
guy rope el viento
gymnastics la gimnasia

H

habit (*custom*) la costumbre
haemorrhoids las hemorroides
hail el granizo
hair el pelo
hairbrush el cepillo para el pelo
hair curlers los bigudíes
haircut el corte de pelo
hairdresser's la peluquería
hair dryer el secador de pelo
hairgrip la horquilla
hairspray la laca
half la mitad
half medio/a
  half an hour media hora
  half past (*see* Time, *page 185*)
half board la media pensión
half price/fare el medio billete
hall (*in house*) el vestíbulo
  (*concert*) la sala
ham el jamón
  boiled ham el jamón York
  cured ham el jamón serrano
hamburger la hamburguesa
hammer el martillo
hand la mano

handbag el bolso
hand cream la crema de manos
handicapped minusválido/a
handkerchief el pañuelo
handle el asa (*f*)
hand luggage el equipaje de
  mano
hand-made hecho/a a mano
hangover la resaca
to hang (up) colgar
to happen pasar
  what has happened? ¿qué ha
    pasado?
happy feliz
harbour el puerto
hard duro/a
  (*difficult*) difícil
hard shoulder el arcén
hat el sombrero
to hate odiar
to have tener (*see page 180*)
  do you have . . . ? ¿tiene . . . ?
hay fever la fiebre del heno
hazelnut la avellana
he él
head la cabeza
  (*boss*) el jefe
headache el dolor de cabeza
headphones los cascos
to heal curar
health la salud
healthy sano/a
health foods los alimentos
  dietéticos
to hear oír
hearing aid el audífono
heart el corazón
heart attack el infarto
heat el calor
heater el calentador
heating la calefacción

heaven el cielo
heavy pesado/a
hedge el seto
heel el tobillo
   (shoe) el tacón
height la altura
helicopter el helicóptero
hell el infierno
hello hola
help la ayuda
   help! ¡socorro!
to help ayudar
her la; le; ella
her (of her) su
herb la hierba
herbal tea la infusión
here aquí
hers suyo/a
hiccups: to have hiccups tener
   hipo (tener, see page 180)

high alto/a
high chair la silla alta
to hijack secuestrar
hill la colina
hill-walking el montañismo
him lo; le; él
to hire alquilar
his su; suyo/a
history la historia
to hit pegar
to hitchhike hacer autostop
hobby el pasatiempo
hole el agujero
holiday(s) las vacaciones
   on holiday de vacaciones
   public holiday la fiesta
holy santo/a
   Holy Week Semana Santa
home la casa
   at home en casa
   to go home volver a casa
   home address el domicilio

homosexual homosexual
honest honesto/a
honeymoon la luna de miel
to hope esperar
   I hope so/not espero que
   sí/no
horrible horrible
horse el caballo
horse-riding la equitación
hose la manguera
hospital el hospital
hot caliente
   I'm hot tengo calor
   it's hot (weather) hace calor
hot (spicy) picante
hotel el hotel
hour la hora
house la casa
housewife el ama (f) de casa
housework los quehaceres
   domésticos
hovercraft el aerodeslizador
how? ¿cómo?
   how are you? ¿cómo está
   (usted)?
how long? ¿cuánto tiempo?
how many? ¿cuántos/as?
how much? ¿cuánto/a?
how much is it? ¿cuánto es?
human humano/a
hungry: to be hungry tener
   hambre (tener, see page 180)
to hunt cazar
hunting la caza
hurry: to be in a hurry tener
   prisa (tener, see page 180)
hurt: my . . . hurts me duele
   el/la . . . (see page 154)
husband el marido
hut la cabaña
hydrofoil el aerodeslizador
hypermarket el hipermercado

I

I **yo**
ice **el hielo**
ice-cream **el helado**
ice rink **la pista de patinaje**
icy **helado/a**
idea **la idea**
if **si**
ill **enfermo/a**
illness **la enfermedad**
to imagine **imaginar**
imagination **la imaginación**
immediately **inmediatamente, en seguida**
immersion heater **el calentador de inmersión**
impatient **impaciente**
important **importante**
impossible **imposible**
impressive **impresionante**
in **en; dentro (de)**
included **incluido/a**
income **los ingresos**
independent **independiente**
indigestion **la indigestión**
indoors **dentro**
industrial **industrial**
industry **la industria**
infected **infectado/a**
infection **la infección**
infectious **contagioso/a**
inflamed **inflamado/a**
inflammation **la inflamación**
influenza **la gripe**
informal **informal**
information **la información**
information office **la oficina de información (turística)**
injection **la inyección**
injured **herido/a**
injury **la herida**

ink **la tinta**
inner **interno/a**
innocent **inocente**
insect **el insecto**
insect bite **la picadura (de insecto)**
insecticide **el insecticida**
insect repellent **la loción contra insectos**
inside **dentro (de)**
instant coffee **el café instantáneo**
instead of **en vez de**
instructor **el instructor**
to insist **insistir**
insulin **la insulina**
insult **el insulto**
insurance **el seguro**
insurance certificate **el certificado de seguros**
intelligent **inteligente**
interested: I'm (not) interested in . . . **(no) me interesa . . .**
interesting **interesante**
interior **interior**
international **internacional**
interpreter **el intérprete**
internal **interno/a**
interval (*theatre etc.*) **el descanso**
interview **la intervista**
into **en**
to introduce **presentar**
to invite **invitar**
invitation **la invitación**
iodine **el yodo**
Ireland **Irlanda**
Irish **irlandés, irlandesa**
iron (*metal*) **el hierro** (*for clothes*) **la plancha**
to iron **planchar**
ironmonger's **la ferretería**

is (*see* to be)
  is there . . . ? ¿hay . . . ?
island la isla
it lo/la
itch la picazón

J

jacket la chaqueta
jam la mermelada
jar el tarro
jazz el jazz
jeans los vaqueros
Jesus, Jesus Christ Jesús,
  Jesucristo
jelly la gelatina
jellyfish la medusa
jeweller's la joyería
Jewish judío/a
job el trabajo
jogging: to go jogging hacer
  footing
  I go jogging hago footing
joke el chiste
journalist el/la periodista
journey el viaje
judge el juez
jug la jarra
juice el zumo
to jump saltar
  jump leads los cables para
  cargar la batería
  jumper el suéter
junction el cruce
just (*only*) solamente

K

to keep guardar
kettle la caldera
key la llave

key ring el llavero
kidney el riñón
to kill matar
kilo(gram) el kilo
kilometre el kilómetro
kind (*sort*) la clase
kind (*generous*) amable
king el rey
kiss el beso
to kiss besar
kitchen la cocina
knickers (*men's*) los
  calzoncillos
  (*women's*) las bragas
knife el cuchillo
to knit hacer punto
  I knit hago punto
to knock golpear
knot el nodo
to know (*someone*) conocer
  I don't know him/her
  no le conozco
  (*something*) saber
  I (don't) know (no) sé
to know how to saber
  I (don't) know how to . . .
  (no) sé . . .

L

label la etiqueta
lace el encaje
  (*shoe*) el cordón
ladder la escalera (de mano)
lady la señora
  ladies and gentlemen
  señoras y señores
lager la cerveza
lake el lago
lamb el cordero
lamp la lámpara
lamp post el farol

land la tierra
to land aterrizar
landlady la propietaria
landlord el propietario
lane (country road) el camino
language el idioma
large grande
last último/a
  (week etc.) pasado/a (see page 184)
to last durar
late tarde
later más tarde
laugh la risa
to laugh reír
laundrette la lavandería automática
laundry la lavandería
law la ley
  (study subject) el derecho
lawyer el abogado
laxative el laxante
lazy perezoso/a
lead el plomo
lead-free sin plomo
leaf la hoja
leaflet el folleto
to learn aprender
learner el/la estudiante
least: at least por lo menos
leather la piel
to leave (message etc.) dejar
  (to go) salir (de); marcharse
left la izquierda
  on/to the left a la izquierda
  on the left-hand side a mano izquierda
left luggage (office) la consigna de equipajes
left-hand izquierdo/a
left-handed zurdo/a

leg la pierna
legal legal
lemon el limón
lemonade la limonada, la gaseosa
to lend prestar
length la longitud
  (duration) la duración
lens la lente
less menos
lesson la clase
to let (allow) permitir
  (rent) alquilar
letter la carta
  (of alphabet) la letra
letterbox el buzón
lettuce la lechuga
level (height, standard) el nivel
level (flat) plano/a
level crossing el paso a nivel
library la biblioteca
licence (driving) el carné de conducir
  (fishing etc.) el permiso
lid la tapa
life la vida
lifebelt el cinturón salvavidas
lifeboat el bote salvavidas
lifeguard el vigilante
lifejacket el chaleco salvavidas
lift el ascensor
light la luz
light (coloured) claro/a
  (weight) ligero/a
to light (fire etc.) encender
light bulb la bombilla
lighter (cigarette) el encendedor
lightning el relámpago
like (similar to) como
  like this/that así
  what is . . . like? ¿cómo es . . . ?

what are . . . like? ¿cómo son . . . ?
like: I like . . . me gusta/ gustan . . . (*see page 16*)
  do you like . . . ? ¿le gusta/ gustan . . . ?
likely probable
limited limitado/a
line la línea
lion el león
lipstick la barra de labios
liqueur el licor
liquid el líquido
list la lista
to listen (to) escuchar
litre el litro
litter la basura
little (*small*) pequeño/a
a little un poco (de)
to live vivir
liver el hígado
living-room el salón
loaf (of bread) la barra (de pan)
local local
lock la cerradura
to lock cerrar con llave
London Londres
lonely solo/a
long largo/a
to look (at) mirar
to look after cuidar
to look for buscar
to look like parecer a
loose suelto/a
  (*clothes*) ancho/a
lorry el camión
lorry-driver el camionero
to lose perder
lost property office la oficina de objetos perdidos
a lot (of) mucho/a

lotion la loción
lottery la lotería
loud fuerte
lounge el salón
love el amor
to love querer (*see page 180*)
lovely precioso/a
low bajo/a
lower de abajo
lozenge la pastilla
LP el elepé
lucky: to be lucky tener suerte (tener, *see page 180*)
luggage el equipaje
lump el bulto
lump of sugar el terrón
lunch el almuerzo, la comid

M

machine la máquina
machinist el/la maquinista
mad loco/a
madam señora
magazine la revista
main principal
make (*brand*) la marca
to make hacer
  I make hago
  he/she/it makes; you make hace
make-up el maquillaje
male masculino/a
man el hombre
manager el gerente
managing director el director gerente
many muchos/as
  not many pocos/as
map el mapa
marble el mármol

margarine **la margarina**
market **el mercado**
married **casado/a**
mascara **el rímel**
masculine **masculino/a**
mask **la máscara**
mass (*church*) **la misa**
match (*game*) **el partido**
matches **las cerillas**
material **la tela**
mathematics **la matemática**
matter: it doesn't matter **no
  importa**
  what's the matter? **¿qué pasa?**
mattress **el colchón**
mature **maduro/a**
mayonnaise **la mayonesa**
me **me; mí**
meadow **el prado**
meal **la comida**
mean: what does it mean? **¿qué
  quiere decir?**
meanwhile **mientras tanto**
measles **el sarampión**
  German measles **la rubéola**
to measure **medir**
measurement **la medida**
meat **la carne**
  cold meats **los fiambres**
mechanic **el mecánico**
medical **médico/a**
medicine (*subject*) **la medicina**
  (*drug*) **la medicina, el
  medicamento**
Mediterranean **el Mediterráneo**
medium (*size*) **mediano/a**
  (*steak*) **medio/a**
medium dry (*wine*) **semi-seco**
meeting **la reunión**
melon **el melón**
  water melon **la sandía**

member **el miembro, el socio**
to mend **reparar**
menu **la carta**
  set menu **el menú**
message **el recado**
metal **el metal**
meter **el contador**
metre **el metro**
microwave (oven) **el (horno)
  microondas**
midday **mediodía**
middle **el centro**
middle-aged **de mediana edad**
midnight **medianoche**
migraine **la jaqueca**
mild (*taste*) **suave**
  (*temperature*) **templado/a**
mile **la milla**
milk **la leche**
milkshake **el batido**
mill **el molino**
mince **la carne picada**
mind: do you mind if . . . ?
  ¿le importa si . . . ?
  I don't mind **no me
  importa**
mine (*of me*) **mío/a**
minister **el ministro**
minute (*time*) **el minuto**
mirror **el espejo**
Miss **(la) señorita**
to miss (*bus etc.*) **perder**
mist **la neblina**
mistake **el error**
mistaken **equivocado/a**
mixed **mixto/a**
mixture **la mezcla**
model **el modelo**
modern **moderno/a**
moisturiser **la leche hidratante**
monastery **el monasterio**

money el dinero
month el mes
monument el monumento
moon la luna
moped el ciclomotor
more más
morning la mañana
mortgage la hipoteca
mosque la mezquita
mosquito el mosquito
mosquito net la red para
  mosquitos
most (of) la mayor parte (de)
mother la madre
mother-in-law la suegra
motor el motor
motorbike la moto(cicleta)
motorboat la motora
motor racing el automovilismo
motorway la autopista
mountain la montaña
mountaineering el alpinismo
moustache el bigote
mouth la boca
to move mover
movement el movimiento
Mr (el) señor
Mrs (la) señora
much mucho/a
  not much poco/a
mug el tazón
to murder asesinar
museum el museo
mushroom el champiñón
music la música
musical musical
musician el músico
must: you must ... tiene
  que ...
mustard la mostaza
my mi; (pl) mis

N

nail el clavo
  (finger/toe) la uña
nail file la lima de uñas
nail polish el esmalte
  (para uñas)
nail polish remover el quita-
  esmalte
naked nudo/a
name el nombre
  my name is ... mi nombre
  es ...; me llamo ...
  what is your name? ¿cómo
  se llama (usted)?
napkin la servilleta
  paper napkin la servilleta
  de papel
nappy el pañal; disposable
  nappies los dodotis
nappy liner la gasa
narrow estrecho/a
national nacional
nationality la nacionalidad
natural natural
naturally naturalmente
naughty travieso/a
navy la marina
navy blue azul marino
near (to) cerca (de)
nearly casi
necessary necesario/a
necklace el collar
to need necesitar
needle la aguja
negative (photo) el negativo
neighbour el vecino, la vecin
neither ... nor ni ... ni
nephew el sobrino
nervous nervioso/a
net la red
never nunca
new nuevo/a

New Year el Año Nuevo
news las noticias
newspaper el periódico
newspaper kiosk el quiosco
next próximo/a
  week/month/year (*see page 184*)
nice (*person*) simpático/a
  (*place etc.*) bonito/a
niece la sobrina
night la noche
nightclub el nightclub, la boite
nightdress el camisón
no no
nobody nadie
noise el ruido
noisy ruidoso/a
non-alcoholic no alcohólico/a, sin alcohol
none ninguno/a
non-smoking no fumador
normal normal
north el norte
northern del norte
nose la nariz
nosebleed la hemorragia nasal
not no
note (*bank*) el billete
notepad el bloc
nothing nada
nothing else nada más
now ahora
nowhere en ninguna parte
nuclear nuclear
nuclear energy la energía nuclear
number el número
nurse el enfermero, la enfermera
nut la nuez
  (*for bolt*) la tuerca
nylon el nilón

O

oar el remo
object el objeto
obvious evidente
occasionally de vez en cuando
occupied (*seat*) ocupado/a
odd raro/a (*not even*) impar
of de
of course claro; por supuesto
off (*switched off*) apagado/a
offended ofendido/a
office la oficina
  (*room*) el despacho
official oficial
often muchas veces
  how often? ¿cuántas veces?
oil el aceite
OK vale
old viejo/a
  how old are you?
    ¿cuántos años tiene(s)?
  how old is he/she?
    ¿cuántos años tiene?
  I am . . . years old
    tengo . . . años
old fashioned pasado/a de moda
olive la aceituna
olive oil el aceite de oliva
on en
  (*switched on*) encendido/a
once una vez
onion la cebolla
only solamente
open abierto/a
to open abrir
opera la ópera
operation la operación
opinion la opinión
  in my opinion en mi opinión

opposite (*contrary*) **contrario/a**
opposite (to) **enfrente (de)**
optician **el óptico**
or **o**
orange (*fruit*) **la naranja**
  (*colour*) **color naranja**
order **la orden**
to order (*in restaurant*) **pedir**
ordinary **ordinario/a**
to organise **organizar**
original **original**
other **otro/a, otros/as**
others **otros/as**
our, ours **nuestro/a**
out (of) **fuera (de)**
  he/she is out **no está**
outdoors **al aire libre**
outside **fuera**
over (*above*) **por encima de**
overcast (*sky*) **cubierto/a**
overcoat **el abrigo**
to overtake **adelantar**
owner **el propietario, la propietaria**

P

package tour **el viaje organizado**
packet **el paquete**
padlock **el candado**
page **la página**
pain **el dolor**
painful **doloroso/a**
painkiller **el calmante**
paint **la pintura**
to paint **pintar**
painter **el pintor**
painting (*picture*) **el cuadro**
  (*art*) **la pintura**
pair **el par**
palace **el palacio**
pale **pálido/a**

(*colour*) **claro/a**
panties, pants (*women's*) **las bragas**
paper **el papel**
paper clip **el clip, el sujetapapeles**
paraffin **la parafina**
parcel **el paquete**
pardon? **¿cómo?**
parents **los padres**
park **el parque**
to park **aparcar**
parking **el aparcamiento, el estacionamiento**
parking disc **el disco de estacionamiento**
parking meter **el parquímetro**
parliament **el parlamento**
  (*Spanish*) **las Cortes**
part **la parte**
parting (*hair*) **la raya**
partly **en parte**
partner (*business*) **el socio**
party (*celebration*) **la fiesta**
to pass (*salt etc.*) **pasar**
  (*exam/test*) **aprobar**
passenger **el pasajero**
passport **el pasaporte**
passport control **el control de pasaportes**
past **el pasado**
past (*time, see page 185*)
pasta **la pasta**
pastille **la pastilla**
pastry **el pastel**
path **el camino**
patient (*hospital*) **el/la paciente**
pattern **el diseño**
pavement **la acera**
to pay **pagar**

to pay cash **pagar al contado**
pea el **guisante**
peace la **paz**
peach el **melocotón**
peanut el **cacahuete**
pear la **pera**
pedal el **pedal**
pedestrian el **peatón**
pedestrian crossing el **paso de peatones**
to peel **pelar**
peg la **clavija**
    (*clothes*) la **pinza**
pen la **pluma**
pencil el **lápiz**
pencil sharpener el **sacapuntas**
penfriend el **amigo**/la **amiga por correspondencia**
penknife la **navaja**
pension la **pensión**
pensioner el **jubilado**, la **jubilada**
people la **gente**
    (*nation*) el **pueblo**
pepper la **pimienta**
    green/red el **pimiento verde/ rojo**
peppermint la **menta**
    (*sweet*) la **pastilla de menta**
per **por**
perfect **perfecto/a**
performance la **representación**
    (*cinema*) la **sesión**
perfume el **perfume**
perhaps **quizás**
period (*menstrual*) las **reglas**
period pains los **dolores menstruales**
perm la **permanente**
permit el **permiso**
to permit **permitir**

person la **persona**
personal **personal**
personal stereo el **walkman**
petrol la **gasolina**
petrol can el **bidón de gasolina**
petrol station la **estación de servicio**
petticoat la **combinación**
philosophy la **filosofía**
photocopy la **fotocopia**
to photocopy **fotocopiar**
photo(graph) la **foto(grafía)**
photographer el **fotógrafo**
photography la **fotografía**
phrase book el **libro de frases**
physics la **física**
piano el **piano**
to pick (*choose*) **elegir**
    (*flowers etc.*) **coger**
to pick up **recoger**
picnic la **merienda**
picture el **cuadro**
piece el **pedazo**
pier el **embarcadero**
pig el **cerdo**
pill la **píldora**
    (*contraceptive*) la **píldora (anticonceptiva)**
pillow la **almohada**
pillowcase la **funda**
pilot el **piloto**
pin el **alfiler**
pineapple la **piña**
pink **rosa**
pipe (*smoking*) la **pipa**
    (*drain etc.*) el **tubo**
place el **lugar**, el **sitio**
    (*seat*) el **asiento**
    (*campsite*) la **plaza**
plan (*of town*) el **plano**
plant la **planta**

plaster (*sticking*) la tirita,
    el esparadrapo
plastic el plástico
plastic bag la bolsa de plástico
plate el plato
platform (*station*) el andén
play (*theatre*) la obra (de teatro)
to play (*instrument, record*) tocar
    (*sport*) jugar
    I play juego
    he/she plays, you play juega
pleasant agradable
please por favor
pleased contento/a
plenty (of) bastante, mucho/a
pliers los alicates
plimsolls las zapatillas
plug (*bath*) el tapón
    (*electrical*) el enchufe
plumber el fontanero

pneumonia la pulmonía
pocket el bolsillo
point el punto
poison el veneno
poisonous venenoso/a
pole el palo
police la policía
police car el coche patrulla
police station la comisaría
polish (*shoe etc.*) el betún
polite cortés
politician el político
political político/a
politics la política
polluted contaminado/a
pollution la contaminación
pool (*swimming*) la piscina
poor pobre
pop (*music*) la música pop
Pope el papa
popular popular
pork el cerdo

port (*harbour*) el puerto
    (*wine*) el oporto
portable portátil
porter el portero
porthole la portilla
portrait el retrato
possible posible
    as . . . as possible lo más . . .
        posible
    if possible si es posible
possibly posiblemente
post (*mail*) el correo
to post mandar por correo
postbox el buzón
postcard la postal
postcode el código postal
poster el cartel
postman el cartero
post office Correos, la oficina
    de correos
to postpone aplazar
pot el tarro
potato la patata
pottery la cerámica
potty (*child's*) la bacinica
pound (*sterling*) la libra
    (esterlina)
to pour echar
powder el polvo
powdery (*snow*) polvoriento/a
power la fuerza
    (*electrical*) la corriente
power cut el apagón
pram el cochecito
to prefer preferir
    I prefer prefiero
pregnant embarazada
to prepare preparar
prescription la receta
present (*gift*) el regalo
pretty bonito/a

price **el precio**
priest **el sacerdote**
prime minister **el primer ministro, la primera ministra**
prince **el príncipe**
princess **la princesa**
print (*photo*) **la copia** (*picture*) **el grabado**
prison **la cárcel**
private **privado/a**
prize **el premio**
probably **probablemente**
problem **el problema**
producer (*radio/TV*) **el realizador, la realizadora**
profession **la profesión**
professor **el profesor, la profesora**
profit **la ganancia**
program (*computer*) **el programa**
programme **el programa**
prohibited **prohibido/a**
promise **la promesa**
to pronounce **pronunciar**
pronunciation **la pronunciación**
properly **correctamente**
property **la propiedad**
protestant **protestante**
public **el público**
public **público/a**
public holiday **el día festivo**
to pull **tirar**
to pump up **inflar**
puncture **el pinchazo**
pure **puro/a**
purple **morado/a**
purse **el monedero**
to push **empujar**
push-chair **la sillita de ruedas**
to put, to put down **poner**
   I put **pongo**
pyjamas **el pijama**

Q

quality **la calidad**
quarter **el cuarto** (*of a town*) **el barrio**
quay **el muelle**
queen **la reina**
question **la pregunta**
queue **la cola**
quick **rápido/a**
quickly **rápidamente**
quiet **silencioso/a** (*place*) **tranquila/a**
quite (*fairly*) **bastante** (*completely*) **completamente**

R

rabbi **el rabino**
rabbit **el conejo**
rabies **la rabia**
race **la carrera**
racecourse/track **la pista de carreras** (*horse*) **el hipódromo**
racing **las carreras**
racket (*tennis*) **la raqueta**
radio **la radio**
radioactive **radioactivo/a**
radio station **la emisora**
raft **la balsa**
railway **el ferrocarril**
railway station **la estación (de ferrocarril)**
rain **la lluvia**
to rain **llover**
   it's raining **está lloviendo**
raincoat **el impermeable**
rainy **lluvioso/a, de lluvia**
to rape **violar**
rare **raro/a** (*steak*) **poco hecho/a**

rash el sarpullido
raspberry la frambuesa
rate (speed) la velocidad
  (tariff) la tarifa
rather (quite) bastante
raw crudo/a
razor la máquina de afeitar
razor blade la hoja de afeitar
to reach (arrive at) llegar a
to read leer
reading la lectura
ready listo/a
real (authentic) auténtico/a
really (very) realmente
  really? ¿de veras?
rear trasero/a
reason la razón
  the reason why el por qué
receipt el recibo
receiver (telephone) el auricular
reception la recepción
receptionist el/la recepcionista
recipe la receta
to recognise reconocer
  I recognise reconozco
to recommend recomendar
record el disco
to record grabar
record player el tocadiscos
red rojo/a
  Red Cross la Cruz Roja
  (wine) tinto/a
reduction la reducción
  (in sale price) la rebaja
refill el repuesto
  (pen) el recambio
refrigerator el frigorífico
to refund reembolsar
region la región
to register (letter) certificar
  (luggage etc.) facturar
registration number la matrícula
relation (relation) el pariente,

la parienta
religion la religión
to remain permanecer, quedar
to remember recordar
  I remember recuerdo
to remove quitar
to rent alquilar
  rent(al) el alquiler
to repair reparar
to repeat repetir
reply la respuesta
report (business etc.) el
  informe
  (newspaper) el reportaje
to report (crime etc.) denunciar
to rescue salvar
reservation la reserva
to reserve reservar
  reserved reservado/a
responsible responsable
to rest descansar
restaurant el restaurante
restaurant-car el coche
  comedor
result el resultado
retired jubilado/a
return la vuelta
  (ticket) ida y vuelta
to return volver
  I return vuelvo
  (give back) devolver
reversed charge call la
  llamada a cobro revertido
rheumatism el reumatismo
ribbon la cinta
rice el arroz
rich rico/a
ride: to go for a ride dar un
  paseo
to ride (a bike/in a car) ir en
  (bicicleta/coche) (ir, see page
  180)
to ride a horse montar a caballo

right la derecha
  on/to the right a la derecha
  on the right-hand side a
    mano derecha
right: you are (not) right
  (no) tiene razón
  that's right eso es
right-hand derecho/a
ring (jewellery) el anillo
ripe maduro/a
river el río
road (main) la carretera
roadworks las obras
roast asado/a
to rob robar
  I've been robbed me han
    robado
robbery el robo
roll (bread) el bollo
roof el tejado
roof rack la baca
room (house) el cuarto
  (hotel) la habitación
  (space) el sitio
rope la cuerda
rose la rosa
rosé rosado/a
rotten podrido/a
rough (surface) áspero/a
  (sea) embravecido/a
round redondo/a
roundabout (traffic) el cruce
  giratorio
  (funfair) el tiovivo
row (theatre etc.) la fila
to row remar
rowing boat la barca
royal real
rubber (material) la goma
  (eraser) la goma (de borrar)
rubber band la gomita

rubbish la basura
  rubbish! ¡tonterías!
rucksack la mochila
rude descortés
ruins las ruinas
ruler (measuring) la regla
rum el ron
  and coke el cubalibre
to run correr
rush hour las horas punta
rusty oxidado/a

S

sad triste
safe (strongbox) la caja fuerte
safe seguro/a
safety pin el imperdible
sail la vela
sailboard la plancha
sailing la vela
sailing boat el velero
sailor el marinero
saint el santo, la santa
salad la ensalada
salami el salchichón
sale la venta
  (reduced prices) la liquidación
sales representative el/la
  representante
salesman el vendedor
saleswoman la vendedora
salmon el salmón
salt la sal
salty salado/a
same mismo/a
sample la muestra
sand la arena
sandal la sandalia
sandwich el bocadillo
  toasted sandwich el sandwich

259

sanitary towel la compresa
sauce la salsa
saucepan la cacerola
saucer el platillo
sauna la sauna
sausage la salchicha
to save (*rescue*) salvar
   (*money*) ahorrar
to say decir
   I say digo
   he/she says, you say dice
   how do you say it? ¿cómo se
      dice?
   people say that ... se dice
      que ...
   that is to say es decir
scales la balanza
scarf la bufanda
scene (*theatre*) la escena
   (*view*) el panorama
scenery (*countryside*) el paisaje
scent el perfume
school la escuela
science la ciencia
scientist el científico,
   la científica
scissors las tijeras
score: what's the score? ¿cómo
   está el marcador?
   final score el resultado
Scotland Escocia
Scottish escocés, escocesa
scrambled eggs los huevos
   revueltos
scratch la raya
   (*on skin*) el arañazo
screen (*TV, cinema etc.*) la
   pantalla
   (*partition*) el biombo
screw el tornillo
screwdriver el destornillador
sculpture la escultura

sea el mar
seafood los mariscos
seasick mareado/a
season (*of year*) la estación
season ticket el abono
seat el asiento
   (*chair*) la silla
seatbelt el cinturón de
   seguridad
second segundo/a
second (*time*) el segundo
secret el secreto
secret secreto/a
secretary el secretario, la
   secretaria
section la sección
to see ver
   I (can't) see it (no) lo veo
to seem parecer
   it seems ... parece ...
self-catering sin pensión
self-service (de) autoservicio
to sell vender
to send enviar
senior citizen el/la
   pensionista
sensible sensato/a
sentence la frase
   (*prison*) la sentencia
separate, separated
   separado/a
serious serio/a
   (*important*) grave
to serve servir
service (*church*) el culto
service (charge) el servicio
set (*group*) el juego
   (*series*) la serie
   (*hair*) el marcado
setting lotion el fijador
several varios/as
to sew coser
sewing la costura

sex (*gender*) el sexo
  (*intercourse*) las relaciones
  sexuales
shade (*colour*) el tono
shadow la sombra
shampoo el champú
shampoo and set el lavado y
  marcado
shampoo and blow-dry el lavado
  y secado a mano
sharp (*edge*) afilado/a
  (*pain*) agudo/a
to shave (oneself) afeitar(se)
shaver la afeitadora
shaving cream/foam la crema/
  espuma de afeitar
she ella
sheep la oveja
sheet la sábana
shelf el estante
shell (*egg, nut*) la cáscara
  (*sea*) la concha
shellfish los mariscos
shelter el refugio
sherry el jerez
shiny brillante
ship el barco
shirt la camisa
shock (*surprise*) el susto
shoe el zapato
shoelace el cordón
shoe polish la crema de zapatos
shoe shop la zapatería
shop la tienda
shop assistant el dependiente,
  la dependienta
shopping: to go shopping
  ir de compras
  (ir, *see page 180*)
shopping centre el centro
  comercial

short corto/a
shorts los pantalones cortos
to shout gritar
show el espectáculo
to show mostrar
shower la ducha
to shrink encoger
shut cerrado/a
shutter la contraventana
  (*camera*) el obturador
sick (*ill*) enfermo/a
  to be sick vomitar
  to feel sick tener náuseas
  (tener, *see page 180*)
side el lado
sieve el colador
sight (*vision*) la vista
sights (*tourist*) los monumentos
sightseeing el turismo
sign la señal
to sign firmar
signal la señal
signature la firma
silent silencioso/a
silk la seda
silver la plata
similar (to) parecido/a (a)
simple sencillo/a
since desde
to sing cantar
single (*room, bed*) individual
  (*ticket*) ida solamente
  (*unmarried*) soltero/a
single (*record*) el single
sink el fregadero
sir señor
sister la hermana
sister-in-law la cuñada
to sit (down) sentarse
  sit down siéntese
  sitting (down) sentado/a

size (*dimension*) **el tamaño**
  (*clothes*) **la talla**
  (*shoes*) **el número**
skate **el patín**
to skate **patinar**
ski **el esquí**
to ski **esquiar**
ski boot **la bota de esquí**
skiing **el esquí**
ski-lift **el telesquí**
skimmed milk **la leche desnatada**
skin **la piel**
skindiving **la natación submarina**
ski pole **el palo de esquí**
skirt **la falda**
ski-run/slope **la pista de esquí**
ski suit **el traje de esquí**
sky **el cielo**
to sleep **dormir**
  I sleep **duermo**

  he/she sleeps, you sleep **duerme**
sleeper/sleeping-car **el coche cama**
sleeping bag **el saco de dormir**
sleeve **la manga**
slice **la lonja**
sliced **en lonjas**
slide (*film*) **la diapositiva**
slim **delgado/a**
slip (*petticoat*) **la combinación**
slippery **resbaladizo/a**
slow **lento/a**
slowly **despacio**
small **pequeño/a**
smell **el olor**
smell: it smells bad/good **huele mal/bien**
  it smells of . . . **huele a . . .**
smile **la sonrisa**
smoke **el humo**
to smoke **fumar**

smoked **ahumado/a**
smooth **liso/a**
snake **la serpiente**
to sneeze **estornudar**
snorkel **el tubo (snorkel)**
snow **la nieve**
snow: it's snowing **está nevando**
so **tan**
  (*thus*) **así**
soap **el jabón**
sober **sobrio/a**
socialism **el socialismo**
socialist **socialista**
social worker **el/la asistente/a social**
sociology **la sociología**
sock **el calcetín**
socket (*electrical*) **el enchufe**
soda (water) **la soda**
soft **blando/a**
  (*flabby*) **flojo/a**
soft drink **la bebida no alcohólica**
sold out **agotado/a**
soldier **el soldado**
solid **sólido/a**
some **algunos/as**
somehow **de alguna manera**
someone **alguien**
something **algo**
sometimes **a veces**
somewhere **a/en alguna parte**
so many **tantos/as**
so much **tanto/a**
son **el hijo**
song **la canción**
son-in-law **el yerno**
soon **pronto**
  as soon as possible **lo más pronto posible**
sore throat **el dolor de garganta**

sorry (*pardon me*) ¡perdón!
I'm sorry lo siento
sort la clase
sound el ruido
soup la sopa
sour agrio/a
south el sur
southern del sur
souvenir el recuerdo
space el espacio
spade la pala
Spain España
Spanish español, española
spanner la llave inglesa
spare (*available*) disponible
(*left over*) sobrante
spare time el tiempo libre
spare wheel la rueda de
recambio
sparkling (*wine*) espumoso/a
to speak hablar
special especial
specialist el/la especialista
speciality la especialidad
special offer la oferta
spectacles las gafas
speed la velocidad
speed limit el límite de
velocidad
to spend (*money*) gastar
(*time*) pasar
spice la especia
spicy picante
spinach las espinacas
spirits los licores
splinter la astilla
to spoil estropear
sponge (*bath*) la esponja
(*cake*) el bizcocho
spoon la cuchara
sport el deporte

spot el grano
(*place*) el sitio
sprain la torcedura
sprained torcido/a
spray el spray
spring (*season*) la primavera
square la plaza
square (*shape*) el cuadrado
stadium el estadio
stain la mancha
stainless steel el acero inoxidable
stairs la escalera
stalls (*theatre*) la butaca
stamp (*postage*) el sello
stand (*stadium*) las gradas
standing (up) de pie
staple la grapa
stapler la grapadora
star la estrella
start (*beginning*) el comienzo
to start empezar
I start empiezo
he/she/it starts, you start
empieza
starter (*food*) el entremés
state el estado
station la estación
station master el jefe de estación
stationer's la librería
statue la estatua
stay la estancia
stay: I'm staying at . . . estoy
en . . .
steak el filete
to steal robar
steam el vapor
steel el acero
steep escarpado/a
step el paso
(*stair*) el escalón
step-brother el hermanastro

step-children los hijastros
step-daughter la hijastra
step-father el padrastro
step-mother la madrastra
step-sister la hermanastra
step-son el hijastro
stereo el estéreo
sterling: pound sterling la libra esterlina
steward (*air*) el camarero
stewardess (*air*) la azafata
stick el palo
to stick pegar
sticking plaster el esparadrapo
sticky pegajoso/a
sticky tape la cinta adhesiva
stiff rígido/a
still todavía
still (*non-fizzy*) sin gas
sting la picadura

to sting picar
stock exchange la bolsa
stockings las medias
stolen: my . . . has been stolen me han robado el/la . . . . (*see page 169*)
stomach el estómago
stomach ache el dolor de estómago
stomach upset el trastorno estomacal
stone la piedra
stop (*bus*) la parada
to stop parar
stop! ¡alto!
stopcock la llave de paso
storey el piso
story el cuento
stove (*cooker*) la cocina
straight derecho/a
straight on todo recto

strange extraño/a
strap la correa
straw (*drinking*) la pajita
strawberry la fresa
stream el arroyo
street la calle
street light el farol
stretcher la camilla
strike la huelga
string la cuerda
stripe la raya
striped rayado/a
strong fuerte
student el/la estudiante
studio el estudio
to study estudiar
stupid estúpido/a
style el estilo
styling mousse la espuma moldeadora
subtitled subtitulado/a
suburbs las afueras
to succeed, be successful tener éxito (*tener, see page 180*)
success el éxito
such tal
suddenly de repente
sugar el azúcar
sugar lump el terrón
suit el traje
suitcase la maleta
summer el verano
sun el sol
to sunbathe tomar el sol
sunburn la quemadura de sol
sunglasses las gafas de sol
sunshade la sombrilla
sunstroke la insolación
suntan cream la crema bronceadora
supermarket el supermercado

supper la cena
supplement el suplemento
suppose: I suppose so/not
  supongo que sí/no
suppository el supositorio
sure seguro/a
surface la superficie
surname el apellido
surprise la sorpresa
surprised sorprendido/a
surrounded (by) rodeado/a (de)
to sweat sudar
sweater el suéter
sweatshirt la sudadera
to sweep barrer
sweet dulce
sweetener la sacarina
sweets los caramelos
swelling la hinchazón
to swim nadar
swimming la natación
swimming pool la piscina
swimming trunks, swimsuit el
  traje de baño
switch el interruptor
to switch off apagar
  (engine) parar
to switch on encender
  how do you switch it on?
  ¿como se enciende?
swollen hinchado/a
symptom el síntoma
synagogue la sinagoga
synthetic sintético/a
system el sistema

T

table la mesa
tablet la pastilla
table tennis el ping-pong

tailor el sastre
to take tomar
  (bus etc.) coger
  (time) tardar
to take out sacar
taken (seat) ocupado/a
to take off (remove) quitar
  (plane) despegar
talcum powder los polvos
  de talco
to talk hablar
tall alto/a
tame manso/a
tampon el tampón
tap el grifo
tape la cinta
tape measure la cinta métrica
tape recorder la grabadora
taste el sabor
tasty sabroso/a
tax el impuesto
taxi el taxi
taxi rank la parada de taxis
tea el té
teabag la bolsita de té
to teach enseñar
teacher el profesor,
  la profesora
team el equipo
teapot la tetera
to tear rasgar
teaspoon la cucharilla
teat (for baby's bottle) la tetilla
tea-towel el paño de cocina
technical técnico/a
technology la tecnología
teenager el/la adolescente
telegram el telegrama
telephone el teléfono
telephone directory la guía
  telefónica

to telephone **llamar por teléfono**
television **la televisión**
to tell **decir**
  I tell **digo**
  he/she/it tells, you tell **dice**
temperature **la temperatura**
  to have a temperature **tener fiebre** (**tener**, *see page 180*)
temporary **provisional**
tender **tierno/a**
tennis **el tenis**
tennis court **la pista de tenis**
tennis shoes/trainers **las zapatillas**
tent **la tienda**
tent peg **la piqueta de tienda**
tent pole **el mástil**
terminal, terminus **la terminal**
terrace **la terraza**
terrible **terrible**

terrorist **el/la terrorista**
thank you (very much) **(muchas) gracias**
that **ese/a; aquel, aquella** (*see page 176*)
that one **ése/a; eso** (*see page 176*)
the **el, la;** (*pl*) **los, las**
theatre **el teatro**
their **su;** (*pl*) **sus**
theirs **suyo/a**
them **los/las; ellos/as**
then **entonces**
  (*later on*) **después**
there **allí**
there is/are **hay**
therefore **por lo tanto**
thermometer **el termómetro**
these **estos/as** (*see page 176*)
they **ellos/as**
thief **el ladrón**
thick **grueso/a**
thin **delgado/a**

thing **la cosa**
to think **pensar, creer**
  I think so/not **pienso que sí/no; creo que sí/no**
third **tercero/a**
thirsty: to be thirsty **tener sed** (**tener**, *see page 180*)
this **este/a; esto** (*see page 176*)
this one **éste/a** (*see page 176*)
those **esos/as; aquellos/as** (*see page 176*)
thread **el hilo**
throat **la garganta**
throat lozenges/pastilles **las pastillas para la garganta**
through **por**
to throw **lanzar**
to throw away **echar**
thumb **el pulgar**
thunder **el trueno**
ticket (*travel*) **el billete**
  (*theatre*) **la entrada**
ticket office **el despacho de billetes**
  (*theatre*) **la taquilla**
tide **la marea**
tidy **ordenado/a**
tie **la corbata**
to tie **atar**
tight **ajustado/a**
tights **las medias panty, el panty**
till (*until*) **hasta**
time (*once etc.*) **la vez**
time **la hora** (*see page 185*)
  there's no time **no hay tiempo**
timetable **el horario**
tin **la lata**
tin foil **el papel de estaño**
tinned **en lata**
tin opener **el abrelatas**

tip (*money*) la propina
tired cansado/a
tissues los pañuelos de papel
to a
toast el pan tostado
toasted sandwich el sandwich
tobacco el tabaco
tobacconist's el estanco
today hoy
together junto
toilet el wáter
  toilets los servicios
toilet paper el papel higiénico
toiletries los artículos de tocador
toilet water el agua de colonia
toll el peaje
tomato el tomate
tomorrow mañana
tongue la lengua
tonic water la tónica
tonight esta noche
too (*also*) también
too (*excessively*) demasiado
tool la herramienta
too many demasiados/as
too much demasiado/a
tooth el diente
toothache el dolor de muelas
toothbrush el cepillo de dientes
toothpaste la pasta de dientes,
  el dentífrico
toothpick el palillo
top la cima
  on top (of) sobre, encima (de)
top floor el último piso
torch la linterna
torn rasgado/a
total el total
to touch tocar
tough (*meat*) duro/a
tour (*excursion*) la excursión

(*visit*) la visita
tourism el turismo
tourist el/la turista
tourist office la oficina de turismo
to tow remolcar
towards hacia
towel la toalla
tower la torre
town la ciudad
town centre el centro de la ciudad
town hall el ayuntamiento
tow rope el cable de remolque
toy el juguete
track (*path*) el camino
tracksuit el chandal
trade union el sindicato
traditional tradicional
traffic el tráfico
traffic jam el embotellamiento
traffic lights el semáforo
trailer el remolque
train el tren
  by train en tren
training shoes, trainers las
  zapatillas
tram el tranvía
tranquilliser el tranquilizante
to translate traducir
translation la traducción
to travel viajar
travel agency la agencia de viajes
traveller's cheque el cheque de
  viaje
travel sickness el mareo
tray la bandeja
treatment el tratamiento
tree el árbol
trip el viaje
trolley el carrito
trousers el pantalón, los
  pantalones

267

trout la trucha
true: that's true es verdad
to try (*attempt*) intentar
  (*sample, taste*) probar
to try on probarse
T-shirt la camiseta
tube el tubo
tuna el atún
tunnel el túnel
to turn girar, doblar
turning (*side road*) la bocacalle
to turn off apagar
  (*engine*) parar
  (*tap*) cerrar
to turn on encender
TV la tele
twice dos veces
twin beds dos camas
twins los gemelos, las gemelas
twisted torcido/a
type (*sort*) la clase
to type escribir a máquina
typewriter la máquina de
  escribir
typical típico/a

U

ugly feo/a
ulcer la úlcera
umbrella el paraguas
uncle el tío
uncomfortable incómodo/a
under debajo de
underground el metro
underneath debajo (de)
underpants (*men's*) los
  calzoncillos
to understand entender
  I (don't) understand (no)
  entiendo
underwear la ropa interior

underwater submarino/a
unemployed en paro
unfortunately
  desgraciadamente
unhappy infeliz
  (*sad*) triste
uniform el uniforme
university la universidad
unleaded petrol la gasolina
  sin plomo
unless a menos que
unpleasant desagradable
to unscrew destornillar
until hasta
unusual insólito/a
unwell enfermo/a
up arriba
upper de arriba
upstairs arriba
urgent urgente
urine la orina
us nosotros/as
use el uso
to use usar, utilizar
useful útil
useless inútil
usual: as usual como siempre
usually normalmente, por lo
  general

V

vacant libre
vacuum cleaner la aspiradora
vacuum flask el termos
valid válido/a
valley el valle
valuable de valor
valuables los objetos de valor
van la camioneta
vanilla la vainilla

vase el florero
VAT el IVA
veal la ternera
vegetable (*green*) la verdura
  (*pulse*) el legumbre
vegetarian vegetariano/a
vehicle el vehículo
vermouth el vermut
very muy
very much mucho
vest la camiseta
vet el veterinario
via por
video cassette la video-cassette
video recorder
  la video-grabadora
view la vista, el panorama
villa la casa, el chalet
village el pueblo
vinegar el vinagre
vineyard la viña
virgin la virgen
  Virgin Mary la Virgen María
visit la visita
to visit visitar
visitor el/la visitante
vitamin la vitamina
vodka la vodka
voice la voz
volleyball el voleibol
voltage el voltaje
to vote votar

W

wage el sueldo
waist la cintura
waistcoat el chaleco
to wait (for) esperar
waiter el camarero
waiting room la sala de espera

waitress la camarera
  waitress! ¡señorita!
Wales el País de Gales
walk el paseo
  to go for a walk dar un paseo
to walk andar
walking stick el bastón
wall (*inside*) la pared
  (*outside*) el muro
wallet la cartera
walnut la nuez
to want querer (*see page 180*)
  would like: I would like
  quisiera
war la guerra
  Spanish Civil War la Guerra
  Civil Española
warm caliente
to wash lavar
washable lavable
wash-basin el lavabo
washing el lavado
washing machine la lavadora
washing powder el jabón en
  polvo, el detergente
washing-up: to do the washing-
  up fregar los platos
washing-up liquid el lavavajillas
wasp la avispa
wastepaper basket la papelera
watch (*wristwatch*) el reloj
to watch (*TV etc.*) mirar
watchstrap la pulsera de reloj
water el agua (*f*)
water heater el calentador de
  agua
water melon la sandía
waterfall la cascada
waterproof impermeable
water-skiing el esquí acuático
wave (*sea*) la ola, la onda

wax la cera
way (route) el camino
  that way por allí/ahí
  this way por aquí
  (method) la manera
way in la entrada
way out la salida
we nosotros/as
weather el tiempo
  what's the weather like? ¿qué tiempo hace?
wedding la boda
week la semana
weekday el día laborable
weekend el fin de semana
weekly semanal
  (each week) cada semana
to weigh pesar
weight el peso
welcome bienvenido/a
well (water) el pozo
well bien
  as well también
well done (steak) muy hecho/a
Welsh galés, galesa
west el oeste
western del oeste, occidental
wet mojado/a
wetsuit el traje de bucear
what lo que
what? ¿qué?
  what is . . . ? ¿qué es . . . ?
wheel la rueda
wheelchair la silla de ruedas
when cuando
when? ¿cuándo?, ¿a qué hora?
where donde
where? ¿dónde?
  where is/are . . . ? ¿dónde está/están . . . ?
which el/la/lo cual

which? ¿qué?; ¿cuál?, (pl) ¿cuáles?
while mientras
whisky el whisky
  whisky and soda el whisky con soda
white blanco/a
  (with milk) con leche
who que
who? ¿quién?
  who is it? ¿quién es?
whole entero/a
wholemeal bread el pan integral
whose cuyo/a
whose? ¿de quién?
why? ¿por qué?
  why not? ¿por qué no?
wide ancho/a
widow la viuda
widower el viudo
wife la mujer
wild (animal) salvaje
  (plant) silvestre
win la victoria
to win ganar
  who won? ¿quién ganó?
wind el viento
windmill el molino de viento
window la ventana
  (car/train) la ventanilla
  (shop) el escaparate
windsurfing el windsurf
windy: it's windy hace viento
wine merchant/shop la bodega
wing el ala (f)
winter el invierno
with con
without sin
woman la mujer
wonderful maravilloso/a

wood (*group of trees*) el bosque (*material*) la madera
wool la lana
word la palabra
work el trabajo
work (*job*) trabajar (*function*) funcionar
world el mundo
world (*of the world*) mundial
  First/Second World War la Primera/Segunda Guerra Mundial
worried preocupado/a
worry: don't worry no se preocupe
worse peor
worth: it's worth ... vale ...
  it's not worth it no vale la pena
would like (*see* to want)
wound (*injury*) la herida
wrap (up) envolver
write escribir
writer el escritor, la escritora
writing pad el bloc
writing paper el papel de escribir
wrong (*incorrect*) equivocado/a
  you're wrong está equivocado/a; no tiene razón
  there's something wrong hay algo que no va bien

yellow amarillo/a
yes sí
yesterday ayer
yet todavía
  not yet todavía no
yoghurt el yogur
you usted (*formal*); tú (*informal*) (*see page 177*)
young joven
your su (*formal*), tu (*informal*), vuestro/a (*informal pl*) (*see page 176*)
yours suyo/a; tuyo/a; vuestro/a
youth la juventud
youth hostel el albergue de juventud

Z

zip la cremallera
zoo el zoo
zoology la zoología

X

X-ray la radiografía

Y

yacht el yate
yawn bostezar
year el año

EMERGENCIES

(*see also* Problems and Complaints, *page 164;* Health, *page 151*)

You may want to say

Phoning the emergency services

(I need) the police, please
(Necesito) la policía, por favor
netheseeto la poleethee-a por fabor

(I need) the fire brigade, please
(Necesito) los bomberos, por favor
netheseeto los bomberos por fabor

(I need) an ambulance, please
(Necesito) una ambulancia, por favor
netheseeto oona amboolanthya por fabor

There's been a robbery
Ha habido un robo
a abeedo oon robo

There's been a burglary
Ha habido un robo en casa
a abeedo oon robo en kasa

There's been an accident
Ha habido un accidente
a abeedo oon aktheedente

There's a fire
Hay fuego
iy fwego

I've been attacked/mugged
Me han atacado
me an atakado

I've been raped
He sido violada
e seedo bee-olada

There's someone injured/ill
Hay una persona herida/enferma
iy oona persona ereeda/enferma

It's my husband/son
Es mi marido/hijo
es mee mareedo/eehho

It's my wife/daughter
Es mi mujer/hija
es mee moohher/eehha

It's my friend
Es mi amigo (*male*)/**amiga** (*female*)
es mee ameego/ameega

Please come immediately
Venga inmediatamente
benga eenmedeeatamente

I am at . . .
Estoy en . . .
estoy en . . .

My name is . . .
Me llamo . . .
me lyamo . . .

My telephone number is . . .
Mi número de teléfono es . . .
mee noomero de telefono es . . .

Where is the police station?
¿Dónde está la comisaría?
donde esta la komeesaree-a

Where is the hospital?
¿Dónde está el hospital?
donde esta el ospeetal

At the police station/hospital

Is there anybody who speaks English?
¿Hay alguien que hable inglés?
iy algyen ke able eengles

I want to speak to a woman
Quiero hablar con una mujer
kyero ablar kon oona moohher

Please call the British Embassy
Por favor, llame a la embajada británica
por fabor lyame a la embahhada breetaneeka

I want a lawyer
Quiero un abogado
kyero oon abogado

You may hear

When you phone the emergency services

¿Qué pasa?   **¿Qué ha pasado?**
ke pasa   *ke a pasado*
What is the matter?   What has happened?

Dígame su nombre y su dirección
*deegame soo **nombre** ee soo direekthyon*
Tell me your name and your address

Vamos a enviar una patrulla
bamos a enbyar oona patroolya
We will send a police patrol

Ahora va el coche de policía
a-ora ba el koche de poleethee-a
A police car is on the way

Ahora va el coche de bomberos
a-ora ba el koche de bomberos
A fire engine is on the way

Ahora le envío una ambulancia
a-ora le enbee-o oona amboolanthya
I am sending an ambulance to you now

The police

Cómo se llama usted?
komo se lyama oosteth
What is your name?

¿Cuál es su dirección?
kwal es soo deerekthyon
What is your address?

¿Qué pasó?
ke paso
What happened?

¿Dónde pasó?
donde paso
Where did it happen?

¿Cuándo pasó?
kwando paso
When did it happen?

¿Puede describir . . .?
pwede deskreebeer . . .
Can you describe . . . ?

Venga conmigo/con nosotros a la comisaría
benga konmeego/kon nosotros a la komeesaree-a
Come with me/with us to the police station

Queda usted detenido/detenida
keda oosteth deteneedo/deteneeda
You're under arrest

The doctor

¿Dónde le duele?
donde le dwele
Where does it hurt?

¿Cuánto tiempo hace que está así?
kwanto tyempo athe ke esta asee
How long have you been like this?/How long has he/she been like this?

Tendrá que ir al hospital
tendra ke eer al ospeetal
You/he/she will have to go to hospital

Help!	Stop thief!
¡Socorro!	**¡Al ladrón!**
sokorro	*al ladron*
Help me!	Look out!
¡Ayúdeme!	**¡Atención!**
iyoodeme	*atenthyon*
Police!	Fire!
¡Policía!	**¡Fuego!**
poleethee-a	*fwego*
Stop!	Danger! Gas!
¡Alto!	**¡Peligro! ¡Gas!**
alto	*peleegro gas*

Get out of the way!
¡Váyase!
biyase

Get a doctor
Llame a un médico
lyame a oon medeeko

Call the police
Llame a la policía
lyame a la poleethee-a

Get help quickly
Busque ayuda, rápido
booske iyooda rapeedo

Call the fire brigade
Llame a los bomberos
lyame a los bomberos

It's an emergency
Es una emergencia
es oona emerhhenthya

Call an ambulance
Llame a una ambulancia
lyame a oona amboolanthya

Emergency telephone numbers

Police (in cities and large towns) **091**

There are no emergency telephone numbers that apply all over
Spain. If you cannot get the police on **091**, look in the tele-
phone directory, or phone directory enquiries (**Información
Telefónica**) on **003**:

I want a number for . . .
Quiero un número para . . .

Police
La policía

Fire brigade
Los bomberos

Ambulance
Una ambulancia

Red Cross
La Cruz Roja (*they can help in any emergency*)

Note: It is intended that emergency telephone numbers will be
standardised throughout the EC.

NOTES

NOTES

NOTES

NOTES

NOTES

NOTES

NOTES

NOTES

ALL-PURPOSE PHRASES

Hello
Hola
ola

Good morning/Good day
Buenos días
bwenos dee-as

Good afternoon/evening
Buenas tardes
bwenas tardes

Goodnight
Buenas noches
bwenas noches

Goodbye
Adiós
adyos

Yes
Sí
see

No
No
no

Please
Por favor
por fabor

Thank you (very much)
(Muchas) gracias
(moochas) grathyas

Don't mention it
De nada
de nada

I don't know
No sé
no se

I don't understand
No entiendo
no entyendo

I speak very little Spanish
Hablo muy poco español
hablo mwee poko espanyol

Pardon?
¿Cómo?
komo

Can you repeat that?
¿Puede repetirlo?
pwede repeteerlo

More slowly
Más despacio
mas despathyo

Again, please
Otra vez, por favor
otra beth por fabor

Can you show me in the
  book?
**¿Puede enseñarme en el
  libro?**
pwede ensenyarme en el leebro

Can you write it down?
¿Puede escribirlo?
pwede eskreebeerlo

BBC Books publishes courses on the following
languages:

ARABIC	ITALIAN
CHINESE	JAPANESE
FRENCH	PORTUGUESE
GERMAN	RUSSIAN
GREEK	SPANISH
HINDI URDU	TURKISH

For further information write to:
BBC Books
Language Enquiry Service
Room A3116
Woodlands
80 Wood Lane
London
W12 0TT

Consultant: Julia Bueno

Cover designed by Peter Bridgewater and Annie Moss

Published by BBC Books
an imprint of BBC Worldwide Publishing.
BBC Worldwide Ltd., Woodlands,
80 Wood Lane, London W12 0TT

ISBN 0 563 40002 1

First published 1991
This edition published in 1995
© Carol Stanley and Philippa Goodrich 1991
Reprinted 1991, 1992, 1995, 1996

Set in Times Roman by Ace Filmsetting Ltd, Frome
Text and Cover printed in England by
Clays Ltd, St Ives plc

SPANISH
Phrase book

Carol Stanley and Philippa Goodrich

BBC Books